JOURNE
WIT
AVIATORS
in New Zealand

Recalling the past, Colin Smith swings the prop of a veteran Fox Moth, ZK-ADI, at the Old Mandeville Airfield in Southland. Gerald Grocott is the pilot.
ROY SINCLAIR

Air Safaris' Nomad 24, ZK-NMD, crosses the Main Divide into Westland while flying the famed tourist route, the 'Grand Traverse of Mount Cook'.
GEOFF MASON

JOURNEYING WITH AVIATORS

in New Zealand

~

Roy Sinclair

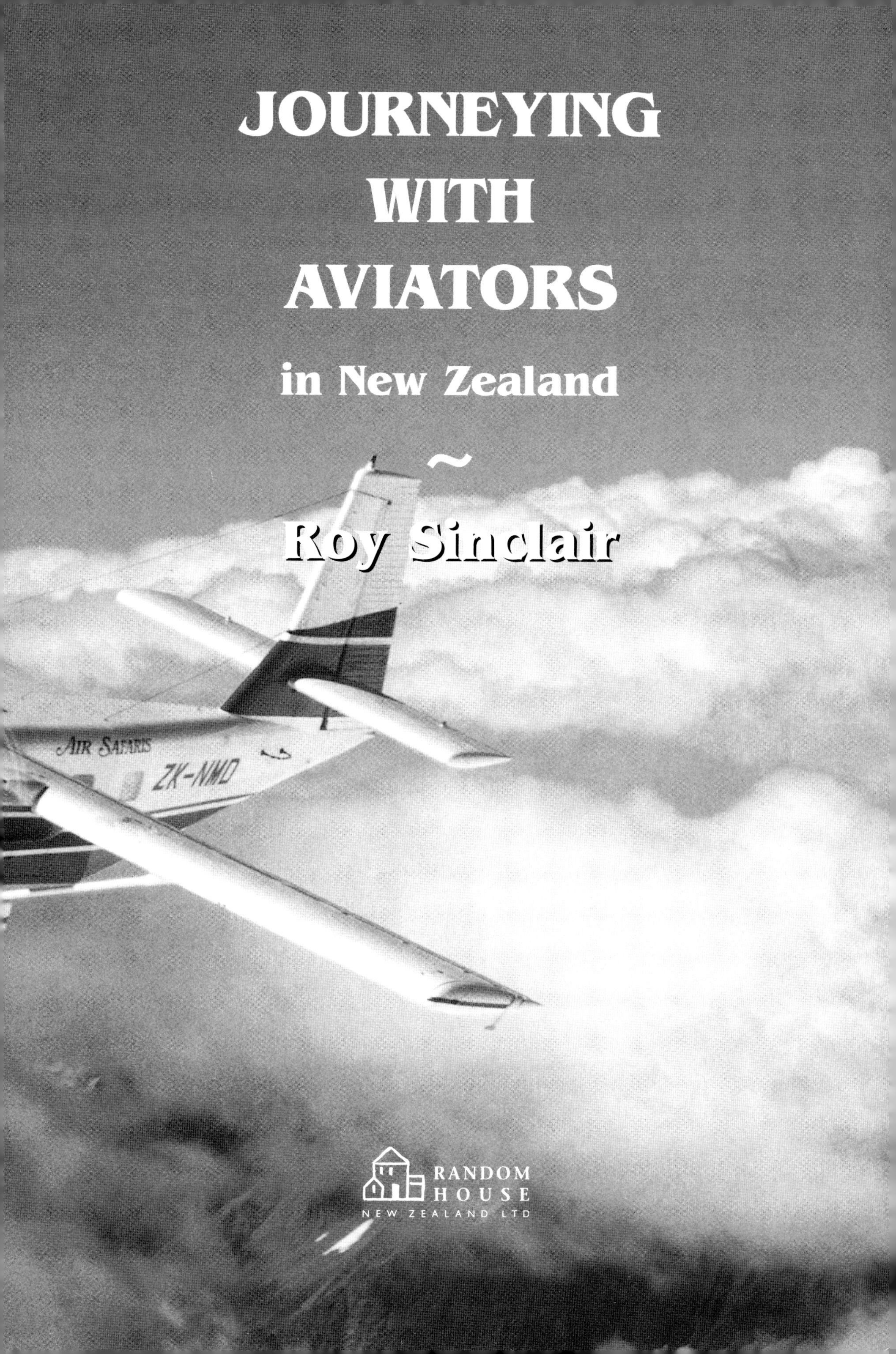

RANDOM HOUSE
NEW ZEALAND LTD

ACKNOWLEDGEMENTS

Many people have helped with this book. Sue Muir of the *Gisborne Herald*, Johanne Buchanan of the *New Zealand Herald* and Dave Wethey of *The Press* helped with photographs. Joanne Diver at *Australian Geographic* helped me contact a wonderful New Zealand aviator living in Melbourne. A special thanks to Ray Gasparich and the other members of the Solent Flying Boat Preservation Society; and to Paul Savage, a private pilot and colleague journalist at *The Press*, for reading the manuscript and offering advice and encouragement.

Ansett New Zealand also deserves special thanks. I suspect those working for the airline have never heard of the author but they always had a favourable airfare offering whenever he went anywhere.

My family should not be overlooked. My wife Helen once again showed her incredible patience as I wrote, on the promise I take her to Europe for a month and forget about my aviators book. The promise has already been honoured. My son Paul was quickly able to solve any problems with computer machinery; Michael, another son, proved to be valuable for his encyclopaedic knowledge of everything to do with aviation; and my daughter, Kirsten, took me flying.

Random House New Zealand Ltd
(An imprint of the Random House Group)

18 Poland Road
Glenfield
Auckland 10
NEW ZEALAND

Sydney New York Toronto
London Auckland Johannesburg
and agencies throughout the world

First published 1998

Printed in Malaysia
ISBN 1 86941 315 6

FRONT COVER: Catching the light, a Pilatus Porter's spinning turbo-prop announces the return of a Mount Cook Airline ski-plane flight from the Tasman Glacier. The pilot is Brent Turner, grandson of FJ (Popeye) Lucas, one of New Zealand's illustrious pioneer aviators. *Roy Sinclair*

BACK COVER: Fox Moth ZK-ADI *Roy Sinclair*

CONTENTS

INTRODUCTION

From a window seat aboard a high-wing Ansett British Aerospace 146 flying between Auckland and Christchurch, the world becomes detached — like a relief map.
Roy Sinclair

Cumulo-nimbus are clouds with ice in them. They are very bumpy. They will kill you. At the aero club we call them CBs for short. CB can also mean 'coffee break'. When CBs are about we drink coffee all day, and leave the aeroplanes in the hangar!

Kirsten Sinclair

MANY PEOPLE, PERHAPS even most people, gazing skyward on a balmy afternoon and watching a small single-engine aero club trainer or a glider passing lazily overhead have dreamed of flying. I am no exception. But my ambitions to fly went into an irretrievable tailspin after just six hours in the air. Perhaps I was a disappointment to my much younger instructors? Perhaps they thought I was going to be a natural pilot? Perhaps they had already forgotten the difficulties they had also experienced when they started flying?

As with all keen student pilots, whenever I arrived for a lesson I was full of hope. Then, each lesson ended in disappointment. I failed to fulfil even my own expectations, let alone those of my flying instructors — and I did have four different instructors for just six hours of flying. Even before I had taxied far on my sixth lesson, somehow I knew it would be my last. I did everything wrong. It got worse and worse, until the toes of my shoes even touched the brakes during the takeoff run. Unforgivable.

Looking confident in a Piper Cherokee, ZK-DUP, teenage pilot Kirsten Sinclair flies above the famed Molesworth Station.
ROY SINCLAIR

The instructor, as always, was far from impressed — and said so. An hour later, back at the clubhouse, I was feeling miserable and yet another $120 poorer. To ensure the morning ended badly, the instructor told me he would discuss my supposed lack of progress with the CFI (Chief Flying Instructor). I knew then that an agreed special deal, enabling student pilots to train as far as solo for a fixed fee, was to be cancelled.

Disheartened, I spent the afternoon pedalling my mountain bike on roads gripping the hills above Christchurch. I almost managed to stop a flow of tears and, on this one occasion, I did not gaze into the rich blue sky whenever I heard a small aeroplane overhead. Nor, as I had often done, did I pause to watch the gliders fly, sometimes close and below where I was riding. Aged in my early fifties, I had become a lapsed flyer.

THE END OF my flying lessons did not mean an end to flying, or the sheer enjoyment of flying in small aeroplanes. My 18-year-old daughter, Kirsten, had been taught to fly exceptionally well at the same aero club — and by the same flying instructors who had bravely attempted to teach me. Kirsten was working towards her Commercial Pilot's Licence, which involved about 100 hours of cross-country flying. She enjoyed the company of a parent passenger, especially one with a bulging back pocket, willing to buy a respectable lunch at Wanaka, Hokitika, Nelson, Wellington, or wherever we landed at the end of the outbound flight.

My six flying lessons had not been entirely wasted. In small aeroplanes — trying to control them myself as we flew further out to sea practising turning, climbing, descending, and wing-drop stalls — an inherent fear of flying had been overcome. I had also gained a good understanding of the principles of flight.

I had given up being a student pilot about the same time as Kirsten obtained her Private Pilot's Licence. I was prepared, and willing, to trust my life to the skills of one of my children. At the time my daughter could not drive a car very well. On the road she was hopeless. Indeed, she did not pass her driver's licence test until she had passed her C-Cat flying instructor's test. By that time she had more than 300 flying hours recorded in her Pilot Logbook.

FLYING WITH KIRSTEN, I soon discovered that the inflight service was excellent. Through my headset I listened to the ATIS (Automatic Terminal Information Service) and the radio calls of all the other air-

A resplendent DH89 Dominie, ZK-AKY, restored in National Airways Corporation colours, flying at the Hokitika air show on 17 December 1994 staged to mark 60 years of New Zealand airline flying. AKY flew from 1947 until 1964.
ROY SINCLAIR

craft flying. I was not stuck in an anonymous airliner cabin with an obligatory view of the seat in front, or being fobbed off with a glass of inferior wine and mediocre lunch. And the person sitting next to me was no longer my little girl; she was a professionally trained pilot working hard towards a rewarding flying career.

Weekend cross-country flights were shared with my wife, Helen, who had also caught the flying bug. But when it was my turn to fly I was always up early, gazing at the sky. Sometimes it looked dubious and a telephone call to the aero club confirmed the worst.

'Cumulo-nimbus in dozens are fast converging on Christchurch,' Kirsten told me one Saturday morning.

'What's that?' I asked as I struggled into my trousers. Somehow I knew the answer would not be congenial to flying a light aircraft.

Also disappointed, she snapped back with, 'They're clouds with ice in them. They're very bumpy. They will kill you. We call them CBs for short.'

'Where I work, CB is for "coffee break," I proffered.

'Exactly. It's the same at the aero club,' she replied. 'We drink coffee all day and leave the aeroplanes in the hangar.'

ONCE KIRSTEN HAD qualified as a flying instructor she encouraged me to take the controls. As much as I enjoyed the flying and everything associated with aviation, I no longer had the heart to fly myself. Kirsten was able to trim an aeroplane expertly once it was in the air and make it fly well. Whenever I took over, the aeroplane became like a knowing delinquent horse — one that takes full advantage of its unwary rider. The aeroplane was clearly flying me!

But as my hours as a flying passenger were gathering, along with memories of views overlooking magnificent landscapes — we flew over Molesworth Station twice when the entire landscape was snowbound — my admiration for those who could fly grew. At some point I decided to go journeying with pen and camera to discover a selection of inspiring New Zealand aviators, especially those who were little known. Sometimes my journeying took me beyond New Zealand. Some of my subjects I already knew before I set out. Others were discovered along the way. Those whose company I enjoyed and whose sometimes heartfelt moments I have shared can now be discovered simply by turning these pages. Recorded with words and photographs, I believe my aviators will be worth knowing.

ROY SINCLAIR

CHAPTER 1

Lone Pioneer of Intercontinental Flight

Aline Quin, aged 94, reminiscing at home in 1993.
Roy Sinclair

My Gipsy Moth was like a Baby Austin — just plywood and four instruments. I was so bitterly disappointed there wasn't one in the Wigram Air Force Museum.

Aline Quin

ALINE QUIN (NÉE BARTON) became the first New Zealand-trained airwoman to make an intercontinental flight when, in 1931, she flew her own Gipsy Moth biplane from Heston airfield in England to Nairobi in Kenya. Jean Batten, perhaps the most celebrated of early New Zealand aviators, was yet to become the Madonna of the skies, but the Englishwoman Amy Johnson and other intercontinental fliers had already made news stories. Aline's flight, momentous as it was, might have passed without celebration.

'The newspaper people were only interested in someone very old, or very young, setting out on a long flight,' Aline said more than 60 years later. 'My sister, Annette, was there. She told them that I was a 19-year-old schoolgirl flying home to New Zealand, just to see what they would swallow.'

And that's the story the newspapers did swallow — and published widely round the world — believing Kenya was merely a stop on the way.

WHEN I MET Aline Quin at her Christchurch home in 1993 she had recently celebrated her 94th birthday. Despite her failing eyesight and her claim to be no more than 'a depressing object and so terribly out of date', I discovered a remarkably alert and almost mischievous old woman who was every bit as charming as she was unrepentant.

With conversation spiced with laughter and quirky humour, she was willing to talk about a charmed life, best described as a series of magnificent adventures. But her outburst when I showed a photograph of a tall, attractive woman and her Gipsy Moth taken at Heston on 19 October 1931 was not what I had expected. At the very least she might have showed a glimmer of pride.

'I was furious over that. The English wanted me to pose looking as if I was starting the plane. I look so self-conscious and indecisive holding the propeller with just one arm. People would have thought, "She won't get very far."'

Her 1931 flight — a remarkable achievement — is not the highlight of her life. Her family apparently never thought much of it, and she is somewhat mystified why suddenly, in her old age, people want to make her into some sort of heroine.

More than 60 years later Aline Quin was still furious about the 'self-conscious and indecisive pose' demanded by the newspaper photographer as she set out on her 1931 flight from England to Kenya.

COURTESY SHIRLEY LAINÉ

She loved motoring even more than flying, and talked with fervour about Jaguar cars she once owned and drove, often alone, to distant, lonely parts of the globe.

ALINE WAS THE third of six daughters born to a wealthy Wairarapa farmer and Cambridge-trained barrister, William Barton, and his wife Lucy, a daughter of John Studholme from Christchurch and South Canterbury's Coldstream Station. The Bartons owned a large sheep and cattle station, 'White Rock', near Cape Palliser on the North Island east coast. They did not live there, however, preferring their large family home, 'Fareham', at Featherston.

Aline was brought up to do nothing more than gainfully amuse herself. 'My father once said, "Aline, it's time you started doing something useful." I said, "All right, I'll take over the farm." To that he laughed and said, "The men will never work for a woman," and that was the end of the matter. I often think of my poor father with all us girls who knew exactly what we wanted to do. He was a kind man

Aline Quin being farewelled from Heston by her sister and friends at the beginning of her flight to Kenya.
COURTESY SHIRLEY LAINÉ

who found it very difficult to say no. He paid for everything. I sometimes regret very much that he was so generous. I was not brought up to do anything useful, or even earn a living. I know I would have become a much better person if I had been a road mender.'

She credits her ancestors with her longevity and ability to revel in adventure. She was born with tremendous strength and always had to be active and busy. The windows and doors at 'Fareham' were thrown wide open, encouraging her to live a healthy outdoor life.

She is passionate about an upbringing when the only sounds to be heard in the Wairarapa were the occasional clip-clop of a horse's hooves on the road leading away from the garden and the whistle of a distant train from Masterton. It was the more wonderful and peaceful world of the New Zealand pioneers; it was like living at the beginning of the world. 'Oh Roy, if you could have heard the birds in the clear wonderful air on a winter's morning.'

FRANCIS CHICHESTER, WHO was soon to make a name for himself for his trans-Tasman and other oceanic float-plane flights, fell in love with Aline. But his considerable efforts to win her were in vain. Aged 30, and slightly older than Chichester, she was 'much too independent to make anyone a good wife'.

'He was a lonely man when he came out here from England. I was not the right woman for him, but I do regret that I was not more sympathetic. He later married Sheila Craven, an Englishwoman who was much more suitable.'

But Chichester, who in 1928 was yet to learn to fly himself, arranged for Aline to have flying lessons at Martinborough. She was taught at first by George Bolt, who later became a successful aviator and engineer in the Air Force and TEAL (Tasman Empire Airways Ltd, now Air New Zealand), then Captain Bill Parke and, finally, a young aero club mechanic, Len Mangham. For Aline, flying was new and exciting. It was something she just had to conquer.

She was a quick learner who never found flying difficult. She went solo after less than six hours of dual instruction, all from a Martinborough paddock.

'Then Captain Parke told me quite suddenly that I must go up and loop the loop. I said, "I can't go up and loop the loop. I don't know how to!"

'"Easy," he said, "you go up about 5000 feet and then you draw the stick into your stomach like this, and your plane will go over and come out again."

'Captain Parke asked Len Mangham to go up with me and he said, "Not on your life!" Len was a very good mechanic, and I liked him a great deal. Later he became chief engineer at Union Airways.

'I was quite frightened so I went up on my own and practised stall turns all over the sky while I was trying to make up my mind to pull the stick into my stomach. I knew they were watching from the ground and I couldn't be a coward so I did quite a good loop and came out the right way up. So I thought I would do a second one just to show I didn't mind.

'But I pulled the stick too suddenly and I went up and was left hanging from my seat strap at the top of the loop. All the dust from the floor and from behind the instrument panel fell into my eyes. Then I was looking straight down 5000 feet to the earth and feeling the plane going out of control.'

When I asked her, 'What happened next?' I watched bemused as a frail old hand was raised as high as it would go before she managed to twist her almost straightened fingers downwards in a half circle. She was demonstrating what my own limited flying experience had already taught me — a spin that is likely to result in a quick and decisive end for any inexperienced pilot.

'I don't know what I did.' She was suddenly laughing back down all those years. 'But I kicked it into control on the rudder pedals before the wind became too hard on my wings. I was not at all frightened. I was too occupied, mentally thinking about how I would save myself.'

Aline qualified for her 'A' licence (No 199) on 15 October 1930 and made several cross-country flights before sailing to England early the following year. On the same ship was Francis Quin, the naval surgeon she later married.

Africa, and Kenya in particular, the beautiful Mt Longido, cumulus clouds sailing above the purple Rift Valley, and a seething mass of magnificent animals on the Nairobi plains were among Aline's treasured memories.

'No one thought I would ever get to Africa when I went to the bank and asked for the £600 to buy my Gipsy Moth. I was certainly not thought of as an accomplished aviator. I never did learn how to navigate. I would go up to about 6000 feet and follow rivers, but rivers in Europe over which I wanted to fly are like canals. I could not rely on being able to follow them.

'I was indignant with the people in the bank when I was told to cable home and ask my father before they would hand over the

Francis Chichester (later Sir Francis), about the time he embarked on his 1931 trans-Tasman flight in a Gipsy Moth floatplane. 'A lonely man when he came out to New Zealand,' he fell in love with Aline Quin.
THE PRESS

money. I even threatened to go to the Jews. I was totally outrageous, wasn't I?'

At a cocktail party she met Bunny Richards, a young surveyor who had been to Kenya and was very keen to get back there. 'He was very trusting because he didn't even know if I could fly. I said, "I'll take you if you can navigate."'

The start of the flight was anything but promising. With no instruments of any significance she flew into a thick fog within 15 minutes of takeoff. 'I turned around very quickly and flew into the clear, and landed back at Heston. I think we all went to the theatre that evening, quite forgetting about the flight until next morning when I started again.'

The flight to Kenya was across Europe to Turkey, and then Egypt, Sudan, Ethiopia and, finally, Nairobi. Bunny Richards set a course, and Aline flew by the compass.

'Bunny was not always very good at judging the wind strength. On one occasion he kept telling me to fly more to the right, making me leave my compass course, until we were lost on the wrong side of a mountain range. We were looking for Sofia, the capital of Bulgaria. It was almost dark. The weather was deteriorating, and the pin on the petrol gauge had almost disappeared, when I saw a very narrow path through the chocolate-coloured earth. The ground was very rough as we landed, and we stayed put for the night.'

A narrow escape and an uncomfortable night spent attempting to sleep in the aeroplane are not the most vivid memories of her forced landing. Next morning Aline was almost stunned by the sight of a small girl aged six or seven.

'She was the most beautiful girl I was ever to see. Dressed in rags, she had wide-apart tiger eyes that were almost orange, and standing out in that valley where everything else seemed to be the colour of mud. She had been looking after a flock of sheep, or pigs. She stood and looked at me as if I didn't exist. She was not frightened, or even fascinated, by the aeroplane, which was undoubtedly the first she had ever seen.'

Aline and her passenger flew about 5280 miles (8500 kilometres) in just over a month, arriving at Nairobi on 22 November 1931. At no stage during the flight was she apprehensive, although she admits that perhaps she should have been. And Kenya, when she arrived, more than lived up to her dreams.

'Ah yes, it had a romantic quality about it. Each morning it was just as if the world had been reborn. I would have liked to live there. That would have been impossible for a young woman on her own with no means of making a living. The morals of the English out there didn't exist, and there were some wonderful scandals. I was once excluded from a famous club because I was a single, unaccompanied woman.

'I was tempted to fly on, but flying was a very expensive pastime and I did not feel justified asking my poor father for any more money. Besides, when we reached Kenya the Gipsy Moth was only just airworthy. A lower wing had warped and a replacement spar would have to be sent out from England.'

Bunny Richards made off soon after they arrived in Nairobi, taking with him Aline's flight route maps. Aline did not see him again. She sold the aeroplane for £450 and, with a friend, went off to China.

Going from one absorbing thing to the next was to be the pattern for the rest of her life. Her marriage to Francis Quin in October 1933, although a very successful relationship that produced a capable daughter, she describes as being 'a leap out of the frying pan and into the fire!' Looking back it was difficult for her to recall when she was in the frying pan, and when she was in the fire. She was always in one or the other.

She lived in many countries and along with other naval officers' wives was stranded in South Africa at the start of the Second World War. With her daughter, Ann, she travelled home to New Zealand for the duration of the war. Francis Quin died in 1958 while they were living in Jersey in the Channel Islands.

In Jersey Aline bought the first of two Jaguar cars she was to own. 'That was in 1959. A little man who was a survivor of the Burma death railway sold it to me. He had great charm and I believe he could have sold me anything.' The same year she arrived back in Kenya, having driven her Jaguar from the Cape in South Africa. Meeting an acquaintance, she asked about her Gipsy Moth.

'I was told that it had been bought by someone who had divorced his wife and married another woman. He set off for his honeymoon in my aeroplane and crashed at a place called Mpika. Distraught at killing his new wife in the crash he shot himself. It was a sad end for the Gipsy Moth. I loved that aeroplane, just as I loved my cars.'

Aline turned the conversation to more philosophical issues and then we paused for a drink. Unashamedly, knowing I would soon be driving home, I took advantage of her near-blindness and poured myself a smaller measure of brandy, disguising it with a larger portion of ginger ale. But I was found out!

EARLY IN 1995 Aline Quin agreed to see me again, but 'for no more than half an hour'. It was to be my last opportunity to talk to someone who had belonged to that wonderful age of pioneer intercontinental flying — an age that launched names such as Amy Johnson, Jim

Chichester's famous Gipsy Moth prior to being converted to a floatplane.

Mollison, Bert Hinkler, Beryl Markham, Charles Scott, Jean Batten, and others, into aviation history.

When I called she remembered my previous visit. 'You are that man who wasted your whole afternoon talking to me. What on earth would you want with me this time!'

Although she was suffering very much from old age, and complaining she had already lived far too long, I was again talking to a remarkably coherent woman — and she was still in control of a delightfully mischievous spirit. Our meeting stretched to more than two hours with scarcely a pause in our chatter.

She talked again about learning to fly and how easy it was coordinating the rudder pedals and the control stick. She had great judgement and knew just when her aeroplane would hit the earth during a landing. She never had to keep a log so was unable to say how many hours' flying she had had in 1931 before setting out for Kenya. In those days regulations were few, if any and aeroplanes were small and simple.

'My Gipsy Moth was like a Baby Austin — just plywood and four instruments. I was so bitterly disappointed there wasn't one in the Wigram Air Force Museum.'

I told Aline about my 18-year-old daughter, Kirsten, who had just gained her Private Pilot's Licence and hoped one day to fly for an airline. Aline was impressed. I told her about one of Kirsten's pre-licence solo cross-country trips when the weather cut up and she was suddenly caught in cloud.

'What did she do?' Aline was suddenly looking alarmed.

'She opened the small Perspex window close to her seat and put her hand outside — to touch a cloud,' I replied.

Aline's aged face suddenly became a broad smile. 'How wonderful,' was all she said.

Aline never met any of the other great aviators of her era, although she almost introduced herself to Beryl Markham when she was dining in the same Nairobi hotel. In September 1936 Beryl Markham made the first east to west solo Atlantic flight and survived a crash-landing arrival in Nova Scotia due to an iced-up fuel line.

New Zealand's Jean Batten, who flew five years after Aline, gained her respect. 'Jean Batten deserved what she achieved. She went minutely into everything and was a pretty fair mechanic of her own. Whenever she flew she never neglected to get her machine checked over by the mechanics — something I never did. I just landed and flew off, hopefully, next morning.'

Aline talked about security and the comfort of always knowing she had a part ownership of the family's huge White Rock property. And she spoke about the Guardian Angel who all too often rescued her from terrible situations: 'I was flying over Portsmouth looking down on one of the navy's big aircraft carriers. I was thinking, "Could I land on it? Could I judge it so I landed so close to this edge that I could stop at the other?"

'I circled round and round saying to myself, "They couldn't kill me if I tried. Shall I have a go, or shan't I?" Then my Guardian Angel intervened. It's a real shock to think that I ever thought about it. I might have been like the German boy (Matthias Rust) who, many years later (in 1989), landed in Red Square and thought he would get away with it.'

'But could you have landed on that ship?' I asked, and once again saw that mischievous grin.

'I've often wondered,' she mused. 'Even a few days ago I was wondering. Could I have managed my speed well enough and landed just at the right moment?'

Nearing the end of an enviable and adventurous life, if Aline Quin had any regrets they were for her long-suffering father who longed for his daughters to achieve something useful. 'I really think he wanted me to become someone like Jean Batten. He must have been so disappointed.'

ALINE QUIN, AGED 97, died on 12 November 1996.

Pilot Gerald Grocott flies his DH83 Fox Moth ZK-ADI over the Old Mandeville Airfield in March 1997. Almost 63 years earlier, ZK-ADI inaugurated airline flying in New Zealand.
ROY SINCLAIR

CHAPTER 2

Dreams Take Flight Over the Old Mandeville Airfield

I guess I was just fascinated by the things people who flew veteran biplanes were talking about — the wind in the wires, the unbounded freedom and that sort of thing. It was something worth preserving for another generation.

Colin Smith

As early morning mists burn away to reveal a lush Southland countryside, a beautifully presented de Havilland Fox Moth biplane is pushed out of a hangar and onto the grass. The fuselage is the colour of the marigold flower — orange, with green lettering. Four wood and fabric wings, and the tail sections are silver. A small crowd gathers. Among them is Gerald Grocott, a stocky pilot who normally flies an MD 11 jet airliner for Swissair. Remarkably, his red-orange hair and green T-shirt almost match the veteran aeroplane he is preparing to fly for the first time. He asks several questions before climbing into the open cockpit.

The pilot will do three takeoffs and landings with the unladen aircraft. He will then do three more, this time carrying a load of two passengers. When he lands for the sixth time he will have fulfilled Civil Aviation Authority regulations for a Fox Moth type rating. Everything is checked — carefully — and as the last mists roll away the pilot shouts, 'Throttle set, contact.' The prop is swung, and the Gipsy Major motor bursts into life. Soon the tail wheel is lifting from the grass and we watch as the aeroplane makes an uncertain leap from the ground, climbs away, and turns to circuit the airfield.

Among those anxiously watching is Colin Smith, who moments earlier had been swinging the prop. 'He's got it,' he says, sounding just a little relieved. Smiling, he turns to us. 'This is the beautiful thing about these old aeroplanes. We can restore them and then see them fly.

'The aeroplane flying now is ZK-ADI. It is one of New Zealand's most significant historic civil aeroplanes. It's a national treasure. It was the last British-built DH83 Fox Moth, and from December 1934 it was flown by Captain JC (Bert) Mercer when he established New Zealand's first licensed airline, Air Travel (NZ) Ltd, on the South Island's West Coast. It represents the very beginning of civil flying in New Zealand.'

Colin Smith is a former merchant navy marine engineer and Southland farmer. In 1986, with his wife Maeva, he established the Croydon Aircraft Company to restore vintage de Havilland aircraft at the Old Mandeville Airfield, about 16 km west from Gore. Although not well known in New Zealand when I visited the airfield in March

1997, the Croydon Aircraft Company had already restored several historic aeroplanes, some for discerning overseas aviation devotees.

I found Colin Smith working on two almost completed Tiger Moth restorations. My opening remarks suggested the Tigers looked like new and, with an endearing modesty I was beginning to discover, he replied, 'Some would say better than new.' He told me that his interest — others would say his passion — for aeroplanes was rather latent.

'I had parents who believed that if I was going to fly I would have been born with wings. My interest was fostered while I was at sea working as a marine engineer. My senior, Arthur Moultby, was a pilot and a brother of the Moultby of *Dam Busters* fame.'

Rather than having the sailor's obligatory girl in every port, Arthur Moultby usually found access to an aeroplane.

'We went flying in Ceylon, India, Malaya, and anywhere else where we could lease a light aeroplane from a local flying club,' Colin said.

His first flight was in a de Havilland Tiger Moth and it was like 'riding on a motor bike but high up off the ground'. He still recalls the thrill of the wind in the wires, and the unbounded freedom of that flight. He had experienced the fascinating things he had often heard the early aviators talking about. Later, it became his dream and ambition to restore old wood and fabric aeroplanes and have them airworthy for another generation. He had been collecting any old de Havilland pieces he could find and doing restoration work for some years while making a name for himself as a farmer and stud sheep breeder. Then, he and Maeva had an unexpected opportunity to sell their Chatton North farm for a good price.

'I was not so keen to sell, although we had probably achieved everything we had wanted to do with stud sheep. One day when I arrived home from a farming business trip Maeva said, "Colin, you can now go and do what you have always wanted to do."'

Restorer of veteran biplanes and founder of the Croydon Aircraft Company, Colin Smith is preserving the fascination of pioneer flight for another generation.
ROY SINCLAIR

They considered setting up a hangar to restore aeroplanes near Queenstown or at one of the other popular tourist areas, but family and historic associations were closer to home — in a paddock beside Mandeville's former Railway Hotel, which has since been magnificently transformed to become The Moth — an aviation-theme restaurant and bar.

Maeva's uncle, John Crombie, who learned to fly in England during the First World War, had always kept an aeroplane in a T-hangar he had built at Mandeville. Crombie was also an alpine guide at Mt Cook during the early 1950s, when Ed Hillary (later Sir Edmund) was learning his mountaineering skills, and a great friend of pioneer aviator and tourist operator Rodolph Wigley.

'The licensed Railway Hotel at Mandeville was on the outskirts of Gore's "dry" area,' Maeva told me later. 'There was also a store that had fuel. When the Avro 504ks barnstormed around Southland from about February 1921 they would land in my uncle's paddock and taxi up to the store for fuel. A drink or two were enjoyed in the hotel before flying off to Riverton or Lumsden.

'My uncle was a bit of a romantic with his aeroplanes, and he always liked to tell us that he taught Ed Hillary how to climb mountains. We listened intently to all his stories, not quite knowing what to believe, and we used to help push his aeroplane out of the hangar. But we weren't allowed to go flying. Those days you did what your mother told you, especially when she could see the airfield, and everything, from her kitchen window!'

Colin told me Mandeville is now probably the oldest operating airfield in New Zealand. 'For our present airfield we had to buy a lot of

New Zealand's only airworthy de Havilland Gipsy Moth, ZK-AEJ, flying over Central Otago. The aeroplane was restored by Temple Martin, a well-known Moth expert, for Gerald Grocott.
SHARON HENDRIKS

land, in addition to John Crombie's paddock, for a reasonable length of grass runway — more than 800 metres — and for the restoration hangars.'

Much of the land was in quarter-acre lots, and roads criss-crossed the planned airfield complex, which included the former Railway Hotel. To complicate matters even more, during the 1870s the New Zealand Land Company, in England, had arranged for Mandeville to be surveyed as one of the proposed grandiose railway towns between Gore and Lumsden. More than a century later — the railway having long gone and the town having never having achieved more than a handful of buildings — Mandeville still had land remaining in the original land company's name.

'This left doubts about ownership of some land we wanted and it became a real legal complication. The lawyers were able to do very well out of it all,' Colin recalled.

THE CROYDON AIRCRAFT Company, employing 11 people, has become the largest restorer of vintage civil aircraft in Australasia. About 140 people throughout New Zealand belong to the Croydon Aviation Heritage Trust, which assists the funding of specific restoration and building projects, and takes care of aeroplanes kept or stored at Mandeville. The Trust will also enable the Croydon Aircraft Company to continue even if any of the present key people step out.

Colin had to get other people involved and teach them restoration work they had not done before. 'There was no point in establishing a company if it did not have the capability to do what Maeva and I wanted it to do,' he said.

Adele Scott is one of three women working at the Old Mandeville Airfield. She started by helping her father, Russell Scott, with fabric work and airframe assembly. For a time she drove herself to Mandeville each day from Owaka, the round trip taking three hours. According to Maeva, Adele's fabric work is excellent.

'We took Adele to the Warbirds Over Wanaka air show where she was shown some of the very good restoration work being done there. Adele was impressed with the Wanaka work and then she surprised us with, "But I don't know what all the fuss is about. I could do better!"'

Gerald Grocott, a New Zealander, became involved when he wanted someone to look after his Gipsy Moth, ZK-AEJ, while he went to live in Europe and fly for Swissair. Gerald is now a director of the Croydon Aircraft Company, and his Gipsy Moth is part of the Mandeville collection.

'This is New Zealand's only airworthy de Havilland Gipsy Moth and also the oldest registered aircraft,' Colin Smith told me as his gaze fixed on the silver sculpture of the aeroplane, stored with its wings folded. 'The Gipsy Moth biplane was the first really reliable aeroplane and the type flown by Jean Batten, Francis Chichester, Aline Quin, and all those early intercontinental aviators. AEJ is a special DH60M metal racing Moth made for Alan Butler, an employee of de Havilland, who wanted to compete for the 1930 King's Cup in the Round Europe Challenge de Tourisme Internationale. The aeroplane had various modifications and streamlining features which probably contributed to Butler finishing second in the race. The same year this aeroplane, with a new French owner, won the Coupe Zenith race around France.

'It was rebuilt in New Zealand for Gerald Grocott by Temple Martin, who is a well-known Moth expert, and started flying again in July 1987. We are rather lucky to have this aeroplane at Mandeville. It was a special one-off Gipsy Moth and we believe it is almost original, as it was when it was built for Alan Butler.'

The economic viability of the Croydon Aircraft Company relies on Colin Smith finding owners for many of the aeroplanes he restores. He sources fine old aeroplanes in New Zealand or from overseas, and finds people who will pay to have them rebuilt. A restored Tiger Moth with an overhauled engine ready for another 1500 flying hours will cost about $150,000. Completed aeroplanes may either leave Mandeville or remain to be cared for and displayed by the Croydon Aviation Heritage Trust, and flown by Croydon Air Services to earn income for the owner and the trust.

'We've avoided restoring the heavy military machines as they do at Wanaka, and have stuck to the light civil aeroplanes. These are priced in a bracket many more people can afford. And early civil aeroplanes, especially, interest me the most. They are definitely lovely old aeroplanes,' Colin said.

'We have so far completely restored nine aeroplanes from the ground up. Others have involved major work but not a total restoration. We also make assemblies or singular components such as a set of wings or fuel tanks. At the moment we have aeroplanes here from India, Canada, France, and all sorts of places. We are restoring a Fox Moth that was once used by the Flying Doctors in Australia. The owner lives in Perth.

'A recent addition to the hangar infrastructure has been an engine overhaul shop where we have employed an engineer with the necessary Civil Aviation Authority licences. This makes us completely self-sufficient. You would have to go to the United States or the United Kingdom to see veteran civil aircraft restoration on this scale. And Maeva, as a Croydon Aircraft Company director, has played as big a role in all this as I have.'

An early project was rebuilding another former Air Travel (NZ) Ltd Fox Moth, ZK-AEK, completed in May 1993. The aeroplane had originally belonged to the Prince of Wales (later King Edward VIII) before arriving in New Zealand in October 1935. It had an illustrious life in New Zealand that included a crash on Franz Josef Glacier in October 1943 (see Chapter Three). Its flying days supposedly ended in 1957 when its airworthiness certificate was suspended after another crash while joyriding in Fiji.

'The remaining components of AEK were found in Fiji and in Wellington, and we were asked if there were sufficient pieces for a restoration. It presented us with quite a challenge but most parts had been located except for the wooden fuselage, which had rotted away like an old tea chest. The restoration was commissioned in 1990 by an Englishman, Roger Fiennes, who wanted to fly the aeroplane back to England via Japan, China, and across Russia. He also knew that Captain Mercer's original Fox Moth ZK-ADI was in England, owned by Brian Woodford, and was flying with the historic registration G-

Jet airline captain and owner of veteran aeroplanes, Gerald Grocott, poses with his Fox Moth ZK-ADI. The de Havilland Fox Moth 'was one of the great designs of the 1930s. It still looks great.' ROY SINCLAIR

ACDD and in the Prince of Wales Guard's colours. Fiennes thought this misrepresentation was a sham and to settle a wager he wanted to arrive in England flying the real historic aeroplane.

'We got to know Roger Fiennes when we supplied fuel tanks for a group of Tiger Moths that flew from the UK to Russia. He was one of those pilots. As it turned out, more recently, he wasn't able to get a clearance to fly the Fox Moth across Russia owing to the chaotic conditions created there by the former Soviet Union. So we shipped the aeroplane to the United States where Roger flew it extensively and ended up at the famous Oshkosh '93 air show in Wisconsin. He then shipped the aeroplane to the UK. The following year AEK was purchased by Sir Tim Wallis and returned to New Zealand to become part of the Wanaka civil aircraft collection. Sir Tim had visited us during the three years we spent restoring AEK and expressed considerable interest in the aeroplane. We said if he was prepared to be patient AEK could be up for sale once Roger Fiennes had proved his point.'

OUTSIDE, AS WE stand in the warm autumn sunshine, the Fox Moth ZK-ADI, now expertly controlled, flies back across the airfield, slip-turns onto final approach, and touches the grass briefly before taking to the air once again. Gerald Grocott had purchased ZK-ADI a year previously from Brian Woodford. The Fox Moth had been in flying condition, but when it arrived at Mandeville (disassembled for shipping) in September 1996 Colin Smith found it needed more work than was anticipated.

1934 or 1997? ZK-ADI reenacts the past as it flies near the Haast Pass in South Westland while en route to an air show at Westport in February 1997.
SHARON HENDRIKS

Veteran Fox Moths, ZK-ADI and ZK-AEK, in formation over the South Westland coast. Both aeroplanes, as part of Captain Bert Mercer's Air Travel (NZ) Ltd fleet, flew people and supplies to isolated South Westland settlements during the 1930s. SHARON HENDRIKS

'It had apparently been involved in a few accidents, and repairs had been done with the focus on localised areas that had been damaged, with little regard for the alignment of the whole aeroplane. As a result, we had an aeroplane that was out of "truth". I knew it would not fly nicely as it was. We started in October and ended up spending four months working on it instead of the expected two. It is not a complete restoration but we wanted to bring it up to a standard of safety where we could carry passengers.

'When we replaced the exterior fabric (the material used is linen, cotton, or ceconite) small pieces of the old fabric were sent out with our Croydon Aviation Heritage Trust newsletters. All our members have a piece of the old ADI.'

The restoration was completed in time for a special air show at Westport in February 1997. ZK-ADI was flown to Westport via South Westland, accompanied by ZK-AEK (still in its Prince of Wales navy blue), and a twin-engine Dominie ZK-AKY. ZK-ADI was flown by Rob Hall-Jones of Te Anau.

'We landed at Big Bay to experience what must have been a real miracle in the mid-1930s when Captain Mercer flew supplies, including *The Press* newspaper, from Hokitika to those isolated South Westland settlements,' says Colin.

WHEN ZK-ADI MAKES its third landing and taxies back to the hangar, the pilot is looking smugly pleased. Gerald Grocott has about 14,000 airline flying hours recorded in his Pilot Logbook but admits 12,000 of those were made with a cup of coffee in one hand. Airline flying, according to Gerald, is just a means to an end. He goes to work in his 'office' like anyone else. The only difference is that Gerald's 'office' happens to go along at 500 knots. 'When you fly big aeroplanes everything's organised for you. If you fly IFR (Instrument Flight Rules) it's even easier.

'That's not real flying, is it? Here, you have got to think about everything quite differently: what is the weather doing? Or, how much lift will I get off that hill? There's no autopilot; you're polling (driving) the Fox Moth along yourself. You can't even see straight ahead to where you're going, especially on approach to the airfield. What you need to see is hidden by the engine cowling. That's a bit daunting. You have two choices; you either don't see at all, or you move the nose one way or the other, have a wee look, and put it back where it should be. You have to do that with all biplanes but this one's worse because it has a guppy belly. If you make a curving approach and slide-slip a bit it helps a little, otherwise it's by guess and by God. And you don't see anything during the last little bit of the landing anyway. You wouldn't want to do your first solo in a Fox Moth!

'There's added stress whenever you land a valuable old aeroplane on a small strip. It's easier on the long strip we have at Mandeville.'

But none of the difficulties detract from the sheer enjoyment of flying a veteran de Havilland. Just one exhilarating hour in the air can wipe out the memories of hundreds of hours spent airline flying. And

ZK-ADI at Big Bay, South Westland, in February 1997. The pilot is Rob Hall-Jones.
SHARON HENDRIKS

as he continues to talk about 'real flying' my heartbeat quickens in anticipation of the words I have been wanting to hear. Finally, in his quiet, reassuring voice Gerald says, 'Well Roy, how about a flight?'

Helen and I are strapped into a seat in ADI's cramped but enclosed cabin, supposedly designed to carry four passengers. It is best described as like sitting inside a slightly enlarged baby's pram while being pushed backwards — and it would probably not be a good place to be during an overshoot! The cabin, in a sense, is an add-on to the Tiger Moth; the Fox Moth was the brainchild of de Havilland's designer, Arthur Hagg, who also had a passion for yachting and wanted to carry his family quickly to the coast. Hagg had, in effect, designed the world's first mini-airliner, which was used to begin several of the world's great airlines, including Air New Zealand.

We are separated from the pilot, who sits behind and above us in an open cockpit equipped with its basic instruments — airspeed indicator, altimeter, RPM gauge, oil pressure gauge, compass, and turn-and-bank (slip) indicator. ADI also has a radio for use when flying within controlled air space. Soon the grass is rushing past the orderly maze of wires and struts strung between upper and lower wings. Fixed to one strut is an ancillary airspeed indicator operated by the rush of air. It indicates 60 knots as we leap into the sky.

It is our first flight in a veteran aeroplane and despite our airline pilot being off the leash and using us to complete his type-rating, it is very much like flying in any other small aircraft as we cruise jauntily along tree-lined rivers, past small lakes, and beside low hills. We predictably slip-turn to line up with the runway; the throttle is closed, briefly, then opened as we accelerate and climb out from the second takeoff. The landing, a little rough and followed by a steep climbing turn, adds some excitement to the flight. Once we are levelled out our pilot promises 'no more frights' through a porthole window he opens between his cockpit and the passenger cabin. All too soon we land after the third takeoff and circuit. Swissair's Captain Gerald Grocott has renewed his Fox Moth type-rating.

DECIDEDLY UNASSUMING, GERALD Grocott is not the archetypal airline captain. He talks quietly but confidently. The only give-away is the professionalism learned from years of strict airline training, which emerges as he talks endearingly about flying the old aeroplanes. Despite the dashing slip-turn approaches and steep climbing turns, his ultimate goal is to fly well and for his passengers to feel exhilarated but secure.

'I really had to concentrate to fly ADI well,' he told us. 'The only other Fox Moth I have flown was AEK at Wanaka, on a gusty day. ADI is much more sensitive — more so than a Tiger Moth. It was even more difficult to fly well when you people came for a ride. Passengers must change the centre of gravity and that reacts differently on the control surfaces.'

Gerald Grocott was born in Palmerston North in 1950 and said he eventually went to university with the idea of being an accountant. 'Then one day while I was sitting in this accountant's office I thought, "Holy shit. Is this going to be my life?" I promptly struck being an accountant off the list.

Flashback. Children rush to greet Captain Mercer who has just stepped from his cockpit after landing ZK-ADI on Bruce Bay beach in 1935.
LEO WHITE

'My Dad was fascinated by aeroplanes and he had a lot of friends at the nearby Ohakea Air Force Base. We went to a lot of flying events there. When my Dad died I had to think seriously about doing something rather than goofing around for the rest of my life. I worked out what options were left — after accounting — and figured flying would be fun.

'Eric Dalcombe had a flying school at Wanganui so I clocked in and started early one January. By the end of October I had my Commercial Pilot's Licence and instrument rating, the whole deal costing $2400. Those days everyone wanted to get into NAC (National Airways Corporation) but I was turned down because I

Captain JC (Bert) Mercer, right, who pioneered airline flying in New Zealand, and one of his pilots, JD Hewett, with the Fox Moth ZK-AEK at Waiho (Franz Josef) in the mid-1930s. THE PRESS

needed more experience. I did a flight instructor's rating and worked at the Hawke's Bay Aero Club and the East Coast Aero Club at Hastings. NAC had another intake at the beginning of 1973 and they were silly enough to accept me.'

Gerald was flying Boeing 737s when he left, about the time of the NAC merger with Air New Zealand in 1978; an unhappy time for former NAC people. He was single, earning a lot of money, paying a lot of tax and itchy-footed. 'I shot through to enjoy a holiday in Europe and saw this rare opportunity to join Swissair. The airline is not normally allowed to employ foreigners. I joined with 29 others and began flying DC-9s.

'I liked the idea of living in the centre of bustling Europe where there's a lot of interesting world to look at. Mandeville is quite the opposite. My friends in Switzerland just don't understand why I spend a month of my year down here at a little grass airfield in the middle of nowhere, and where the nearest town is a place you wouldn't stop at anyway. "What's the attraction?" they ask, and I say, "I don't really know; it's just nice. It's a neat little spot. You will have to come along and have a look." Mandeville is away from controlled air space. You can take off and do whatever you want without having to ask anyone. You can't do that in Europe.'

Gerald became a shareholder of the Croydon Aviation Company after his first visit to Mandeville in 1990 during a north-to-south Tiger Moth rally. He believed Colin Smith's expertise should be recognised and he saw the Old Mandeville Airfield as a venture that needed to become financially secure. Over the next seven years the Croydon Aircraft Company changed from being hobby-minded to a worthwhile commercial enterprise that could pay its bills.

'These days the people at Mandeville don't make a fortune, but they don't lose a fortune either,' Gerald said.

He had attempted to buy the historic Fox Moth for the Air Travel (NZ) Ltd 60th anniversary air show, which was held in Hokitika in December 1994, but that was not to be. Later he heard that Brian Woodford was experiencing some marriage turbulence and was unsure what to do with some pieces of a large de Havilland aeroplane collection.

'I needed another aeroplane like a punch in the whatevers, but I couldn't let this one go. If you like, it was Air New Zealand's first aeroplane. I called the Woodfords and found them to be very agreeable people. I told them I would be interested in the Fox Moth because of its New Zealand heritage and I knew about Colin Smith's enthusiasm for de Havillands. Nothing more happened and just when I was getting used to the idea that the opportunity to buy ADI was probably gone, I bumped into these people again at Nairobi while on a trip with Swissair. I was having breakfast before flying off to Singapore.

'Brian said to me, "What do you intend to do with the Fox Moth, young man?" He said he had been waiting to hear from me.

'I said, "And I've been waiting to hear from you!" Six weeks later I owned the aeroplane.

'I bought the Fox Moth on a promise to Colin that if ever I were

Colin and Maeva Smith, with an almost completed Tiger Moth restoration, ZK-CCH.
ROY SINCLAIR

Beer mat from The Moth restaurant and bar at the Old Mandeville Airfield.

to sell it, it would be to the Croydon Aviation Heritage Trust. Mandeville is exactly the right place for it. I hope that one day the trust will have the funds to buy ADI from me. In the meantime it doesn't matter who owns it. We can have a bit of fun in it and experience what it was like to fly in pioneer New Zealand.'

Gerald describes the Fox Moth as one of the great designs of the 1930s, and almost 70 years later it still looks great.

'Not every aeroplane design of that era was perfect. There are very few planes around these days that people agree were great, and they were that way because of good design or good fortune. Something was right about them. The Beechcraft Staggerwing biplane was one aeroplane that was way ahead of its time. You could probably say the same about the Fox Moth.

'They have a very nice fuselage form and that is one reason why the Fox Moth was such a good workhorse. The Fox has the same 130 horsepower engine as the Tiger Moth, and the same wings, but carries about another 600 lbs and flies at the same speed. One has to ask, how does it do it?

'It has that guppy shape and the rounded teardrop front tapering off. It's the perfect aerodynamic shape for reduction of drag and creation of lift. Many aeroplanes have been a boon and have then been forgotten. This one has survived and that's amazing. Just imagine when ADI was introduced to South Westland all those years ago, painted marigold and silver to show up against the bush and the snow. There were no roads. People moved on pack horses and steam barges. God help us! Captain Mercer and this aeroplane were a huge leap forward for civil aviation in New Zealand.'

PETER HENDRIKS IS Croydon's chief pilot and flying instructor. With his wife Sharon (who has a talent for air-to-air photography) he also manages The Moth restaurant and bar, the sumptuous hospitality arm of the Old Mandeville Airfield.

'We opened The Moth in November 1996 to provide a restaurant with an aviation theme that didn't go overboard. We have our "Moth" image, which is catching on. Moths are seen on all our crockery,' Peter told us. And we even discovered the ubiquitous moths in the bottom of our coffee cups as we sipped them dry.

An intriguing Moth Clock with a rotating Gipsy Moth aeroplane is projected onto the wall above the bar. It was discovered in Europe by Gerald Grocott, who had its computerised workings slightly modified to comply with the aviation theme. A Tiger Moth wing without its fabric covering sits above the bar. A variety of aviation souvenirs including leather helmets, original French flying goggles and Moth Pot beer mugs are for sale. Very little of the old Railway Hotel is evident in The Moth, which just five months after opening was already enjoying brisk business despite its apparent isolation. Overseas visitors have said that The Moth is as stylish as any restaurant and bar in Europe.

The aim, Peter said, is to provide excellent cuisine at reasonable prices. 'We like to be affordable. Reasonable pricing also applies to the flying. A 10-minute flight in the Fox Moth or a Tiger Moth costs $45. You can have a gentle flight, or experience one or two aerobatic loops. Elsewhere it might cost $130 or more for a similar flight.

'We are getting more calls from coach tours. We can provide a convenient lunch stop and also offer flying. We can take a group of eight people in the twin-engine Dominie for $25 each.'

When he is not working in the restaurant Peter is flying and, as with everyone else working at Mandeville, he is passionate about everything he does. Aged in his mid-thirties, and with about 3000 flying hours in his logbook, and a B Cat instructor's rating, he could have become an airline pilot. But he had already turned down attractive offers of multi-engine instructing, and flying Nomads and Britten Islanders with a tourist airline.

When I asked about his aspirations he replied, 'Me? I'll probably grow old here. I have no other ambition. I am lucky to be here where I can fly many types of interesting old aeroplanes. Soon we will have a Chipmunk and a high-winged Leopard Moth. We also expect to get a twin-engine Dragonfly — one of Colin Smith's favourites — which will be one of only two in the world.

Restaurant and bar manager, as well as chief pilot and flying instructor, Peter Hendriks combines the exquisite cuisine at The Moth with the thrills of veteran aeroplane flights.
ROY SINCLAIR

'A different type of people come through here. Some trained on Tiger Moths during the Second World War and you can see tears in their eyes as they remember back through all those years and tell you, "I used to do this once," and they know it will be their last opportunity to fly in their lifetime. It's great to be a part of all that. You become very sentimental; that's what the Old Mandeville Airfield is all about.

'Younger pilots come here to do a type-rating in a Tiger Moth, or even learn to fly one from scratch and go for their first solo in a Tiger.'

WHILE COLIN SMITH is teaching another generation the skills associated with restoring old aeroplanes, Peter Hendriks is restoring an art of flying small aeroplanes, which, he said, had been lost in today's aero clubs where the focus on flying training is to prepare pilots for airlines.

'Many pilots are losing the fundamentals of aircraft handling. Modern aeroplanes almost fly themselves. Here, we are talking about footwork on rudder pedals, and stick coordination. You have to fly these aeroplanes. You can't just sit there and let the aeroplane do it all for you. We are also talking about the care and maintenance of aeroplanes. In an aero club flight line operation pilots finish their flight, hop out, and are gone. Pilots here will pull the aeroplane out of the hangar, fill it up with fuel and oil, start it up, warm up the motor and then go off and enjoy the flying. Later, they will clean down the aeroplane with an oily rag before pushing it back into the hangar.

'All our aircraft are tail wheel types and most do not have wing flaps. We have to retrain pilots to land a tail wheel aeroplane. A pilot who can master a tail wheeler will get into a modern aeroplane and land it sweetly every time.

'We don't use the radio very much, just hand signals. While exposed to the airflow of an open cockpit, hand signals are easier to understand.'

Peter talked about taking the veteran aircraft on longer flights such as to the Westport air show. 'We landed at Big Bay and people came out of the bush carrying their letters for posting. They had seen "Royal Mail" on ADI's fuselage. We said we would take their mail and we posted it at the next town.'

Finally, Peter told me the Old Mandeville Airfield with its Croydon Aircraft Company was Colin Smith's dream. 'He's the granddad of the whole thing. We are here to help him fulfil his dream to restore and fly what may become the world's largest collection of beautiful old de Havilland aeroplanes — perhaps even with the twin-engined DH88 Comet, and the DH89 Mosquito.

'Gerald and I have absolutely no problems with flying aeroplanes Colin has rebuilt. A test flight is always a non-event. We have watched him work. He is meticulous. He knows all about the art of rigging an old biplane and he will say, "I can tell by the way it rigs, the way it will test fly." I enjoy helping Colin whenever I can, even if it is just sweeping up the floor.'

The DH90 Dragonfly, one of Colin Smith's 'prettiest aeroplanes', may one day join the Mandeville aeroplane collection. This one, ZK-AFB, was photographed in December 1946 when it belonged to the Canterbury Aero Club. In 1961 it was bought by Brian Chadwick. The following year it disappeared while on a flight to Milford Sound.
VIC BROWNE/THE PRESS

Always keen to recall the fascinating era of flying boats, Gerald Brown demonstrates the autopilot engagement control on the Solent ZK-AMO flightdeck at Auckland's MOTAT. Roy Sinclair

CHAPTER 3

AUTOPILOTS, FLYING BOATS AND A FLEDGLING AIRLINE

Show a New Zealander an aeroplane, and a path will be beaten to the door.
Gerald Brown

A CHANCE REMARK while visiting Auckland's Museum of Transport and Technology (MOTAT) early in 1995 introduced me to a truly remarkable man whose experiences touch New Zealand's fledgling aspirations for international aviation. I was in a dingy but cosy shed beside the aviation hangar and enjoying a cup of tea with Ray Gasparich, Eddie Tredrea, Jack and Mary Shorthouse, Geoff Freer and others involved with the restoration of the world's last Short S.45A Solent Mark 4 flying boat. ZK-AMO *Aranui* had run the famous TEAL Coral Route from Suva to Tahiti until September 1960. Most members of the Solent Flying Boat Preservation Society had worked with ZK-AMO when it was flying. The Wednesday morning get-together and working bee had attracted a good turnout of people who were mostly strangers to me. As one of them filed past, Ray Gasparich said casually, 'Oh, that's Gerald Brown. In August 1939 he flew to New Zealand on the delivery flight of the first TEAL Empire-class flying boat *Aotearoa*.'

I made a note of Gerald's phone number. Two days later I arrived on the doorstep of a neat Mt Roskill apartment where I was greeted by a tall Englishman of impeccable speech and manners. His welcome

TEAL's flying boats under construction at the Short Bros' workshop in Rochester, Kent, in February 1939. The prow of Aotearoa *is on the right.*
THE PRESS

was as genuine as his enthusiasm for aeroplanes, and a cup of tea immaculately presented in a china cup was soon dissipating the effects of a sultry Auckland morning. Then began a fascinating story of graceful four-engined flying boats plying the famous Far Eastern Imperial Route from England, down to Australia and, finally, New Zealand.

Gerald had been a specialist technician working for Smiths Aircraft Instruments Ltd, manufacturers of the autopilot fitted to the early TEAL flying boats. Aboard *Aotearoa* he arrived in Auckland on 28 August 1939, just five days before the Second World War was declared. He soon realised he was in for an involuntary stay, which he was able to put to good use assisting TEAL as the airline prepared for its trans-Tasman air services, and meeting and marrying Jeanne Gray, the chief engineer's secretary. In 1942, with Jeanne, he returned to England to work through the remainder of the war at Farnborough's Royal Aircraft Establishment. But he had been so impressed by what he had seen of New Zealand, and the capabilities of New Zealand airmen — especially Captain John Burgess, who had piloted *Aotearoa* — he knew he would have to return.

'Show a Kiwi an aeroplane and a path will be beaten to the door,' Gerald told me. 'Kiwis have always been infatuated by aeroplanes. You have only to look at the numbers of New Zealanders who joined the Royal Air Force during the Second World War. It was disproportionate to the population of their country.'

DURING THE LATE 1920s and 1930s Gerald Brown was growing up in Sussex. He became a frequent visitor to the Cinque Ports Flying Club at the Lympne aerodrome. It was a very old First World War aerodrome used by people like Jean Batten, Amy Johnson, Jim Mollison, and other early intercontinental aviators. Being so close to the English Channel, it was the last hopping-off point from England for anyone doing those early intercontinental flights.

'My father was a club pilot when my brother and I were schoolboys. Taking turns in the front seat, we grew up with Gipsy Moth biplanes. It became a family ritual each weekend, travelling from our home near Hastings, and over Romney Marsh to the aerodrome. In 1935 my brother got a flying scholarship with the *Daily Mail*. The newspaper saw that England was not very well prepared for anything to do with the air and 10 scholarships were offered for the whole of Britain. My father then bought his own monoplane and I learned to fly, and took my Private Pilot's 'A' licence in 1936.'

It was Gerald Brown's flying experience that helped to get his first job in an east London company, making autopilot units for the Air Ministry. 'The job I got was in a test laboratory. We worked at three or four oscillating tables tuning or adjusting these units so that hour after hour they would plug away and work within the very strict limits required for acceptance by the Air Ministry.

'What we were really looking at was the very early development of the flight simulator. Some Royal Air Force heavy bomber squadrons were using our autopilots. It was the early days of such flying control equipment. Smiths made one of only two autopilots in the world. The other was the American Sperry, evolved by Elmer Sperry and first used in the Curtiss flying boat in 1912.'

Gerald was working with the Smiths Aircraft Instruments Mark IA autopilot, which had three axis controls, for elevator, rudder and ailerons, and two gyroscopes. One gyroscope controlled the rudder and elevator, and the other the ailerons. It was all driven by compressed air at 35 psi. Each gyro was spun 12,000–13,000 rpm by air. Servo motors were operated through a system of valves, also by air, to apply actual pressure onto the aircraft controls.

'After working for a year or two for Smiths, the firm sold a licence to the Italian Fiat company to manufacture the English Mark 1A autopilot. So when I was aged 21, in 1937, I was sent to Italy with a young RAF Flying Officer who, having been invalided with ear trouble from a bomber squadron, had joined the Smiths company.'

Gerald's colleague was Patrick Talbot. The two young men were instructed by Smiths to check the autopilot installations as they worked with the Italian engineers and flight crews. The autopilots were being fitted to a variety of military and civil aircraft.

'We effectively became the installation and testing department, sometimes working at the Italian Air Force's research, development and test centre, Guidonia, near Tivoli. This was Italy's equivalent to Britain's Farnborough Royal Aircraft Establishment. We were commuting to and from Italy for a couple of years as the Second World War was brewing up. One day when Patrick and I were relaxing in a Rome coffee shop he said, "No other people would have a job like this anywhere in the world. There are hardly any autopilots about anyway, and here we are working with them in a foreign country."

'Mussolini, the Italian Fascist dictator, had said very clearly that he was on Hitler's side, and there we were in this most unusual situation — fitting and checking autopilot installations, ground testing, and flying with the Regia Aeronautica. The only way to get the autopilot adjusted in a new aeroplane was to fly with it, so we got to know some of the Italian Air Force pilots pretty well.

'We worked with a very impressive Savoia-Marchetti SM.79 tri-motor monoplane bomber; the Fiat BR 20 twin-engine bomber; Fiat G 18, a twin-engined airliner similar to the Douglas DC-2; and various other transport aircraft.'

GERALD SAID IT helped to know how to fly an aeroplane when setting up an autopilot, and it was all somewhat complicated. The autopilots performed exceedingly well when everything was running smoothly but they could also become temperamental. Air is a very good medium but at high altitudes any moisture in the systems would freeze up. By this time an autopilot had become known, informally, as 'George'. In England a popular household appliance of the 1930s was being promoted in a flying magazine and the catchline was, 'Let George do it.' Once the RAF pilots cottoned on to the catchline they would quote it whenever they engaged the autopilot, and the name has stuck.

'In Italy, the Italian engineers and air crew were very pleasant to work with. The only nasty side of being in Italy was Mussolini and his Fascists. They were a real pain in the neck, making it as difficult as possible for anyone English or French. It was eventually suggested we had

Two veteran flying boats, the British Empire-class G-ADUT and the ill-fated Pan American Sikorsky Clipper II, on Auckland's Waitemata Harbour in December 1937. Both aircraft had just made survey flights to New Zealand. NZ HERALD

better return to England for the last time in April 1939. On the eve of our departure the Fiat management presented both Patrick and me with a 24-inch-tall model of Christopher Columbus's ship, the *Santa Maria*. The beautifully hand-carved models had been made by a talented Fiat employee who was an enthusiast of Columbus's ship and his fifteenth-century voyages to the New World. My model of Columbus's ship has also been round the world.'

As soon as Gerald and his companion arrived back at Smiths in England they were told, 'You two had better get down to Rochester in Kent. New Zealand has bought three Short Brothers long-range flying boats and they are fitting them out with Smiths' autopilots.'

The flying boats were going to fly to New Zealand and start the TEAL airline service across the Tasman Sea between New Zealand and Australia, the last link along the Far Eastern Imperial Route from England. By 1939 flying boats from England were going right down to Sydney, with Qantas people flying them beyond Singapore. They were the high-winged Short S.23, C class Empire flying boats, the largest and most advanced British aircraft of the mid-1930s. Imperial Airways, being in a hurry to introduce services across the Atlantic and

Captain Edwin Musick, second from right, arriving ashore in Auckland with his Pan American crew, in 1937. Musick was soon to become a martyr of pioneer intercontinental airline flying.
NZ HERALD

to the Far East, ordered 24 from a design on Shorts' drawing table. This was despite Shorts' protest that they should first build a prototype to see how well it flew. *Canopus*, the first S.23, took off from Rochester's River Medway in July 1936. Four 920 hp Bristol Pegasus gave a maximum speed of 200 mph over a range of 700 miles. Just 18 months later *Centaurus*, a special long-range version, piloted by Captain John Burgess, made a survey flight from England to New Zealand.

'We were in on the early testing of another new type of long-range S.30 Empire flying boat, even as the first one, *Australia* — the one that never got to New Zealand — came off the slips. Lankester Parker was Shorts' test pilot. He was a very experienced pilot, having flown since the First World War. When the first two flying boats, *Australia* and *Awarua*, were delivered to Imperial Airways they made a number of flights as far as India and back.

'These flying boats for TEAL had slightly less powerful but more economic 890 hp Bristol Perseus engines, new long-range tanks, and quite a bit of different equipment. So I went "down the line" to India and back several times with *Australia* and Patrick went on *Awarua*.

'At that time Imperial Airways crews were not familiar with the Smiths' pneumatic autopilot. They had previously had the Sperry. We always claimed, rightly or wrongly, that the slight elasticity you get when air pressure is applied to the controls via the servo motors was an advantage, being easier on the aeroplane. The Sperry, which was also a very good autopilot, used oil as a medium, which we reckoned applied a much more solid pressure.

'It was quite uncanny when an aeroplane was flying under autopilot; the rudder pedals and control column, without any human assistance, moved as if they had a mind of their own. You could give the control column a good shove and the aeroplane would, of course, respond but it would immediately come back to datum again. Those early autopilots were very accurate and were able to pick up a fraction of a degree in deviation.'

SKIPPER BURGESS, AS Gerald Brown called him, never got a great deal of publicity but 'without a doubt he would have been New Zealand's No 1 flying boat pilot'. He was very experienced and extremely able. He attended Wellington College, and then went to England early in the 1930s for a short-service commission with the RAF. He was among many young South Africans and Australians who were also looking for an opportunity to get into flying. He was able to get quite a bit of flying boat experience with the RAF so when he resigned his commission he joined Imperial Airways and was soon flying the London–Paris route.

'I flew quite a lot with Skipper Burgess and he was a magnificent natural pilot. His navigation was faultless. In 1937 he had been picked to fly *Centaurus* on the entire survey route to New Zealand. He was chosen from all the Imperial skippers, and there were a lot of them. But he arrived in Auckland disappointed to discover that *Centaurus* was not to be the first large flying boat to land on Waitemata Harbour. Two days earlier Captain Edwin Musick had arrived flying his Pan American Airways Sikorsky Clipper II. Pan American was also using a flying boat to open up a route through the South Pacific from San Francisco.

'A famous photograph shows Burgess and Musick together in Auckland. It was a terrible disaster when the American flying boat blew up soon after taking off from Samoa on its return flight. No one is sure what happened, but it is thought they were trying to jettison fuel after an engine failure, and the fuel ignited. They had reported engine trouble soon after takeoff. It was the early days of fuel jettison. We had no facility to jettison fuel on our flying boats. It's a common thing these days, of course, but it was a highly dangerous thing to do then. Skipper Burgess was flying back to Australia when he heard of the disappearance of his American counterpart and offered to go and look for the Clipper. But it was soon realised there would only be a few bits to be found anyway. Captain Musick became one of the martyrs of pioneer intercontinental flying. Musick Point in Auckland is named after him.'

'I WAS ABOUT to go to India again with *Australia* in August 1939 when TEAL's flagship *Aotearoa* arrived at Hythe from Shorts' with all the final mods and so on, and was to be delivered to New Zealand by Skipper Burgess. Someone from Smiths was to go to New Zealand to monitor the autopilot and, as Patrick was married, I volunteered. We left from Southampton on 16 August, and arrived in Auckland on 28 August. Then, war broke out in Europe.'

In a sense, flying to New Zealand was just another job for the young technician from Smiths. He boarded *Aotearoa* with a pile of technical literature and his special tools for 'George'. He expected he might need to stay in New Zealand for a while, until the new airline, TEAL, got going and the crews familiarised themselves with the autopilot. He would then be on his way back to England where

Smiths would find him another job to do. For some people, flying 12,000 miles (almost 20,000 km) on barely established air routes might have been a nerve-racking experience.

'Oh no, it was not nerve-racking,' Gerald assured me. 'When you look back you might say, "Gosh we were stretching our luck a bit." But, those days, I was always mad keen on aeroplanes and I was only too happy to be engaged in a very interesting occupation. And the reliability of engines was getting pretty good. Four engines were considered an absolute necessity, and became the fashion. An aeroplane could stay up on three engines, and later, on two.'

The early starts were the worst part of the flight: 'Shaving at 3.15 am is a poor way to start a day.' *Aotearoa* was at Southampton's berth 108, close to where the famous liner *Queen Mary* berthed. In the gloomy pre-dawn light and the slight sea mist, which would not help the takeoff, the flying boat looked somewhat sinister.

'We (the nine delivery flight crew) were soon piling in after our considerable luggage, and the Imperial Airways engineers were wishing us "bon voyage". Then, with all doors and hatches closed, the starting-up patter began. Cabin lights went out, leaving us in darkness as, one by one, the props revolved and caught. Then all four motors were running. We were free from the buoy and warming up for

Heralding a new era of international aviation and the founding of New Zealand's Tasman Empire Airways Ltd, Aotearoa, *piloted by Captain John Burgess, arrives in Auckland on 28 August 1939.*
WHITES AVIATION

taxiing. We strapped in, the last S-turn brought us into the wind, the four engines bellowed up to takeoff boost, and in a matter of seconds we were off the water and on our way towards France.'

TEAL's S.30 flying boats were designed to carry 19 passengers on a lower deck. A flying crew of four — skipper, first officer, flight engineer, and radio operator were located on the upper deck. Flying boats, having no need for land-based airfields, were thought to be the key to future international aviation. Being half boat and half aeroplane, they were referred to as a 'ship' as often as they were called an aircraft.

During the delivery flight, which went 'down the line' to Greece, Palestine and the Middle East, India, Burma, Siam, Singapore, Darwin, Sydney, and Auckland, Gerald Brown's job was to monitor the autopilot and make any necessary adjustments and repairs.

'After about 10 minutes I climbed aloft to check that "George" had engaged properly. It had. Skipper Burgess and first officer Bill Craig, also a New Zealander, were letting the "ship" fly itself as they set about their other duties. On the upper deck the noise was considerable and the engines in the darkness were an amazing sight. The pipes running into the exhaust collector rings were ruby red and the main exhaust stacks were blasting out solid sheets of blue-white flame. Reflecting,

Captain JW Burgess arriving in Auckland on 28 August 1939.
THE PRESS

morbidly, how close these flames were to our long-range 1750-gallon fuel tankage, I went below to doze as flight steward Ray Phillips, a Tasmanian from Imperial Airways, checked out his pantry.'

More welcome was the clear dawn, and breakfast, before landing in bright morning sunlight at the marine airport of Marseilles. Gerald Brown was required to provide a daily report of the flight to Smiths. He went one better and kept a detailed diary, which has since been printed and sold to raise funds for the Solent Flying Boat Preservation Society. The diary recalls an idyllic, albeit challenging era of aviation during those final uncertain days of peace as the world prepared for war.

IT TELLS OF landing on sheltered marine waterways marked out by launches, taxiing among ships of the Royal Navy's Mediterranean fleet and stopping close to the towering bows of the aircraft carrier, HMS *Glorious*. At Palestine, skipper Burgess collects a bottle of Galilee water to take to New Zealand for the christening of his new baby. Nights are sometimes spent in grand hotels. Flying over desert in hot bumpy weather, in an aeroplane devoid of any wheeled landing gear, is one of the more uninviting aspects of the flight. It is a good time to keep busy and not look out the window until, when almost at Baghdad, '*a particularly large bump causes "George" to cut out and nearly puts us on our ear*'.

They touch down on Baghdad's Lake Habbaniyeh to make adjustments to the autopilot, and end the day at Basra where, a few days previously, *Australia* had ploughed into a sandbank during her takeoff run. Gerald records his sadness at seeing the crippled flying boat that had taken him on his previous trial flights. '*I manage to get taken over to* Australia *to check that her "George" installation is all right, which it is. I feel sad to see her like this, but she will be repaired and flown back to England.*'

(*Australia*, ZK-AMB, originally intended for the TEAL fleet, was repaired and taken over by Imperial Airways. It was subsequently lost during enemy action at Lisbon.)

A 15-hour day flying 2000 miles (3200 km), taking *Aotearoa* from Calcutta to Singapore, breaks all the early-rising records.

> *When we assemble in the hotel vestibule at 2 am everyone seems a little on edge. Paddy Cussans, our radio operator, is missing and the skipper threatens to leave without him. At the last minute, down rushes Paddy, still dressing, and off we go. The day also ends in darkness as we circle Singapore, losing height and peering down at a tiny flare path looking ridiculously inadequate for our needs.*

A final circuit brings *Aotearoa* over the city:

> *the mass of lights rush by, throttles come back, a ship's mast seems to flash by below the wing then, through the side windows, a smear of orange light shows we are on our flare path. The welcome swishing noise heard as we touch increases to the harsh drumming and thumping of water as the keel dips in, and we've arrived in Singapore.*

I HAD BEEN able to get a copy of the diary before I met Gerald, and I was keen to ask him about his entry on 26 August as they flew from Darwin to Sydney. Despite flying being a serious business, it appears ex-RAF flyers were not averse to a bit of fun, especially when the skipper was not about. Skipper Burgess had gone down with Dengue fever; under normal circumstances they would have stayed in Darwin for a few days until he recovered.

'He certainly had a high temperature,' recalled Gerald Brown, 'but we had heard that a Boeing Clipper flying boat was also on its way to Auckland from San Francisco. Skipper Burgess had been pipped two years before by Captain Musick and, not wanting to be beaten again, was all for pressing on. He was there for the takeoff and then went below to rest on his bunk. I was asked to be supernumerary first officer and, naturally, I was very pleased to do so as I took the second pilot's seat next to Bill Craig.

'At Mackay, a small coastal town in Queensland, they were having a special pageant to open some harbour facility. The authorities had wired the skipper asking if we could show them *Aotearoa* as we flew over. Well, Craig was quite a character and he would enjoy few things more than a good beat up. Our flying boat, despite its size, had enough power to perform quite an impressive beat up once the pilot yanked it up with the control column and kicked on the rudder. It was definitely not the sort of thing that was done with passengers aboard, that was for sure.

'Arriving over Mackay, "George" was disengaged and for the next five minutes the even tempo of our flight was broken as Bill pulled the flying boat into a steep turn round the town at 1000 feet. We saw the official ship decorated and moored and Bill said, "That'll do for a start," and down goes the nose, and down goes *Aotearoa* with quite a lot of engine. The ship had two masts and a lot of bunting strung between them.

'With the air speed indicator climbing through 200 mph we swept across the ship. I can't recall how low we were because we had a little problem with the trailing aerial, which was causing us some alarm.

Paddy Cussans, our radio operator who had been seconded from Imperial Airways for the flight, had forgotten to wind the aerial in and was frantically starting to do so. By this time Craig already had the nose up and was making a tight turn before diving towards the main street running from the harbour. I was craning my neck to see if the bunting was still there. It was, but I will never know why, for we were plumb across the two masts as we pulled up and the aerial must have swung down.

'In a shallow dive *Aotearoa* picked up a lot of speed and went straight up the street.'

When I asked Gerald how low they were flying he replied, 'Very low.' From the right-hand second pilot's seat it appeared as if they were just clearing the rooftops on either side. The very deep hull of the flying boat would have been even lower!

'I will never forget watching a cyclist right ahead of us. At first he was unaware and then he turned his head to see where all the noise was coming from. We were clocking 170 mph as he looked up in amazement, unable to take his eyes off this large flying boat that was apparently following him along the street. He swerved and fell to the ground, bike and all! Bill pulled the nose up and did a final circle of Mackay at 2000 feet. Back on course, we engaged "George" and continued on our way.

'We later found out that when the skipper heard the engines change note he had tried to get out of his bunk. When you do that sort of caper the skipper will want to know what's going on. However, he had some difficulty leaving his bunk, and by the time he got up to the flight deck we were sedately back on course, on our way to Brisbane. In any event, the skipper did a very impressive low-level beat up himself when we arrived over the Auckland waterfront two days later.'

ON THE FINAL day of the delivery flight they were all predictably assembled at Rose Bay, Sydney, well before dawn. 'We were by now accustomed to seeing each other in our pre-dawn state of mind but on this morning everyone seemed keyed up and keen to be off on the final leg, a 1400-mile ocean crossing to Auckland. We were airborne after a 20-second run and started on a long climb, the lights of Sydney receding into the distance.'

Gerald climbed aloft and sat between the two pilots. The autopilot had performed admirably since he adjusted it in India. Paddy Cussans was busy contacting ships and weather stations for bearings. Skipper

Aotearoa's delivery crew RS Peek, left (engineer), ER Macnamara (engineer), Mr B Knee (chief engine inspector), SJ Bardshaw (instrument engineer), G Brown (instrument engineer), Captain JW Burgess, WJ Craig (first officer), WG Cousins (senior radio officer), and RA Phillips (flight clerk).
THE PRESS

Burgess, meanwhile, had left his seat for the chart table. A missed landfall would have them ending somewhere out in the Pacific. At 6000 feet, droning above unbroken cloud, it was a monotonous flight, relieved for a short time by breakfast and, later, lunch (Sydney oysters) served by an untiring steward.

Eventually they saw a thin line on the horizon and agreed it was the coast of New Zealand, and made a landfall a little south of a direct course.

'We had been forced down by the low cloud base, and as we crossed the coast someone said, "It's just like England." And so it seemed. It was the first really green countryside we had seen since France. Cows and sheep were everywhere, and as we were below 1000 feet we were causing frequent stampedes.

'In the cabin we got busy tidying everything up and packing our clothes, which had been hung around as if the "ship" were a second-hand shop. Then we were over Auckland and, as the skipper started his fast low-level beat up, the tidying-up gang was thrown to the floor. There followed yet another faultless landing, as the skipper showed off *Aotearoa* to thousands of his fellow New Zealanders who had turned out in the rain for the arrival.

'Eventually, when I walked up from Mechanics Bay, I glanced back to see *Aotearoa* peaceful and quiet at her pontoon, almost as if she had never seen Europe, Egypt, India, and all those faraway places. She seemed to belong here.'

ONCE THE SECOND World War had been declared on 3 September 1939 the British Government was not very interested in new airlines. Gerald Brown said he would not have been at all surprised had they been told to fly *Aotearoa* back to England. But that did not happen.

'Fortunately common sense prevailed. Without *Aotearoa* New Zealand was cut off from the rest of the world, except by ship. In 1939 New Zealand did not have one other aeroplane that was capable of flying out of the country. It was 1400 miles to Sydney or up to Fiji. There was nothing else within a range of more than about 500 miles.

But the fledgling airline was almost cut off as far as spares were concerned. The British Government was not going to bother very much about TEAL's aeroplane when all the spares were needed back in the United Kingdom.

'Tasman's people at Mechanics Bay had to make things here in New Zealand they had never made before. They set up all sorts of test rigs they normally would not have had to bother with. We had to build up a whole repair organisation for the airframe, and for the engines. This all took quite a while. Then on 30 April 1940 *Aotearoa* finally got going on the first trans-Tasman service. By that time a second S.30 flying boat, *Awarua* ZK-AMC, had arrived in Auckland on 3 April 1940, flown to New Zealand by Captain Oscar Garden. The two flying boats became New Zealand's air link with the world. They plugged on right through the war.'

Gerald told me he thought it was a marvellous effort that the airline was run so successfully for four or five years in wartime — and without killing anybody. He laughed when I asked should they have killed anybody?

'Well, in those days, any airline that could say, "We've being flying five years and we haven't killed anybody," was most unusual. If you read the history of Imperial Airways, even before the war, four or five of their flying boats were lost. One ran into a hill in France. Another crashed at Brindisi, near the south of Italy. Yet another crashed in the bay at Athens, and so on.

'Navigation equipment was relatively crude. There were no long-range beacons or control towers to provide instructions for landing. Imperial Airways did have motor boats to clear a landing path but there was nobody to give you ground control approach or anything like that. You would take off from Hythe in England and the first stop would be Marseilles in France, then Rome, Brindisi, Athens, and so on. Crews had to be familiar with all the landing areas, sometimes harbours, or lakes and rivers. Landing on water required special skills. You

A-M

Despite the rain, after its delivery flight from England, Aotearoa *predictably draws a huge crowd of curious onlookers to the Mechanics Bay mooring on 28 August 1939.*
NZ Herald

would arrive and do a circuit. If you weren't quite sure where you were you would ease down a little to see, and it was very easy to run into a mountain or something else.

'In New Zealand the flying boats were running scheduled services on one of the world's longest ocean crossings, and it was stretching the capabilities of even the long-range Empire-class flying boats. They had been designed for landing on sheltered waters, and their hulls would not have survived a forced landing in the Tasman Sea in rough weather.'

In 1940 TEAL had a staff of about 70 people. Captain Burgess became TEAL's chief pilot. When a chief engineer was appointed he wanted a secretary. 'One of the young chaps working in the traffic control was a friend of Jeanne Gray, the girl I would soon marry (and who would later accompany me to a wartime Britain). He suggested she put in for this secretary's job. She had worked in a law office and although she said she didn't know anything about aeroplanes or engines, she applied for and got the job.'

After a flying boat had made a return flight to Australia it was one of Jeanne's jobs, as chief engineer's secretary, to phone up an Air Force flight lieutenant in Hobsonville and advise that the aircraft had landed in Auckland. She would say it was available until such and such a time when it would be required for its next scheduled service.

'The flying boat could then be taken over for long-range coastal command reconnaissance. We had a changeover kit that involved hanging temporary bomb racks under wings and mounting a Lewis gun on one of the upper hatches. Finally, a TEAL air crew would change into RNZAF uniform. The armament was manned by RNZAF staff.'

The air service that enabled government and military people to get to Australia in just a few hours was very important during the war. Gerald Brown went on the second flight to Australia, and on the return trip TEAL made the first trans-Tasman night flight.

'I was with *Aotearoa* and Skipper Burgess again. While we were in Rose Bay there had been a bit of bother with one of the engines. It was too late to do the normal daylight flight, so Skipper Burgess said we would fly at night. The forecast was quite good, and there would normally be following winds from Sydney to Auckland. But two hours out we ran into the dirtiest electrical storm I had ever encountered. At about 5000 feet we were right in it. It was pouring rain and the pilots' window screens were streaming. I don't think I ever flew in worse weather. St Elmo fireballs, caused by static electricity, could be seen going off under the wings. I had never seen anything like it.

'The radio operator had to wind in the trailing aerial, which meant we had no radio contact. I was worried about "George" so I went up and sat between the pilots. Bill Craig was once again our first officer and second pilot. Skipper Burgess was following the control column while Bill Craig had his feet on the rudder bar just monitoring that. They daren't risk any possibility of "George" failing and not being ready for it. If the worst happened, they could whip "George" out and still work on the blind flying instruments. We went on like that for an hour or two with no visibility and no radio signals. After a time, feeling happy that "George" was doing his job, I walked back to the navigator's table and asked, "How are we doing?"

'He said, "How the hell would I know. With no visibility and no radio, I just hope that gadget of yours is working well or we are way off course."'

Gerald said he went down into the cabin and actually slept for an hour and then went back to the flight deck.

'How are we doing now?' he asked, and Burgess replied, 'Have a look.' One starboard engine was just windmilling around. 'We've lost an engine.'

The last bit of the flight, in much improved weather, was made on three engines. The flight had taken 11½ hours, just inside the range of the flying boat.

Gerald explained that the autopilot is particularly good in rough flying conditions. 'Just imagine the strain of flying hour after hour on

Aotearoa *in Auckland after her final TEAL flight in November 1947. Over almost seven years the flying boat made more than 440 Tasman crossings.*
THE PRESS

night flying instruments. The autopilot could pick up each deflection just that little bit quicker than a human pilot could.'

These days autopilots on large airliners are integrated into sophisticated flying control and navigation systems. Gerald said whenever he flies he can tell if the autopilot is engaged, even when sitting in the passenger cabin. 'The trailing edge of the aileron is on the move all the time. It's continually on the job correcting the tiniest of deflections that would put the aeroplane off course, and often providing a smoother flight than can be achieved by hand flying.'

GERALD BROWN DID not continue working in aviation after the war. As he was married to an Aucklander, he welcomed an opportunity to return to New Zealand in 1948. His father also emigrated and established a small engineering business, which Gerald took over until 1952 when he became an engineer with a water filter company.

'New Zealanders, I already knew, were very much like English people. They were crazy about such things as aeroplanes, MG cars, and steam locomotives.'

One day in 1980 he read in the newspaper that a small group of retired TEAL and Air New Zealand people were trying to save an old Short Bros' Solent flying boat at MOTAT's Keith Park Memorial Airfield in Auckland.

'I then remembered my diary of daily notes to Smiths I had made during *Aotearoa*'s delivery flight. I had kept the diary through the war, and still had it. I went along and met Ray Gasparich, Geoff Freer, and the team. I asked these folk if they were interested in the diary, and if I could join them and give them a hand. The Solent Flying Boat Preservation Society has since given me quite an interest. Once you get bitten by aviation it never leaves you, even if you do not continue to work in it.'

IAN SEXTON OF Pukekohe, a former radar mechanic, can recall a day in September 1942 when a TEAL flying boat was approaching Auckland with apparent engine trouble. He was stationed at the RNZAF Radar Unit No. 4, at the south end of Piha beach, west of Auckland:

'I was in charge of the afternoon radar watch when our commanding officer from Whenuapai phoned to say a TEAL flying boat was coming in with engine trouble. He said the flying boat was only 20 miles out and wanted to know why we were not plotting it. I told him that we had nothing at that range. He replied that as it was only

20 miles out we should have located it. I insisted that there was nothing at 20 miles, and we got into quite a heated argument until I told him that if it was only 20 miles out then it must be down in the drink.

'"EH! WHAT'S THAT, WHAT'S THAT??!!" he roared down the phone. Just then I heard a shout from the operator on the range tube who had found a weak echo 60 miles to the west. I reported this to the commanding officer, who calmed down a little, and we plotted the plane as it came in. As it turned out it was the TEAL flying boat and when it came close I was instructed to go outside to look at it and report. As far as I could see all engines were going and it had sufficient altitude to get over the Waitakeres. It landed safely on Auckland harbour. It seems the TEAL crew were working on dead reckoning and had miscalculated their distance out when they reported being only 20 miles from Auckland.'

Gerald Brown with the carved model of Columbus's Santa Maria *presented to him by the Fiat management in April 1939. The model was an appreciation for Gerald's work fitting autopilot equipment to Italian military and civil aircraft.* ROY SINCLAIR

CHAPTER 4

The Last Great Airline Adventure

Artwork by Philip West recalls the magic of a flying boat taking off from Evans Bay, Wellington, bound for Sydney. The depicted flying boat is ZK-AMO Aranui, *now displayed in the Aviation hangar at Auckland's MOTAT.*

AIR ART PUBLICATIONS

Our Wednesday morning working bee is known as the 'Wednesday morning playcentre for veteran aviators'. But we have saved a Solent flying boat, the last of its kind in the world.

Ray Gasparich

IF, WHEN I was a teenager, I had been asked, 'What is the world's most appealing journey?' I would have said, 'A flying boat journey to a Pacific island.' Regrettably, my experiences with flying boats are limited — and I have never been to a Pacific island. I *have* watched an RNZAF Sunderland take off from Evans Bay in Wellington harbour. I *have* climbed aboard two land-bound flying boats: a Sandringham VH-BRC *Beachcomber* at Southampton's Hall of Aviation, and a Solent ZK-AMO *Aranui* in the aviation hangar at MOTAT.

Decked out in its TEAL livery, MOTAT's Solent is impressive. For size, and sheer beauty, it even overpowers a nearby immaculately restored Avro Lancaster bomber. I have visited the Auckland aviation hangar on three occasions. Each time I left with some important little task wilfully undone, as if I was ensuring a return — to take that simple additional photograph, or to talk to a particular member of the Solent Flying Boat Preservation Society.

One can climb aboard the Solent and quietly let the imagination off its leash. The inside, on two decks, is set out rather like an upmarket 1950s milk bar, or a millionaire's yacht. On the lower deck, passengers once sat around the fixed tables. The seats have provided comfort for film stars, captains of industry, royalty, and others belonging to the rich and famous set. Their hand luggage — hats and ladies' fur coats — was stored overhead in string racks, rather like those found on a first-class British railway carriage. There is a bar. And a galley is a silent witness to the great days of airline meals, when even bacon and eggs could be cooked to order.

On my most recent visit I sat in the left-hand pilot's seat for the first time. I made myself comfortable before stretching out my legs and placing my feet on huge rudder pedals. I glanced at the complex instrument panel, looking for the handful of instruments I could identify: altitude indicator, air speed indicator, slip-and-turn indicator, and a few more. I put my hands out to take a firm hold of the control column. I was there on my own. And I wondered what sort of superhuman flew such a wonderful flying machine which became a boat once it was earthbound.

ALMOST HALF A century ago, TEAL inaugurated an airline journey that was without peer. It was the Coral Route from Auckland to Tahiti, flown by Solent flying boats. By today's jet-age standards it was a leisurely flight of nearly 20 hours in the air, offering travellers long stopovers at idyllic islands. TEAL's flying boats had a certain glamorous style that was missing from other aircraft of the day. They flew as low as 3000 feet and, at a cruising speed of just 200 miles per hour, passengers were treated to magnificent views as each island appeared beyond tropical coral reefs.

The experience is one that, these days, can only be imagined — a dream that will never become a reality. But my imagination has been enhanced, even embellished, by a small number of magnificently enthusiastic people who were there.

'We would land in a spray of sea to be welcomed by the islanders with their leis and what the Tahitians call *couronnes*, or rings of scented flowers. It was all so fabulous,' recalls Irene Kingwill, a former flying boat hostess.

Surrounded by an abundance of aviation memorabilia, the world's last Solent Mk S.45 Mark 4 flying boat ZK-AMO forms the centrepiece at MOTAT's aviation museum. 'The flying boat looks very much as it did when it was on service,' says Ray Gasparich who, with other veteran aviators, has spent many years working on MOTAT's Solent project.
ROY SINCLAIR

Ray Gasparich samples 1950s airline comfort aboard the MOTAT Solent flying boat ZK-AMO. He was a ground engineer in Auckland when ZK-AMO flew the famed Coral Route to Tahiti.
Roy Sinclair

Former TEAL aviators, and members of the Solent Flying Boat Preservation Society, Captain Eddie Tredrea, left, in-flight hostess Irene Kingwill, and Flight Engineer Geoff Freer recall memories of the Coral Route as they try out the flightdeck of ZK-AMO. 'Working on the flying boats, we always felt we were important,' says Geoff Freer.
Roy Sinclair

Irene (née Zimmerman) was aged 23 when she flew the Coral Route. That was during the early 1950s when TEAL offered the sole scheduled passenger service to Tahiti, an island almost untouched by European civilisation. 'We would tell our passengers to bring their bathing costumes with their hand luggage. We stopped for about two hours at Akaiami, a small uninhabited atoll in the Cooks, while the flying boat was refuelled. Akaiami was said to be the world's only uninhabited island with an international airport. Passengers would swim in the lagoon where the water was a rich emerald green, contrasting with the deep blue of the ocean.'

Irene, a member of the Solent Flying Boat Preservation Society, has been involved with the restoration work on ZK-AMO, the world's only surviving Solent S.45 Mark 4 flying boat.

'Most of our members worked on this Solent and three others operated by TEAL on Pacific, trans-Tasman and Chatham Island routes,' says Ray Gasparich. Ray had joined TEAL in July 1941 as an engineer's assistant. He had been a ground engineer during the 1950s when the Solent *Aranui* was flying the Coral Route. In 1981 he founded the Solent Flying Boat Preservation Society, soon after retiring from Air New Zealand's training school where he was chief technical instructor.

'Sheer unadulterated enthusiasm by our members over many years has got the Solent to its present condition, where it is the centrepiece of MOTAT's aviation museum. The aircraft looks very much as it did when it was on service. If we had another $6 million we could fly it, but most of our 200 members would be against that. We have the world's last four-engine boat that went into regular passenger service. We would not want to lose it. If the aeroplane were to fly it would be necessary to modernise some of the flight deck fittings and instruments. We would no longer be able to show people what a 1950s Solent flying boat was really like.'

Ray puts the success of the Solent preservation group down to the fact that he never learned how to control people. He believes that an organisation like the Solent Flying Boat Preservation Society needs to be very social. 'We began with a Wednesday morning working bee, and we still meet every Wednesday. We are now known as the Wednesday morning playcentre for veteran aviators.'

THE BASIC SOLENT design derived from the Short Bros S.25 Sunderland, primarily a military flying boat, used extensively during the Second World War. The civil version was the S.25 Sandringham.

ZK-AML, Aotearoa II, *one of four Solent S.45 Mark 4 flying boats that plied TEAL's trans-Tasman and Pacific Island routes. ZK-AML flew with the airline from 1949 to 1955.*
SOLENT FLYING BOAT PRESERVATION SOCIETY

By the mid-1940s Short Bros were building a larger military flying boat, the Seaford. But when hostilities ceased, the company once again turned its attention to civil aviation and the Seaford became the S.45 Solent, Mark 2 and Mark 3.

Then, in 1949, Short Bros of Belfast, Northern Ireland, built four Solent S.45 Mark 4 flying boats for TEAL. They were built to strict specifications laid down by the late Sir George Bolt, who was then TEAL's chief engineer. The Mark 4 Solents were the last and most successful of the British flying boats.

'Some of the earlier flying boats, the Sandringhams in particular, failed TEAL rather badly,' recalls Ray Gasparich. 'The Sandringhams were converted Sunderlands and their American Pratt & Whitney Twin Wasp engines suffered a lot of overheating problems while on the long trans-Tasman flights. On more than one occasion TEAL came near to disaster with a Sandringham.

'When an engine failed and fuel was running low during a flight to New Zealand in December 1947 (ZK-AME *New Zealand* was returning to Sydney), a lot of passengers' luggage and bits and pieces were thrown overboard — including a bishop's garments. Some people say that by throwing away the bishop's garments the aeroplane was saved. I don't know whether that saved the aeroplane or not, but later the crew said they were "surplice" to requirements.'

The Solent represented new technology. George Bolt insisted on every piece of the flying boat being treated to protect against corrosion. For that reason the Solent has remained in excellent condition despite being stored outdoors for many years.

'But other important modifications included fitting the more powerful 2050-horsepower Bristol Hercules 733 twin-row 14 cylinder sleeve-valve piston engines, with fully feathering propellers. When an engine failed, the propeller blades could be set at right angles to the airflow to prevent drag and windmilling. The early Solents had a problem with tail heaviness, which was corrected by inserting a three-degree wedge in the wing root which moved the centre of lift rearward, but caused the engine's centre line to point outward three degrees.

'Bolt had the set of the engines changed so that their thrust line was parallel to the aircraft centre line, putting power where it was required to reduce the built-in drag of earlier Solents.'

TEAL's Solents were the first civil aircraft to arrive in New Zealand with a full Certificate of Airworthiness from the British Civil Aviation. The new flying boats considerably reduced the flying time of earlier Short Bros Empire-class, Sunderland, and Sandringhams. TEAL's Empire-class of 1939 carried 19 passengers and five crew. The Solent carried 45 passengers and six to eight crew. With a still-air range of 3000 miles, the Solent offered comfortable margins on TEAL's Tasman and Pacific routes.

TEAL inaugurated a fortnightly Auckland–Papeete service via Fiji, Samoa, and the Cook Islands on 27 December 1951, partly to create goodwill among the South Pacific island people. In May 1954 the Auckland to Suva sector was taken over by DC-6 land planes, and the Solent ZK-AMO was retained for the remainder of the flight to Papeete. In September 1960 the world's last scheduled flying boat service on an international route ended. ZK-AMO, replaced by a DC-6 aircraft, sat outdoors, forlorn, for the next 20 years.

'IT TOOK TWO and a half days to fly the Coral Route from Auckland to Tahiti,' recalls Irene Kingwill. 'In that time we got to know our 45 passengers and they would follow the crew around the island. We knew all the best nightspots. No one had much sleep the first night in Tahiti.'

In the 1950s international air travel was for the well-heeled — few New Zealanders flew the Coral Route. Irene met the Norwegian anthropologist Thor Heyerdahl of the *Kon-tiki* expedition; and in 1953 she met Sir Edmund Hillary, on his way back from climbing Mt Everest. Others were Martine Carol, the siren of the French movies, Gary Cooper, Paul Brickhill, author of *The Dam Busters*, Mr and Mrs Reynolds from Camel Cigarettes, and Harry Miller, who she describes as 'a real larrikin'.

'Passengers travelled in considerable luxury. Meals were all cooked in a full-sized oven on board, and cutlery and everything was set up on the aircraft,' says Irene. 'It was the second steward's job to do the cooking. The hostess used to set up a butter plate and little jam dish for each passenger. Every bit of cutlery had to be accounted for, as were the rugs and magazines. And woe betide if you lost one, or one was missing. We had to wash up all dishes — they were all breakable — ready for the next flight.'

FIVE FLIGHT CREW worked in a somewhat spacious flight deck. Eddie Tredrea was aged 33 when he first flew the Coral Route. He flew TEAL's flying boats for several years, starting in 1946, and retired from Air New Zealand after completing his DC-10 training in 1972. Geoff Freer was a flight engineer on Solents. He married a flying boat hostess, Jean Stanich, and also retired from flying in the DC-10 era.

'It took a lot of power to get a flying boat into the air,' Eddie tells me. 'Water went everywhere and thumped against the hull until we got up on the step. Then the drag went right away. In about 50 seconds we would cover 7000 feet of water. Fortunately, in those days when we took off from Mechanics Bay we had no Auckland harbour bridge to worry about. It was a different story at Rose Bay in Sydney. We often had to turn away from the bridge.

'Our maximum wave height was four feet, but we could drop into six-foot seas with no trouble. A short sea, when the waves were close together, often caught us out.'

During the start of the takeoff run the propeller torque tended to rotate the flying boat towards the right. To maintain a straight run the pilot would throttle back the port outer engine until, at a certain speed, the torque was negated by the forward motion. The port outer was then put up to full power. The flying boat was by then getting up on the step, having gained 90 per cent of the takeoff speed.

Geoff Freer sat in a seat facing aft, almost underneath the astrodome (a Perspex bubble above the flight engineer's position). He monitored the engine instruments, air conditioning and lighting, and kept a log of fuel consumption. Starting each engine was a two-man job. While the captain or first officer operated the starter and throttle, the flight engineer held a finger on a fuel-priming button until the engine ran smoothly. He would be standing with his finger on the primer while watching the engines through the astrodome.

If a ground engineer had inadvertently already primed an engine, it would backfire with an impressive sheet of flame. Geoff Freer says the captain would use the throttle to suck the flame back.

Occasionally the flight engineer had to go below and clean a spark plug — similar to that fitted to a lawn mower; this was an integral part of the Janitrol air-conditioning units.

'On the water, we got used to using marine terminology. We talked about port and starboard, and the bow line that tied the hull to the buoy. And, of course, our flight times were from buoy to buoy. Typical buoy-to-buoy times on the Coral Route were Auckland to Suva, 7 hours 15 minutes; Suva to Samoa, 4 hours; Samoa to Akaiami, 5 hours; and Akaiami to Papeete, 3 hours 30 minutes. It was quite an adventure. We left Auckland in this relatively small flying boat — a speck in the ocean really — going to Tahiti and back, landing at these isolated islands knowing that we had to cope with any problems and combat weather that was not always as we would expect to find among our tropical islands.

'Captain Ian Patterson had to turn back twice on one trip while flying between Akaiami and Tahiti — once because of debris in the harbour, and then because of the weather. On the third attempt there was a mechanical problem. My wife was the hostess. She returned home from that trip with ghastly recollections of passengers getting hungry and tired. When they finally landed back at Akaiami a launch came over from the main island with food.

'Don Le Beech, who ran a famous restaurant in Honolulu, was one of the passengers. He took over the cooking and everyone had a ball. Trouble was, the crew were so damn tired after all the worries associated with getting the Solent back into the air and up to Tahiti.'

Tahitians in canoes flock around the Solent flying boat Aparima at Papeete in 1951 while on a proving TEAL Auckland to Tahiti flight.
THE PRESS

At island stopovers fuel was pumped from 44-gallon drums floating on a barge. The flight engineer had a big metal funnel and filtered the fuel through a chamois leather. As much as 270 gallons would be hand-pumped.

'We used to measure fuel in the tanks by dipstick rather than rely entirely on instruments,' says Geoff Freer. 'We had to tell the captain how much fuel we had "by the dip" — 2000 gallons or whatever it was. That practice continued with DC-6s and Lockheed Electras.

'The island moorings were the most awkward of places to carry out any repairs. We had excellent facilities at Mechanics Bay in Auckland, and at Evans Bay in Wellington. But up there you were really out on a limb. Everything had to be makeshift. A spanner could become too hot to hold. And if you dropped a spanner into the tide that was the end of it. You couldn't go into a workshop and ask for another. Having a float knocked off was always a problem. Cross winds and big seas were hazardous. It was easy to knock off a float sideways. We had to hold down the other float with sacks of sand roped together to stop the aircraft overturning while we repaired the damaged float,' he says.

Irene recalls being stranded at Akaiami for seven days when a float was damaged. The passengers were rescued next day but the crew stayed on the atoll. 'We had such a wonderful time swimming on the reef. We weren't too keen on leaving once repairs were made.'

Dennis Marshall flew as chief steward with TEAL through the 1950s. He flew the Coral Route when the Solent ZK-AMO started the flight from Suva.

'If we got up to Tahiti and back to Suva without incident we gave ourselves a slap on the back. I will never forget arriving at Akaiami very early in the morning and seeing the bright iridescent lagoon with palm trees growing to the water's edge. I thought Akaiami was the most beautiful place in the entire South Pacific.'

One Akaiami stopover was especially memorable. The aeroplane was loaded, ready to go, when a defect was discovered in one of the engines. Captain Joe Shephard got permission to take off with three engines and fly on to Tahiti for repairs. But first he had to unload his passengers and leave them behind.

'Suddenly we were castaways, looking forlorn amongst large piles of alligator-skin baggage. We watched the Solent take off and vanish. Captain Shephard had promised to be back in three or four days. We had unloaded all the catering equipment, the little remaining food, and blankets.

'I was afraid of being lynched as I prepared the first meal on our island. The passengers were not equipped mentally or physically for such an adventure. A German passenger was complaining bitterly about his round-the-world bookings being wrecked. I can still hear him demanding, "Venn do ve get off dis island?"

'We had to move over to the inhabited main island to get more food. With no hotels, we slept in huts. In a plantation I killed my first pig, and we caught fish by throwing spears into the sea from the coral reef. We broke into a wine cellar in the resident agent's house. A New Zealander, he was away, but his wine was excellent. TEAL later paid to restock his cellar. Martine Carol was on the flight. She was very beautiful. With temperatures up in the 80s and 90s in the shade, Martine amused us by always wanting to swim in the nude.

'As the days went by, the passengers became less and less interested in the return of the aircraft. When it did finally return they were reluctant to leave. I was aged 22. It had been a great learning experience. Many of the passengers were still writing to me and sending Christmas cards many years afterwards.'

Eddie Tredrea, co-pilot and navigator (foreground), is part of the crew of TEAL's Solent flying boat ZK-AMN Awatere. *Other crew members are Pat Murphy, radio operator (middle distance) and Captain Ian Patterson.*

Aggie Grey was one of the delightful characters of the Coral Route. A flamboyant elderly lady, she ran the hotel in Samoa where TEAL crews stayed to catch up on a few hours' sleep.

'Aggie is believed to have been the model for "Bloody Mary" in James Michener's *Tales of the South Pacific*,' says Dennis Marshall. The stopover at Aggie Grey's hotel was a highlight of the Coral Route. But for many years she refused to fly with us, preferring instead to go by ship. Then, Captain Joe Shephard did get her to fly home from Suva. She had been visiting her nephew, John Wisdom, who was TEAL's Suva manager. At 1500 feet the Solent had an engine failure and returned to Suva. That did not boost her confidence too much at the time, but Aggie did eventually fly with us again on several occasions.'

SOLENTS, WITH THEIR sleeve-valve engines, were generally reliable, but there were occasions when engines malfunctioned, often as a result of poor quality oil. During a storm Eddie Tredrea was flying trans-Tasman in a Solent ZK-AML when it lost power in two engines on one wing. Telling me about it, Eddie flips through a pile of his log-books until he finds the details.

'That was flight TE 481344, on 7 June 1952, from Auckland to Sydney,' he says. 'The flight plan was 7 hours 35 minutes, which was reasonable for a Solent. Just after our critical point of no return, just on half way, we passed through a large cold front. It was a *real* cold front. We experienced a dramatic temperature change going from the warmer Auckland side to the colder Sydney side of the front. Those days we had no radar but used the radio compass to tell where the thunderstorms were. We would tune it in to a weak station and it would be pulled away by the thunderstorm. Even so, we still often had to fly through the storm, hoping we were going to miss the worst of it.

'At 8000 feet we experienced turbulence as we went into the front. Then, as the temperature dropped, the oil pressure light on No 4 engine came on. We were trained to push a button to stop and feather the engine as soon as the light came on. That was normal procedure. A few minutes later the No 3 oil pressure light came on. Not wanting to lose two engines completely, we didn't feather that one. It was vibrating like nobody's business so we throttled it right back to where it was giving just a little kick. We had about 100 hp, which meant we were a little better off than feathering the engine. It was running a bit rough, like a motor car that has a spark plug out.'

The real problem then was one of fuel consumption. With one engine out, the remaining three will use more fuel. The crew had calculations for three-engine fuel consumption, and additional fuel was always loaded accordingly. Because no one anticipated losing two engines on a flight, there were no fuel calculations for a flight continuing on two engines.

'Jim Goldie was flight engineer that day. I had never seen him work so hard. We had no idea how much fuel we needed to get to Sydney. We knew we didn't really have enough. At this stage TEAL's ops manager, Captain Ken Brownjohn, came up and said, "I see you have an engine out." I showed him what was happening to the one next to it and when he saw all the red lights he merely said, "OK," and went straight back to his seat.

'Maurice McGreal was first officer. He was on the blower telling them in Sydney we had lost an engine and were having trouble with another. We were asked if we wanted to put out a Mayday. The sea was completely white and there was no hope of landing on the water. I said, "Tell them we don't want to send a Mayday." I didn't want to write all those letters of explanation when I got back. We were later told that the HMAS *Arabus* had put out to sea and was standing off North Head in case we ditched.'

Continuing on at cruise power, the Solent descended on a long glide path from 8000 feet to 1000 feet. 'That took us a couple of hours. We were flying at quite a reduced speed. Even then Jim thought the fuel situation was still dicey. Our other problem was wondering what our two supposedly good engines were like. Having two crook engines on one wing meant we had to trim with the rudder. That was also creating drag.

While on navigation duties, Eddie Tredrea uses a hand-held sextant from a Solent flying boat.

Watched by Fijian police, TEAL's flying boat ZK-AMO gets up on the step during a takeoff run from Lauthala Bay. 'It took a lot of power to get a flying boat into the air,' recalls Eddie Tredrea.
SOLENT FLYING BOAT PRESERVATION SOCIETY

'We continued on at 1000 feet till speed started to sag off — down to about 120 knots of indicated air speed. Then the nose started to come up, increasing the angle of attack and creating even more drag. The wind on the deck had started to decrease a little, and went a bit further round from the north-west to the south. Flying conditions were starting to become a bit more favourable.

'The flight engineer made some more calculations and said he thought we might just make it. So we put No 2 engine up to climb power, lowering the nose and increasing speed a bit as the drag reduced. Lift also increased a little. We flew on for another hour like that until Jim said he thought we would arrive with fuel for another five to 10 minutes' flying. We had about an hour to go so we put another engine, No 1, up to climb power and that increased the speed again. With two engines on climb power we had about the same speed as four on cruise. We landed 9 hours and 20 minutes after leaving Auckland. The flying boat was grounded for a while after that flight. Only much later did I hear through the grapevine that when we had landed, No 4 and No 3 engines were stuffed, and No 2 was marginal. Unbeknown to us, we had only one really good engine out of the four!'

Eddie says he did not alarm the passengers with the details, apart from the fact that one engine was feathered, and the flight would take a little longer. The stewards, who were also unaware of the true situation, just kept on serving food.

'During that last hour of the flight, when we were starting to feel reasonably confident, I rang the steward and said, "You had better send up a cup of tea for the crew."

'He said, "Oh, I'm too busy serving the passengers."

'Then I said, "Well we've had a pretty rough time of it up here with nearly two engines out."

'He was somewhat alarmed at hearing that, and sent up a tray for us to pour our own tea. We had all been feeling the strain. Joe McVicar, the radio operator, wasn't very happy at all.

'Joe started to pour the tea, but he couldn't concentrate. He was pouring the tea into the milk, and someone else was putting sugar into the teapot. It was quite a pantomime.

'The last thing on my mind was thinking we would not get to Sydney. I would have been tossing all the luggage out, but it didn't come to that.'

Ray Gasparich recalls a time when the oil company delivered four drums of incorrectly labelled oil to Rose Bay. 'It was later discovered that the expected engine lubricating oil was in fact tanning oil. In the meantime the tanning oil was put into the engines. Captain Ian Patterson just got ZK-AMM off the water, in very rough conditions, when he lost one engine. He got into the climb and was starting to turn to go back, over Sydney's South Head, when he lost two. He then lost three and, as he dropped the last 10 feet onto the water, he lost four.

'The engines were considerably damaged. They were subsequently removed and we had to get them back to New Zealand for overhaul. At the time Qantas had an old Lancaster bomber that was brought in for the job. It hadn't been flown for some time but no one was too worried about that because it was used only for freight. They took the bomb bay doors off and made a special sling, and slung one of the Solent engines hanging out underneath.

'They gave the Lancaster full power at the end of the runway at Mascot and when it got up to 60 or 70 knots the undercarriage collapsed and the aeroplane sat down on our engine. TEAL made the oil company pay for that damage also. It cost the oil people quite a lot of money. Fortunately, despite it being a near disaster with the tanning oil, nobody was hurt.'

On another occasion while flying to Tahiti a load of apples wrongly stowed caused a problem. 'The aircraft wouldn't get up to speed once we levelled out on cruise power,' recalls Eddie Tredrea. 'At first I was mystified. I had to keep applying power to make the aeroplane fly level. Then I had a look at the load sheet. The apples had been loaded in the aft hold instead of one in the nose section, under the flight deck. Fortunately, the holds on Solents were accessible and the steward was able to transfer the load, case by case, through the passenger cabin.'

GEOFF FREER SAYS that one of the less memorable events of the Coral Route was when the aeroplane was sprayed on arrival at Papeete. 'They were worried about the rhinoceros beetle getting into Tahiti. It was found mainly in the Samoan area. A fellow came on

Front cover of a TEAL Coral Route brochure commemorating 10 years of Solent flying boats, 1949–59.

Vic Hodgkinson, a former RAAF Wing Commander and BOAC flying boat captain, takes care of another former TEAL flying boat at Southampton's Hall of Aviation. ROY SINCLAIR

board wearing a gas mask. But he also sprayed all of us. We used to cough like mad. We arrived at a buoy close to the shore and the aeroplane was later dragged off some distance to moor. It would have been too far, I expect, for the rhinoceros beetle to fly ashore from the mooring.'

Ray Gasparich says it was a sad occasion when the last flying boat was grounded on 15 September 1960. But aviation had to give way to progress. 'We couldn't fly these things forever and we couldn't fly them a very long way either. They weren't pressurised so we couldn't get up above the weather, and we had no beacons or approach aids on water. The flying boats had five technical people, including the pilots, who were all probably getting too much pay — more than us ground engineers, anyway. All the passengers were looked after by up to three cabin crew. The flight hostess ran up and down the stairs taking care of the passengers and all their documentation. That must have been very tiring in an aeroplane that was not pressurised.

'In those days, after the war, flying was very expensive. A return trip from Auckland to Sydney cost £75. An average wage then was about £5 a week, which meant the trip cost 15 weeks' gross salary. A lot of people these days would do the trip on just one week's wage. That says a lot about the efficiency that has been built into modern aviation.

'Whenever we went onto new aircraft, right through to Boeing 747s, it was always very stimulating. But looking back, the Solent flying boats were much more memorable than many aircraft that followed.'

Says Geoff Freer, 'The flying boats belong to a romantic era of air travel and, of course, we were all a lot younger then. We felt important. We will look at our restored Solent here and tell one another that "those were the days". We saw beautiful coral reefs and scenery you don't see from 35,000 feet. Those days will never come back. If you leave Auckland for Tahiti today, the flying time on a jet is about five hours, and you are there. There is no romance at all. You will probably arrive in the middle of the night and the locals, so used to seeing aeroplanes and passengers, couldn't care less. In the flying boat we were always met with a great welcome. People often took the day off work when the flying boat arrived every fortnight.'

But were there times when romance waned? 'The generous Perspex windows above the Solent's flight deck leaked like hell,' says Geoff. 'Sometimes, in heavy rain while waiting to take off, we had to sit there half drenched in our overcoats.'

ONE DAY IN October 1997 I was peering through a window of Southampton's Hall of Aviation, staring at a former TEAL Sandringham flying boat. Ray Gasparich had told me I would find it there. But it was Monday. The English have a damnable habit of closing tourist attractions on selected weekdays. Even more frustrating were the people I could see working inside. Could I attract their attention? I had come so far, but could not get in!

Then, from behind me I heard a friendly, 'Are you interested in aviation?' I turned around and told the stranger I was from New Zealand and I had been associated with the Solent Flying Boat Preservation Society in Auckland. Next thing I was inside and almost overwhelmed. Here I was, on the other side of the world, talking to a bunch of aviation devotees who were so much like Ray Gasparich and all the others at MOTAT.

And the Hall of Aviation is similar to the museum hangar at MOTAT. Jammed full of fighter and civil aircraft of varying vintages, the impressive centrepiece is also a flying boat. In its present Ansett guise, the Short Bros Sandringham is VH-BRC *Beachcomber*. Back in October 1947 the same aeroplane had arrived on Auckland's Waitemata Harbour to become TEAL's resplendent ZK-AMH *Auckland*.

Among the Southampton enthusiasts was a tall former Wing Commander, Vic Hodgkinson, an Australian who had flown flying boats during the war and, later, for British Overseas Airways Corporation (BOAC, now British Airways). Vic is the museum's flying-boat expert. RAAF-trained, in December 1939 he was posted to England to form a Sunderland squadron. Two years later he returned to Australia to fly Catalinas and Sunderlands. He joined BOAC in 1946, and finished his airline flying (on Boeing 707s) in 1971.

'Flying boats represent the very best times of my life,' he says. 'They were far more challenging than land planes. These days you have tricycle undercarriages, nose wheel steering, nice brakes and so on.'

We gaze up at *Beachcomber* as Vic continues searching back down the years. 'An aeroplane like this wanted to weathercock all the time. It was often as difficult to fly as the old taildraggers I was brought up on.

'In BOAC we flew Sandringhams and then Solents from Southampton. We went mostly to Singapore and Africa, and everywhere in between. Those days nobody else flew aeroplanes over Africa. We could fly any height we liked, and anywhere we liked. We flew low over the pyramids in Egypt. We sometimes wandered 200 miles off course to hunt game. At the Murchison (Kalabega) Falls in Uganda we could guarantee seeing huge herds of elephants. We would fly up and down this river with the passengers almost hanging out the side. Elephants didn't like flying boats very much. We then flew over Lake Victoria to the Victoria Falls. Flying boat passengers really had a Cook's tour on their way to Johannesburg.'

Vic says he was trapped into staying in England when he retired. 'The kids had grown up here. We still live close to Southampton. About once a week I come down here to work on *Beachcomber*. I will be 81 in two days' time.'

In a small publication on sale at the Hall of Aviation Vic has written the history of *Beachcomber*. His research also includes other former TEAL flying boats.

Beachcomber had been built in 1943 as a Sunderland Mark 3 for the RAF. Later it was upgraded to a Mark 5 and fitted with Pratt & Whitney engines. Following the war several Sunderlands were sent to Northern Ireland for conversion to Sandringham Mark 4 civil aircraft. Vic tells me the Sunderlands were taxied about 50 miles across the Irish Sea.

'During a pre-flight inspection of the first aircraft an elevator fell off. The delivery crews, therefore, considered it lethal to chance providence. Having recently survived the war, the pilots chose not to fly the aircraft to Belfast.'

Four converted Sunderlands, fitted with upgraded 14-cylinder Pratt & Whitney engines, became TEAL's Tasman Class Sandringham flying boats. But they were dogged by engine overheating problems on long trans-Tasman flights. In 1950 they were sold to Australian airlines. Two went to Qantas, and two to Barrier Reef Airways (later Ansett Flying Boat Services).

Engine overheating problems were finally overcome in Australia by fitting the Pratt & Whitney engines with baffle plates between the staggered front and back rows of cylinders. The airflow from the front cylinders was previously transferring heat to the rear cylinders. Vic believes TEAL should have been able to fit effective baffles to prevent overheating during trans-Tasman flights.

'Without the baffle plates the rear banks of cylinders were getting very hot. The heat also built up the oil temperatures,' he says.

In Australia, *Beachcomber* was put in storage while Barrier Reef Airways flew another former TEAL flying boat, ZK-AME *New Zealand* — the Sandringham that had been involved in a mid-Tasman drama in December 1947. ZK-AME had become VH-BRD *Princess of Cairns*.

'In 1952 *Princess of Cairns* sank in the Brisbane River. It was all

Former TEAL Sandringham flying boat, ZK-AMH Auckland *(preserved in its Ansett VH-BRC* Beachcomber *livery), forms the centrepiece of Southampton's Hall of Aviation.*
ROY SINCLAIR

loaded up and waiting to take off at sunrise. There's not much room in the river. A tug collided with the flying boat, leaving it to sink and settle on the bottom. It was some time before the passengers could be taken off. In the meantime the crew opened the bar. By the time a rescue launch arrived no one wanted to leave the aeroplane.'

Princess of Cairns, no longer in flying condition, was sold to become a night club at Coolangatta. But while it was under tow, a dummy float came off. The flying boat capsized at sea near the border of Queensland and New South Wales.

'The event was seen by the crew of another Ansett flying boat who had come down low to watch it being towed. While they were looking at it, it turned over and sank. It was never recovered.'

Beachcomber was recommissioned to carry on the flying boat services. In 1953 it joined Ansett. When, in 1974, Australian flying boat services ceased, *Beachcomber* was bought by Captain Charles Blair of Antilles Air Boats in the West Indies, and renamed *Southern Cross*. In 1976 *Southern Cross* crossed the Atlantic to Ireland where Blair's actress wife, Maureen O'Hara, had a summer residence near Bantry Bay. *Southern Cross* was then flown to England, landing at Poole in Dorset. The landing completed a round-the-world flight that began 29 years

A realistic display shows a mechanic working on one of Beachcomber*'s Pratt & Whitney engine at Southampton's Hall of Aviation.* ROY SINCLAIR

Charted by Dudley Pictures of the United States to film a two-hour South Pacific Cinerama presentation, Beachcomber, *in November 1957, visits Port Lyttelton near Christchurch.*
THE PRESS

previously when the flying boat, as ZK-AMH *Auckland*, had set out for Marseilles on its delivery flight to New Zealand.

Captain Blair was killed in 1978 when a Grumman Goose amphibian he was flying to the Virgin Islands crashed into the sea. Antilles Air Boats folded and *Southern Cross* was sold to the Science Museum in London.

Vic says the flying boat was named *Southern Cross* when it arrived at Southampton for restoration work in 1983. 'It was seen by visiting Australians, who objected to the name. '*Southern Cross*' is sacred to the memory of Australia's Sir Charles Kingsford Smith.'

When the Southampton Hall of Aviation opened in 1984, the Sandringham was back in its Ansett *Beachcomber* livery. It might have been returned to its TEAL colours but, as Vic says, it had spent most of its flying years as *Beachcomber*.

Jack Shorthouse displays some of the model aircraft he has made over the years. His collection will eventually represent all the types he flew between 1939 and 1980. In his left hand is the Fairey Battle he flew in France in 1939 and 1940. His right hand holds a nimble Messerschmitt Bf 109 that shot him down!
ROY SINCLAIR

CHAPTER 5

SKIES OF WAR AND PEACE

Antoine Allard was a wonderful man. He had saved my life. He remembered my name. He then spent years looking for me. We met again and talked, almost non-stop, for three days.

Jack Shorthouse DFC

JACK SHORTHOUSE MIGHT have recently stepped from one of Captain WE Johns' Biggles stories when I discovered him one day in February 1995. I had made the long busride through the suburban labyrinth of Auckland's North Shore on Ray Gasparich's suggestion. But Jack's gruff — although not entirely unfriendly — greeting was not quite what I had anticipated:

'Ray said you were a reputable journalist,' he told me at the door. 'There's no such thing!'

Initially, I just wanted to talk to a former Air New Zealand captain who had trained in Tiger Moths and eventually retired from the flight deck of a Boeing 747; someone whose experiences almost spanned the entire history of civil aviation, from the late 1930s to mid-1980s. Jack Shorthouse fulfilled these expectations, and more. He is also a celebrated Royal Air Force pilot of the Second World War. In October 1943 he was awarded the Distinguished Flying Cross and, a year later — at the ripe old age of 24 — he attained the rank of Wing Commander, to form and command 189 Squadron of Lancaster bombers. He is adamant that his lofty promotion was no sorry case of 'dead man's shoes'! He is believed to have been New Zealand's first member of the famed Caterpillar Club when, in 1940, he successfully baled out from a blazing single-engine Fairey Battle light bomber during the Battle of France. The so-called club awarded a special pin to pilots whose lives were saved by a parachute jump using one of the Irvine Air Chutes.

As an airline pilot — he joined TEAL in 1947 — he has flown all manner of celebrities: Prince Philip, Queen Salote, a variety of prime ministers, and even raving pop singers whose names he has trouble remembering. I soon discovered his forthright gruff manner was admirably equalled by an endearing quirky humour, and an obvious satisfaction with life, derived partly from a long career spent in a succession of pilot's seats, and an enjoyment of living with his Canadian-born wife, Mary, on the North Shore.

Stepping inside the Shorthouse home, and still reeling from the doubt cast on my journalist reputation, I was sucked in (as are all visitors) by the somewhat unusual clock on the wall. The hands were decidedly going backwards. Jack was laughing. I had been put in my

Captain Jack Shorthouse DFC.

place and I was now yet another unsuspecting visitor set agog by his ludicrous clock. 'It's a perfectly normal clock,' he said, sounding almost apologetic. 'I saw one in a bar in Switzerland after I had been drinking a lot of Swiss beer. At the time even I didn't realise it was supposed to go round backwards! It certainly gives us a lot of laughs.'

His aviation career can be partially followed in a display of model aircraft, most of which he made himself. Almost every one he has flown is represented, from the Tiger Moth at the Wanganui Aero Club in 1939 to the Qantas B747 used to train Air New Zealand crews in 1980. In between are the Vickers Vildebeeste, Fairey Gordon, Fairey light bomber, Avro Anson, Avro Manchester, Hawker Hurricane, Spitfire, Avro Lancaster bomber, Liberator, Solent Flying Boat, Douglas DC-6, Lockheed Electra, Douglas DC-8 and DC-10, and quite a few others.

'I had hopes of becoming a vet, but at that time you had to go to Australia for training and my parents couldn't afford that,' he said. 'During 1938 and 1939 a war was coming on so I thought maybe I would like to be a pilot, perhaps even an airline pilot if I survived the war. I went into the Royal Air Force on a short-service commission, training initially in New Zealand at the Wanganui Aero Club, and then Wigram.'

If wanting to become a vet was one handicap to becoming a competent airline captain, his erratic first hours learning to fly a Tiger Moth were another.

It appeared that he spent an abnormal number of hours before going solo. I asked him why.

'Ah, that's very interesting. This is a story some people believe and some don't. You see I'm left-handed. We had been flying this Tiger Moth at Wanganui for about 10 hours when my instructor, Harry Tancred, said, "What's wrong with you when you get near the ground?" I said, "I have no idea," and he said, "You fly this thing very well in the air and you should be going solo but you're so erratic on your takeoffs and landings.'

'I said, "I don't know why." Eventually he told me to sit in the rear cockpit while he stood on the ground and we would go through the motions of a takeoff.

'So I'm sitting in the cockpit with my left hand on the control column. When he tells me to go through the takeoff procedure I push the throttle forward, lock it, and put my hand back on the control column. When I imagine I should be in the air I ease the column back, then, with my left hand pull the throttle back to reduce power as I level out.

'He says, "What on earth are you doing that for?"

'I say, "How else do I do it?"

'He says, "What's wrong with your right hand?"

'"Nothing," I say. "I'm left-handed. Nobody ever told me to fly this thing with my right hand!"

'A much-relieved flying instructor then took me off to celebrate

Wanganui Aero Club in 1939.

A detail from a painting by John Chrisp showing Pilot Officer JS Shorthouse parachuting from his Fairey Battle on 11 June 1940.

at Rutland's Hotel. Next morning I went solo. It was just as simple as that. Nobody had told me you could fly an aeroplane with your right hand, while your left hand is on the throttle. I, being left-handed, had got into the aeroplane and naturally did everything with my left hand. As I changed my left hand from the control column to the throttle and back again, the aeroplane flew erratically. It was a funny experience really. If my instructor hadn't asked for a "dry run" and found the problem, I would probably have never gone flying.'

Looking back, he said learning to fly during the 1940s was not so ritualised as it is today where it's all precise instruction and you get pieces of paper telling you to do this or that exercise.

'I don't know if pilots learn any better today or not. There was no technical book written about a Tiger Moth. You were told to push the stick (or control column) to go down, pull to go up, and so forth. You were told that if you start a turn with no power on you will stall, and what to do if the engine stops.

'The RAF basic air manual was the Air Publication 1234. I understand it's still in use. Some of the instructions were: How you start off flying; How you fly an aeroplane; What you must look for; When you are flying you must observe the wind on the ground, flat areas of ground, which way the grass is blowing to tell you the wind

direction, what it's doing in the trees; Are there any telegraph lines or big fences or wild cattle — in case your engine stops and you have to force land.

'That sort of thing was written years before the war when engines were not so reliable and you had to think all the time, "What will I do if this engine stops? What do I do if the engine stops just after I lift off the ground and I've got to force land?"'

Jack looked at me, almost taking on the guise of the old flying instructor. 'You don't turn back, do you?' he said.

'Apparently that's fatal,' I suggested.

'Absolutely fatal, because you are going to stall. You must go straight ahead and land, and hope you get away with it. If you start doing a turn with no power on you are going to crash. That old basic manual, it's fascinating reading.'

JACK SHORTHOUSE WENT overseas in December 1939 and ended up in No 12 Squadron, in France. 'We were either the "Shiny Twelve" or the "Dirty Dozen", whichever suited the occasion. Early in 1940 we were sent on missions dropping propaganda leaflets. That seemed pretty harmless. Then, when the balloon went up, they gave us real bombs to play with — which was really dangerous. And I did the traditional Biggles trick, and got shot down in flames while flying out from our base at Souge to bomb the advancing German tanks in the Forêt du Gault. I've still got the scars on one hand, and I've still got the little gold Caterpillar pin the parachute company gave you when one of their parachutes saved your life.

'It really was a Biggles world, I'm not kidding. If you got shot down and killed, that's what happened. There wasn't any great recrimination about it, or weeping and wailing. I was 20 years old and was not conscious of what was going on outside my immediate circle of activity. I soon discovered that an aeroplane on fire, with smoke and flames filling the cockpit, was pretty uncomfortable.'

The German culprit was a nimble Messerschmitt Bf 109, against which the Fairey Battle was no match. Jack Shorthouse was flying an aeroplane that was hopelessly outdated. It was underpowered and undergunned. Armed with a 'toy' Lewis Gun, it had a top speed of 150 knots and that was achieved only with 'a tail wind and going down hill'.

The exact date of the bale-out is uncertain. Jack's own Pilot Logbook has it as 11 June 1940. But W R Chorley, in his book *Royal Air Force Bomber Command Losses of the Second World War*, has it as 13

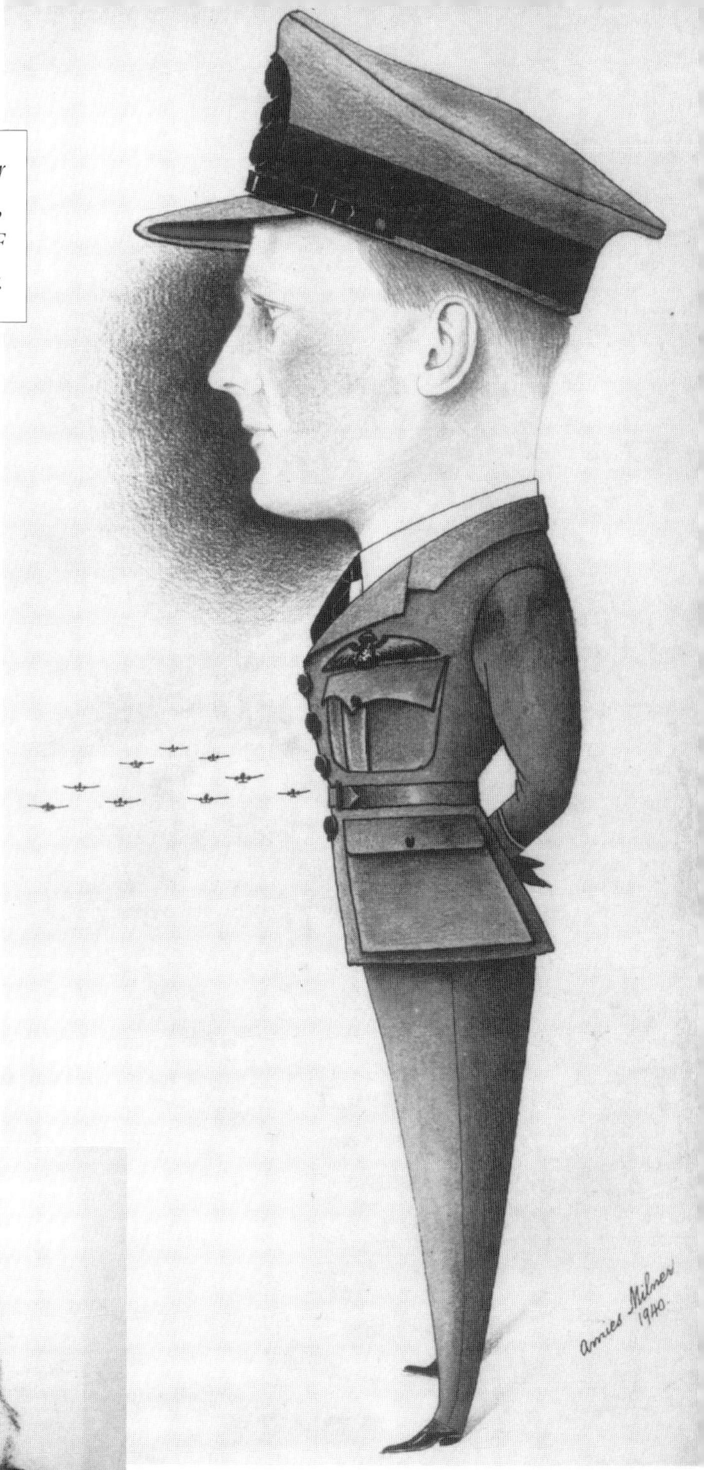

A caricature of Pilot Officer JS Shorthouse at Uxbridge, England, 1940, by RAF artist Arnies Milner.

Antoine Allard, a self portrait. 'He saved my life and he remembered my name,' says Jack Shorthouse.

June. Chorley also records the fatal casualty of the navigator, Sergeant NC Cotterell, and the survival of the wireless operator/air gunner, LAC Copley. Pilot Officer JS Shorthouse is, recorded as injured. The Fairey Battle, shot down when flying a little more than 1000 feet, crashed near St-Bartholémy, 26 km NNE of Provins.

'I was pretty lucky really. I was burned up a bit and shot through the leg. I had no idea where the front lines were or anything like that. There were Germans here, the French were there, and the British were somewhere else. I staggered through a wood, away from the Germans, and lay in a ditch for a day or so. I was worried at the prospect of being found in RAF uniform by the Germans until, as luck would have it, I saw an Allied ambulance come up the road. I hailed it and a Belgian ambulance driver speaking fluent English asked, "Where do you want to go?" I said, "Anywhere, but away from here."

'We shot off towards the west coast until we were running out of petrol. By that time we were near our airfield and I knew where the fuel dump was, so we went there. He had said his name was Antoine Allard and that he was some sort of baron. I was in no mental state to remember his name. He had saved my life. It was as simple as that.'

JACK SHORTHOUSE EVENTUALLY arrived back in England and spent six weeks in a Plymouth hospital. When he returned to his squadron, at Binbrook in north-east Lincolnshire, there was nothing doing there so he was posted to a Photographic Reconnaissance Unit, at Heston, flying Spitfires at high level. They were pale blue Spitfires, highly polished with no guns and no radio. Just petrol tanks and cameras.

'It was interesting flying. We were flying at about 30,000 feet to photograph targets over Germany and France. But I wasn't very good at it. The Spitfire with its Rolls-Royce Merlin engine was a wonderful aeroplane to fly, even if it wasn't so easy to land with its nose stuck up in the air. You needed to land with a curving approach path to see where you were going. You had to judge the approach just right.

'I suspect I was suffering from an early case of what they later called LMF — Lack of Moral Fibre. It was a nice name for being a coward. I did get sick in the Spitfires. It was put down to oxygen sickness, but there was more to it than that. I was still a bit shattered from being shot down in France. I had been the only pilot up at Binbrook. The other personnel were administration staff, who were at a loss to know what to do with an odd pilot who turned up out of nowhere. I had been lonely, but I was more so at the Photographic Reconnaissance

'Early Morning Arrival' is the title of a Robert Taylor paining of a Lancaster bomber, with one failed engine, over a friendly English countryside after a night bombing mission over Germany. The image was found among Jack Shorthouse's Skies of War *memorabilia.*

Unit where many of us were billeted privately. Most of my spare time was spent either sitting in my room or down at the pub. I was having a bit of a thin time.

'Eventually I was asked what I wanted to do, so I said I wanted to go to the Middle East. My burn scars were painful in the cold weather. I wanted to be somewhere warmer. They thought that was wonderful. They had been trying unsuccessfully to get volunteers to go out there. I was to go on the next boat.

'As it turned out, a fortnight later I was on another boat, on my way to Canada. I arrived in mid-winter and spent a year on the prairie at the City of Moose Jaw, Saskatchewan, training young pilots on Harvards. But the main significance of that venture was acquiring a wife — the same one I've got now. I was in effect snared on the prairie. I went on a blind date.

'A fellow flying instructor came to me one evening and asked if I was doing anything that night. I said, "Not really," and he said, "Well how about going on a blind date? You can take my place. I've got to go and fly."

'I accepted, and was later having a few drinks at a friend's house while waiting for the rest of the party to arrive. Two girls then turned up. I was apparently going to have a choice. One had a bottle of gin under her arm, and the other a six-pack of Coke. I thought, My God,

I'd better go for the six-pack of Coke. And I did. That was Mary.

'Much to her astonishment, and mine, I rang her a couple of weeks later. We said we must get together, and we did. Her mother did a lot to encourage me. She did wonderful roast beef and Yorkshire, and steak and kidney pud.'

A year was spent at Vancouver Island training pilots to fly torpedo bombers, Bristol Beauforts and Handley Page Hampdens.

'In October 1942 I was back in England. I was asked what I had been doing and when I mentioned torpedo bombers the squadron leader said, "Yes, yes, wonderful. You can go to torpedo squadron."

'I said, "No, no, that's far too dangerous, thank you very much."

'He said, "Oh, you have already heard."

'And I said, "Yes, I have heard."

'You can't weave if you are dropping a torpedo. You go straight into the battleship to get maximum target area. Then what are you going to do when you've dropped it? You can't turn so close to a ship. You go over the top with all those big guns busily shooting at you. If one of them drops a shell into the water, the water spout will knock you down. There's not a hell of a lot of future in that, Roy.'

A small problem was that by this time he had married, and Mary was still in Canada. Jack went down to London to see Group Captain Leonard Isitt. (Isitt was knighted in 1944 and went on to become a chairman of TEAL.)

'We investigated ways of getting Mary across to England. She eventually arrived but had no idea of where I was. She spent three

Captain Jack Shorthouse enjoys a friendly Tahitian welcome after inaugurating the Auckland to Tahiti DC-6 landplane service.
AIR NEW ZEALAND

days in the large Adelphi Hotel in Liverpool, feeling rather upset. She had sent a telegram to New Zealand House in London, only to have it forwarded to me by post. That took a couple of days. In the meantime, Mary was using up handkerchiefs and listening to string quartets. She has never liked string quartets since. It had taken a lot of guts for her to cross the war-torn Atlantic and find me.'

Jack was subsequently attached to various units including No 44 (Rhodesia) Squadron at Waddington and Dunholme Lodge where he flew Avro Lancaster bombers. Early in 1944 he was posted to No 5 Lancaster Flying School, Syerston, as Chief Flying Instructor. Then, on 15 October 1944, he was promoted to Wing Commander and posted to Bardney to form his own 189 Squadron of Lancasters. Prior to his war duties ending, and a transfer to the RNZAF in July 1945, he was involved with Transport Command, flying Liberators carrying troops from India.

THIS CHAPTER IS gleaned from two visits to the Shorthouse home. The second, in August 1997, found Jack and Mary living in a Browns Bay retirement village. Jack was on crutches awaiting a hip replacement operation. That did not restrain his good-natured bantering, or his quirky storytelling. We all laughed about my first visit when I had arrived as the so-called reputable journalist, only to be 'shot down' by the Wing Commander. This time, my arrival was greeted with a gruff, 'Just you wait till you hear all the lies I'm about to tell you.'

We spent an entire rainy day talking pleasurably. Next morning I was left in the house on my own while my hosts took off for a hospital appointment.

Mary had spent many hours since my previous visit gathering the memorabilia of Jack's flying career. Photographs, wartime medals, telegrams, newspaper clippings, and all manner of other souvenirs have been lovingly assembled into four amazing albums. A small album tells the story of the war. Three larger albums tell the story of TEAL and Air New Zealand. These were left out for me to look through.

ALMOST REVERENTLY, I turn the pages that reveal the poignant Skies of War. The house, some distance from traffic, is uncannily quiet. Halfway through the album is the Irvine Chute's Caterpillar. It is about a centimetre long and curved, almost as if the gold-plated creature is on its way somewhere. Its two eyes are red. The parachute had saved the pilot from a burning aeroplane. Other gold Caterpillars, Mary had told me, have blue eyes.

I turn back to the beginning of the album. In front of me is the silver Distinguished Flying Cross. It stands out on its black background and I refrain from touching it. It seems too precious. It belongs to an age, and an event, in which I have no place. Simply to gaze at it is intrusion enough. Yet my feelings are in stark contrast to the story I had already heard from my ever modest and, sometimes, debunking storyteller.

'It was quite funny,' Jack had told me the previous day. 'But the citation recommending my DFC, it reads quite well:'

> *Squadron Leader Shorthouse was Captain of a Lancaster aircraft detailed to attack Mannheim on 5/6 September 1943. About 70 miles from the target the starboard inner engine caught fire owing to a fractured oil pipe, but the airscrew was feathered, and the fire finally subsided. The height of the aircraft at this time was 16,000 feet, and in the circumstances could be climbed no higher . . . Although the engine was useless Squadron Leader Shorthouse flew on to the target and . . . although engaged by flak and searchlights . . . bombed it. He displayed great determination which has been such a noteworthy feature of the many sorties he has undertaken . . . against some of the heaviest defended targets . . . including 14 attacks on the Rhineland and attacks on Berlin . . . Squadron Leader Shorthouse is an extremely efficient and gallant flight commander.*

'THE SIMPLE FACTS are that I was in the front wave of bombers when an engine got hit by flak and caught fire. We wrestled mightily with that. We got it to stop, which was a good thing, and the fire eventually went out. With the load of bombs we were starting to lose height. As we drifted downhill it was a case of was I going to turn around and go back, or was I going to go on?

'I considered the options and thought that to peel away and return on our own was too lonely, and dangerous. I knew that a single bomber was a sitting target for the fighters and AA fire. I also had to think about the rest of the crew. So I thought the sensible thing to do was to carry on and try and keep up with the other bombers. That's what I did, and I got a gong for it.'

I LEAVE THE small album open. My attention has been diverted by the amazingly neat entries in one of three RAF Pilot's Flying Logbooks that have also been left out for me. It is lying open, silently telling its own abbreviated story of an RAF officer's war. The first entry is 25

May 1940. I glance down the page to find an entry for 11 June: '*L5324, Day Ops. Shot down in flames. Baled out. Badly burnt. Evacuated.*'

In another logbook, for the year 1943, I follow a succession of Lancaster bombing raids to Germany: '*8 Sept, 1943. Operations Mannheim. 1x4000 20xSBC (8,000 lbs). 7 hrs.*' The 8000 lbs is the total bomb weight. The 1x4000 is a large bomb, a 'cookie'. SBC means 'Small Bomb Containers' — usually filled with incendiaries.

22 September, 1943. Operations Hanover (13,240 lbs). 5.20 hrs.
20 October, 1943. Operations Leipzig (11,000 lbs). 6.45 hrs.
22 November, 1943. OPs Berlin (10,000 lbs). 6.25 hrs.

These are just a few entries selected randomly from a large number of wartime operations recorded in the three logbooks.

'The entries are pretty non-committal,' Jack told me when I discussed them later. 'They had to be. A pity though.'

He enjoyed flying the Avro Lancaster that went into service early in 1942. It was, without doubt, by far the most successful heavy bomber of the war.

'It had started out as a Manchester, which was an absolute dog of an aeroplane. It had twin unproven Rolls-Royce Vulture engines that tended to stop unexpectedly. A quick fix was required so the Avro people used the same wing and basic fuselage, changed the tail structure and put in four Merlin engines. Out came the Lancaster. It was

Enjoying TEAL's friendly inflight service aboard a DC-6, Captain Jack Shorthouse and Mary Shorthouse wing their way to a Fiji posting in October 1960.
AIR NEW ZEALAND

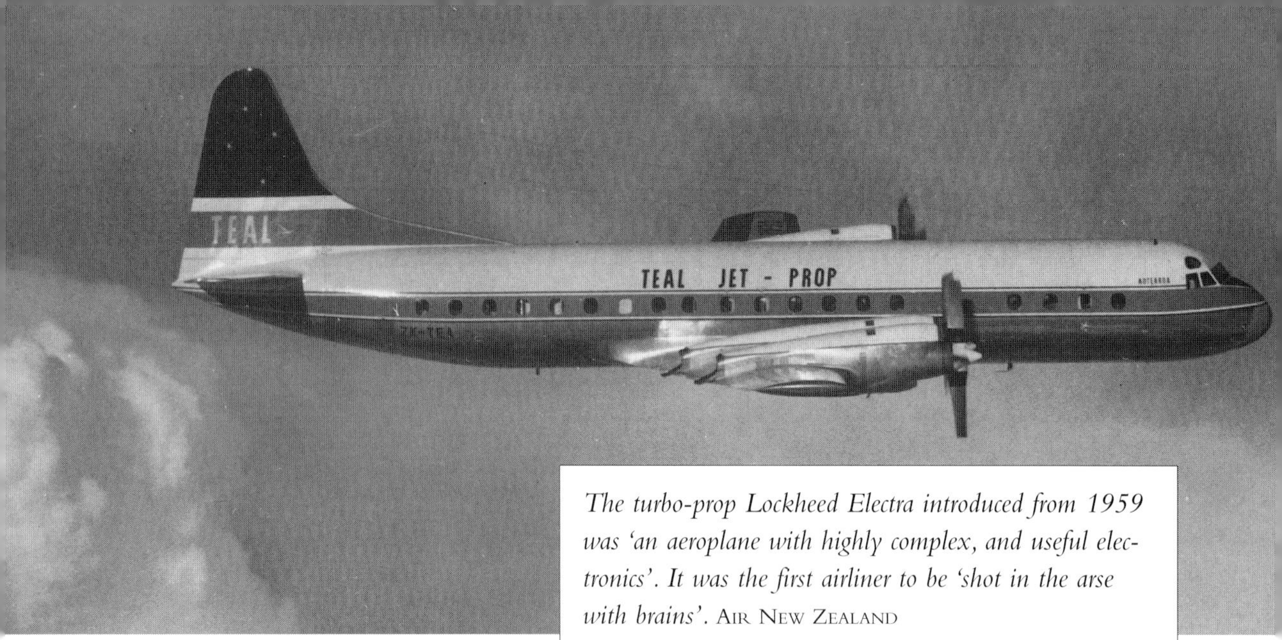

The turbo-prop Lockheed Electra introduced from 1959 was 'an aeroplane with highly complex, and useful electronics'. It was the first airliner to be 'shot in the arse with brains'. Air New Zealand

not difficult to fly. It was a wonderful, wonderful aeroplane that carried an enormous number of bombs.

'One day, on a training flight, we were flying alongside an American B.17 Flying Fortress. They waved to us and we waved to them. We then shut down two engines on the one side — the side facing them — to show them what they were up against. We then put maximum power on the other two engines and slowly drew ahead of them. The look on their faces was amazing.

'The Yanks were staggered by the amount of bombs we could hang on those things. The standard load on a five-hour flight to the Ruhr was about 15,000 lbs, which was a big load in those days. They eventually modified Lancasters to carry the 22,000 lb "Grand Slam". To do that they had to take off the upper turret.

'I have some pieces of flak around the place somewhere — souvenirs from the Mannheim raid,' he said. 'Not very nice to look at; ugly pieces of steel with all sharp edges.'

On my own, I return to the small album of wartime. I find the letter from the Central Chancery of the Order of Knighthood advising that the King will hold an Investiture at Buckingham Palace on 27 July 1945, 'at which your attendance is requested — no later than 10.15 o'clock a.m'.

I look at a Bomber Command medal, the Air Crew Europe Star, cap badges, the epaulettes of various officer ranks, and a Lancaster bomber flying handbook. Near the back of the album I find a reduced copy of a self-portrait of Antoine Allard (1901–1981). The portrait, drawn in 1972, was on a 1985 Christmas card from Elena Allard. A simple inscription reads: *Antoine Allard, your friend of June 1940.* This story I already knew:

BY THE TIME war was over Jack Shorthouse had forgotten the name of the Belgian ambulance driver who had found him in France. He had put his energies into a new life in Auckland, flying TEAL flying boats and settling his Canadian wife into a somewhat antiquated New Zealand — where one's name had to go onto a waiting list to buy a washing machine.

'But the ambulance driver had remembered my name. Years later he was a foundation member of OXFAM and other organisations working for the people who suffered so much injustice in third-world countries. He toured the world and wherever he went he asked people if they knew a man in New Zealand by the name of "Shorthouse", and of course nobody ever did. In about 1965, in Tokyo, he apparently spoke to a man from Auckland. The Auckland man did not know me either but promised he would look in the phone book when he went home. And he did.

'He rang me and asked if I knew a Belgian baron and I said, "No, not really," and he said, "Well, he saved your life in France."

'Then I said, "Yes, yes, I remember." I was given his address, so I wrote to him.

'At that time we were on our way to Hong Kong. I had just been made Senior Route Captain for the Orient, and was being sent out to organise the Orient routes for Air New Zealand when we got the DC-8s. When we got a letter back from Baron Antoine Allard he was in Peking. He was able to change his itinerary and come and stay with us in Hong Kong. We met at the Kowloon railway station one day in June 1966. We did not recognise each other. Twenty-six years previously I was badly burned. The Baron saw only burned flesh, blood and dirt.'

In 1940 Baron Allard, the driver attached to the French Ambulance du Front, had found a man who was very ill and 'tattered and torn'. He took the wounded man aboard his ambulance and headed down the road for St Nazaire on the French coast. The trip took five days. They stopped at farmhouses to beg food, water and petrol. French people were wonderful to them. Much later, the Baron believed the young pilot had died. 'I only knew his name and that he came from New Zealand.'

Jack Shorthouse was delivered on board a British destroyer that was to have taken him to the liner *Lancastrian*, used for evacuating troops. But the destroyer fouled a propeller on a mooring buoy cable and

Captain Jack Shorthouse doing a pre-flight inspection of a Lockheed Electra at Whenuapai.
AIR NEW ZEALAND

failed to reach the *Lancastrian* before it was sunk by the Luftwaffe with a huge loss of life. Another liner eventually took him to Plymouth. In the meantime he had been posted 'missing, believed killed'. He arrived in England still wearing his burnt and tattered uniform, and carrying his wallet, which he still has. He also had a letter the baron had been given by the officer in charge of the evacuation at St Nazaire. It was a 'To whom this may concern' letter simply stating the circumstances associated with rescuing Pilot Officer Shorthouse, and requesting the reader to 'Please assist this gentleman.'

'Meeting Antoine again was a most incredible experience, it really was. I got quite excited about it. He was a lovely man. His wife, Elena, was also wonderful. We must have talked and talked, almost non-stop for three days. Mary and I visited them in Belgium, near Brussels, on about three occasions. It was quite an extraordinary experience after all those years — 26 years later. We kept in touch until he died of a heart attack not so long ago.

'I would probably have been shot if the Germans had found me in my uniform. At the time I did not even know where he had found me, except that it was somewhere in France. I was too shocked to remember his name. He remembered mine and spent all those years finding me again. A wonderful, wonderful man.'

Baron Antoine Allard was also an accomplished artist. On a wall of the Shorthouse residence is one of the baron's paintings of the Great Wall of China. Another, in Jack's den, is the self-portrait original.

In the larger albums Mary has compiled almost every conceivable piece of an air traveller's memorabilia. I go from old timetables and dinner menus recalling the famed TEAL Coral Route to Tahiti, to the fabric used to manufacture airline pilots' shirts. I look at ties, cap badges, pieces of uniforms representing a succession of men's fashions, tiny slippers worn by passengers on long international flights, and photographs of the aircraft types that have taken TEAL and Air New Zealand from primitive, but stylish, flying boats to Boeing 747s. I find plenty of things to ask Jack about.

Civil flying after the war involved the TEAL S.30 Empire-class, S.25 Sandringham and S.45 Solent flying boats. The airline was flying the Tasman to Australia, and starting to expand routes into the Pacific. In a sense, civil flying was a backward step for the still young aviator. He had been a wing commander with his own squadron of Lancaster bombers. Now he was a second officer in a fledgling airline with six aeroplanes, including a Catalina flying boat for crew training. Despite his present-day enthusiastic involvement in the Solent Flying Boat Preservation Society, Jack Shorthouse did not particularly like flying boats — even if moving around on the water was a novel experience.

'In their day the flying boat was a very good aeroplane but you were always getting wet climbing on board from the launch. Taking off from Wellington's Evans Bay, with the wind blowing a bit, you got saturated sitting up the front. Sometimes when it became too rough to take off, you literally had to sail it across the sea and back to the buoy. The Solent was much better than the Sandringham, faster and much more stable.'

There were, however, memorable moments such as trying to land on Sydney harbour when the 18-footers were racing. 'Their huge masts with full sail were very spectacular but they created an interesting hazard for a flying boat on final approach. We had a pilot boat that attempted to clear the water but when an aeroplane becomes a boat on water, who gives way to whom? Who gives way to a flying boat? That was always an interesting question.'

One night an astrodome blew to bits around his head while on a night flight up to Fiji with a Solent.

'I was standing up there admiring the view after taking star sights with the sextant. The astrodome suddenly disappeared and I was slashed across the top of my head. The sudden rush of air and the noise of four Bristol Hercules were incredible. The people (flying crew) up front heard all the din coming from behind the curtains but had no idea what was going on. Fortunately another pilot was able to replace me after I was bandaged up and given a stiff whisky to get over the shock. That was quite exciting.'

The gradual change from enclosed waterways to land-based airports brought the four-engine Douglas DC-6. Pressurised at 19,000 feet, the DC-6 was a real step forward during the mid-1950s. They offered comfort and reasonable speed. They were a very reliable and very tame sort of aeroplane.

'We lost the odd engine, but an engine failure was no great drama. You just scuttled off to the nearest bit of dirt. And on a clear day, 19,000 feet above the Tasman and approaching the South Island, you would see the coastline for a couple of hundred miles, or more when the sun was shining on the snow. Sometimes we would do a circuit around Mt Cook, well above the summit ridge. That was always a great PR exercise, and well worth it if we had time. A DC-6, I expect, provided one of the easiest ways to get to the top of Mt Cook.

'The turbo-prop Lockheed Electra, introduced from 1959, was the first aeroplane we had that was "shot in the arse with brains". It was one of the first to have gone into highly complex, and useful, electronics in a big way. It was a wonderful aeroplane. They had problems in America with Electras losing bits of the wings and one thing and another. For a time until it was all sorted out we flew what was called the "Leap" programme. The aeroplane was limited to about 225 knots, and we were not able to use the autopilot. So it was all hand flying, which was a great experience really, until our aeroplanes were progressively returned to America to have the wings modified.

'We always had plenty of power. The four engines were buried in the wings, or the wings were buried in the engines, as some people used to say. The very big propellers ran at a constant speed. To put power on you just changed pitch on the propellers. They were very noisy on the ground.

'During my time on Electras I had five or six engine failures. A runaway prop was something to be feared. The constant-speed Allison engine ran at 9000 or 10,000 rpm (necessary to produce the power) and a gearbox reduced the rpm to about 1050 for the propellers. A breakdown, reducing the load on those huge propellers, could have them winding up to 10,000 rpm. At that rate they would soon disintegrate and wreck the wing. Fortunately, that was a rare thing to happen. We had a "panic" handle for each engine. It was a great thing on the Electra. It cut the fuel, ignition, and everything. All you had to do was to pull the right handle!

'TEAL crashed an Electra at Whenuapai while on a training flight on 27 March 1965. The pilot was having a check, doing what might be best described as a "kamikaze" approach. The idea was to come in at 1000 feet, or 600 feet if the visibility was really bad, and stick the nose down and round out at the last minute. They didn't round out quickly enough and the aeroplane just sank into the ground.

'The Electra, having such a high wing loading, needed quite a bit of lead time if it was going to pull out of a steep descent. Fortunately nobody got hurt. The company safety officer was on the flight deck. It was an object lesson for him, of course. He was a very nice bloke but he found out that flying on training exercises was not as safe as he had thought it was.

'That type of weird and wonderful approach was given away, very quickly. I had done the exercise but I generally failed. I was too cowardly. I always pulled up too early.'

The following year, on another training flight, at Mangere, a DC-8 crashed while simulating an engine failure on takeoff. 'The power lever was pulled back quickly and the reverse thrust lever, which was part of the same lever, flicked up and put a tremendous amount of horsepower into reverse thrust. There was no way in the world they could have controlled the aeroplane. Had the power lever been pulled off slowly it wouldn't have happened. But the idea was to whip it off to simulate a failure. Heavier springs were subsequently put on the reverse levers so it couldn't happen again. Two crew members were killed. That was a great tragedy.

'Progressing from the Electra to the DC-8 pure jet was quite a jump, especially because we had no simulator. We had to do all our training in the aeroplane. That was pretty exciting. None of us had flown big jets at all.

'The DC-8 was very nice to fly and quite forgiving for a big jet. You had to watch the engines. If you throttled back those early jet engines too far while on final approach, there was quite an appreciable period before they gave full power, if it was needed, for a go around. The DC-8 enabled longer-range flights, especially into Hong Kong, opening up the Orient services.'

Jack and Mary spent about 18 months living in Hong Kong during 1966 and 1967. It was an idyllic life for those who could escape the

An Air New Zealand DC-8 passes a Mount Cook Airlines HS 748 while departing Christchurch for a trans-Tasman flight in 1970. 'The DC-8 was nice to fly and quite forgiving for a big jet,' recalls Jack Shorthouse.
ROY SINCLAIR

obligatory and time-wasting coffee mornings, airline cocktail parties, and poodlefaking.

'We spent some of our leisure time learning about Chinese creeds and customs. By that time I was also a keen yachtsman,' Jack said. 'Peter Allen was my flight engineer. We joined the Royal Hong Kong Yacht Club. Peter and I were inspected very carefully before we were allowed to join. It was very British, and Toc H.

'We had a 12-foot Enterprise class. During one race I made a botch of going around a buoy. Peter abused hell out of me. Later, someone asked why I had let my flight engineer speak to me in such a way. I pointed out that while I was the captain on the aeroplane, Peter was the captain of the boat. He had every right to bully me while we were on the water!'

THE LARGER WIDE-BODIED McDonnell Douglas DC-10 tri-jet, introduced from 1973, was Jack Shorthouse's favourite aeroplane. 'Yes, it was the nicest aeroplane I ever flew. Later I flew up front in the next version, the MD-11, with its so-called glass cockpit and a crew of only two, a captain and co-pilot. It was a new experience for an old pilot like me who was used to having a flight engineer as the technical adviser, and someone who could pass the tea and biscuits. I didn't understand too much about the MD-11. It was certainly very impressive.'

It was a big disappointment when the DC-10s were taken off between 1981 and 1986, partly owing to various problems with the aeroplane and, especially, the Air New Zealand DC-10 crash on Mt Erebus on 28 November 1979, while on a scenic flight. Aviation people, Jack said, will always argue about the cause of the crash, which killed 257 people.

In the original investigation the Chief Inspector of Air Accidents, Ron Chippindale, put pilot error as the probable cause. Captain Jim Collins, uncertain of his position, had descended below the supposedly minimum operating height of 15,000 feet, into terrain of apparent 'poor surface and horizon definition'. A subsequent Royal Commission, headed by High Court Judge Peter Mahon, put the principal cause as a change in navigation coordinates and a failure to notify the crew, combined with the effects of sector whiteout. Unknowingly, a very experienced crew flew into a mountain they did not see.

'I find it hard to accept that Jim Collins showed any lack of airmanship,' said Jack Shorthouse. 'I was involved in his training from time to time and he was a thoroughly conservative, able and experienced pilot.

The DC-10 had an unbelievably accurate inertial navigation system we called "area nav". You put a cassette (like a cassette tape) into the computers. You then dialled up an appropriate number and the aeroplane would fly a course to the nth degree. You could even bang in a waypoint during the flight and programme to fly a holding pattern. Also, at an airport, each parking bay had a specific number and all these were on the area nav tape. It would take you to the hangar if that's where you wanted to go. If you had a latitude and longitude coordinate to take you to the middle of Mt Erebus, that is where it would take you once you pressed the "Go To" button. I believe the principal cause of the DC-10 crash was the inaccurate coordinates that Collins did not know about.

'Even though mechanical or systems failures were not factors in the Erebus crash, the DC-10s had already been involved in other unfortunate incidents. One crashed in Paris as a result of decompression when a cargo door fell off. Another, at Chicago, crashed when an engine flew off a wing moments after takeoff. The engine coming away cut away the hydraulics controlling the wing's leading edge slats. The flaps closed and the plane crashed.

'I think the DC-10 came off the line too quickly. McDonnell Douglas may have wanted to get it into service before the Lockheed L-1011 TriStar. Once all the problems were sorted out the DC-10 became a wonderful aeroplane. I had finished my flying career by the mid-1970s. At that stage Air New Zealand was going forward to a bigger, and better, aeroplane as I suppose the later Boeing 747 was.

'A lot of DC-10s are still flying very well now. The "Big Ten" had a good range and there were only three engines to worry about. When we were training on early Qantas Boeing 747s in Australia, the so-called "new" aeroplane, having less electronic systems, especially for navigation, was somewhat primitive after the DC-10.'

JACK SHORTHOUSE WAS aged 60 when, in 1980, he was asked to be part of the Boeing 747 project. He had finished flying in 1975 and had stayed on with Air New Zealand as a DC-10 simulator trainer.

'Apart from having a crack at the odd light aeroplane, I hadn't done any flying for five years. I was asked to join the Boeing project because of my long experience and instructing. When I expressed some reluctance at the prospect of being away from home for eight weeks, at some location yet to be decided, I was merely told that any pilot wants to fly a new aeroplane. That, of course, is perfectly true.

'So I insisted that I would be paid the same allowances as the flying people involved with the project. I said I wanted to be able to afford to eat the same food, and drink the same amount of beer.'

By 1980 all of his flying licences had lapsed. For the occasion, to make it legal, the Air Department agreed to give him a basic Student Pilot's Licence. It was a licence (now discontinued) that allowed a student pilot to fly solo while training for a Private Pilot's Licence.

'So off I went, down to the Air Department office in Auckland, and asked a young lady for the appropriate application. She looked at me a little suspiciously, and got a form out. She was still watching me as I put my glasses on and started to fill it in. Beside the question asking the number of hours flown I filled in 21,000. She was looking at this. I didn't say anything. Then I heard a strange utterance of, "But, but, but, but . . ."

I then told her about my licences having lapsed. She thought it was quite funny. The form was sent off to Qantas. They said, "We can't let a student pilot fly our 747s!" Air New Zealand said, "You will have to. That's part of the contract."

'"He's a very experienced pilot and instructor," the Air New Zealand people told their Qantas counterparts. In turn, they agreed that I *seemed* to have had quite a bit of experience. They let me join the training. I caused a lot of commotion in aviation circles, I tell you. I caused a lot of giggles too!'

Jack went to Sydney to do all the cockpit simulator training and technical courses. The hands-on flying was at Avalon, near Melbourne.

'It was great to be leaning on the pole (control column) again and flying. I enjoyed it very much. The 747-200 was quite an aeroplane. The Qantas staff called it "Fat Albert". It was a much bigger aeroplane than the DC-10. It had four engines instead of three. We each did five hours of flying and got our 747-200 type rating.'

Jack Shorthouse continued on with simulator training at Air New Zealand until his retirement in 1984.

THESE DAYS JACK has no shortage of interests. He does a little wood carving. He makes fruit bowls and other items from unusual pieces of driftwood found near his home. He helps in the kitchen, and can produce his own respectable blend of smoky bush tea. Yet his flying days are never very far from his thoughts. To anyone who will listen he will talk about the transition from a bomber pilot to airline captain. And he will always be a flying instructor, thinking of ways to produce better pilots and safer operations.

'In modern airline flying there was no room for a one-man band on the flight deck,' he tells me. 'Total team work was something Air New Zealand was very hot on. Those days we had a captain, co-pilot, and flight engineer. If I did something wrong I expected the co-pilot to say something. He was, after all, a professional pilot as well. All he was doing was trying to put the skids under me because I was sitting in his seat. I recall when a Lockheed TriStar crashed at Miami. The captain and co-pilot were both concentrating on one problem, and flew into the ground. Similar mishaps have happened, too often, in New Zealand.

'With teamwork, one person is always flying the aeroplane while someone else is monitoring. Someone is *always* flying the aeroplane.'

Although some long flights — for example, 12 hours from Auckland to Los Angeles — could be a little boring, he could not say there was ever nothing to do. 'There were always other aeroplanes to consider, always a radio to monitor, instruments to check, engine performances to monitor, and fuel flows. Are you ahead or behind on fuel? What is the weather like where you are going? Where are you going to go if something goes wrong, and what are you going to do? What happens if another aeroplane goes into Hong Kong before you and bursts a tyre, blocking the runway?

'High density routes present additional concerns, and losing radio communication, when you can't talk to or hear anybody for an hour, can be something you can get a bit worried about. That used to happen between Los Angeles and Tahiti.

'Forecasting is a damn sight better than it used to be. I remember approaching Whenuapai in a DC-6 one night at about 10 o'clock. I called them up on the tower when I was about 100 miles out and a bloke said, "Don't waste too much time, the fog is starting to form."

'So I hastened on and called up the tower again, and said, "Oh well, ask the Met people what they think it's going to do." I was thinking about a diversion. He came back a couple of minutes later. He sounded quite surprised and I could almost hear the disbelief in his voice.

'"The forecaster said, and I quote, 'I'm not really surprised. We have had a lot of rain lately.'" I wasn't very impressed. It wasn't a hell of a lot of use, really. We did get in. At the first opportunity, I told the Met people all about it.'

He says airline flying used to be a glamour occupation. 'There weren't very many of us, and the business of pushing a heavier-than-air machine through the sky seemed to have some appeal to the young blokes in particular.

Jack Shorthouse's favourite, the Douglas DC-10 tri-jet. 'It was the nicest aeroplane I ever flew.' AIR NEW ZEALAND

'Pilots talked about being up there, free of the ground, in blue skies, dodging clouds and all that nonsense. It's just a tough job now. It's lost a lot of its glamour. Today's pilots are involved with checks all the time: six-monthly proficiency checks, route checks, emergency drills, and medicals. Then, maybe, suddenly you've got no pilot's licence — you've harmed your hearing or lost an eye — and you're no longer any use to the airline.

'Pilots are constantly under pressure. Procedures keep changing. You're learning about a new airfield. New equipment comes out on each new type of aeroplane. You are away from home for many days at a time. You can never allow personality clashes on the flight deck. Airline flying takes a lot of time out of your life.

'We were sometimes facetiously called "bus drivers". Next thing, we hear that a bus driver has become a "coach captain". I suppose we should have demanded to become an admiral or commodore! What does it matter? We were driving a big airborne bus but it was never as easy as it might have looked. We spent six weeks at ground school learning to fly a new type, understanding different flying characteristics, emergency procedures and systems.

'I recall meeting a captain of a cruise ship at some function Mary and I attended in Hong Kong. I was introduced as a TEAL captain. That seemed to trigger him. He obviously didn't like airline pilots. He told me my aeroplane, then a DC-8, carried only about 150 passengers; he was responsible for 2000 or so people on his cruise ship.

'I asked him what happened when he got into trouble coming into a harbour, or if he was in fog with no visibility. He said he could put out his sea anchors and, in any case, he would have a harbour pilot on board. I told him that I had no such thing as a sea anchor and that I had to think at 580 mph and, if I ran out of fuel, I crashed.

The last aeroplane Jack Shorthouse flew was a Qantas Boeing 747-200 at Avalon, near Melbourne. The year was 1980. ROY SINCLAIR

He had only to think at 25 mph.

'Soon we both got tired of arguing and, once our differences were sorted out, we got on quite well.

'Increasingly there are women on the flight deck. Not so long ago Mary and I flew with Continental to the United States. We were disappointed not to have had any women pilots on our flights. Continental has employed women pilots for quite some years now. Several have become captains in the left-hand seat. You never hear of them having any problems — or accidents.'

Jack tried gliding, briefly, after he left Air New Zealand. 'It was nice and quiet. But that is disturbing when you have spent so long believing that three or four big jet engines were the answer for flying. I have had three helicopter flights. I didn't enjoy them. Helicopters are not meant to fly at all.'

He will always have another story to tell. One starts at 3 am, at Tahiti. He had gone out early to 'kick a few tyres and other things' in preparation for the DC-10 flight to Auckland.

'I was met on the steps by the head purser. Despite the ungodly hour, he was looking very pleased with himself.

'"Do you know who is on this flight?" he asked.

'"No idea," I said. "Who?"

'"Glen Campbell," he said, his grin widening.

'"Who's he?" I said, feeling as if I was about to spoil his day. The purser looked at me. Other cabin crew joined him. They were all looking at me as if I was indeed a "poor bugger". How was I to know he was a favourite American pop singer of the 1970s? Mary, of course, would have known. She would probably have one of his records. I knew something more about classical music.

'To help make amends I invited Glen Campbell onto the flight deck. He was a really nice bloke. He was just earning his living by the sweat of his brow, I guess.'

LOOKING BACK ON the 'Skies of War', Jack Shorthouse says it's just something that happened in the past. History. He has corresponded with a German who had written an article in a Bomber Command publication. It was about the raid on Mannheim the particular night that earned Jack Shorthouse his Distinguished Flying Cross.

'We have exchanged photographs and Christmas cards. He keeps saying, "Come over and see us." I don't think there is much bitterness between people these days. Some people still go on about the POW camps and the Japanese. There's not much point in it really. The present generation, on both sides, thinks about things a little differently.

'But I still keep in touch with wartime friends, belong to several associations and have attended many reunions over the years.'

Waving a hand towards his collection of models, he says model-making has been just something for him to do. He is still building a Fairey Gordon, Liberator, and Catalina. 'Trouble is,' he says, 'I'm a bit impatient.'

MARY LISTENS AND says nothing as we enjoy an excellent evening meal. There is a break in the conversation. It is quiet. We have been talking about the Skies of Peace. The silence is eventually broken by Mary's softly spoken Canadian accent. 'Jack always loved his flying,' she says. 'He never complained, like some other pilots did, about being on the long international routes. It was difficult for us to arrange to go to a concert or the ballet. Sometimes he would agree to do something for the children at some school function, only to find that the schedules were changed and he had to be away somewhere. That used to disappoint him. But I know, given half a chance, he would do it all over again.'

The Fairey Gordon, one of the model aeroplanes Jack Shorthouse is still to finish building. 'I'm a bit impatient,' he says.

It's just like old times for veteran aviators Murray Thomas (sitting in the rear cockpit) and Ken Paterson as they check out an old Tiger Moth used to give joyrides at Wigram.
ROY SINCLAIR

CHAPTER 6

The Forgotten Crash of ZK-AND on Franz Josef Glacier

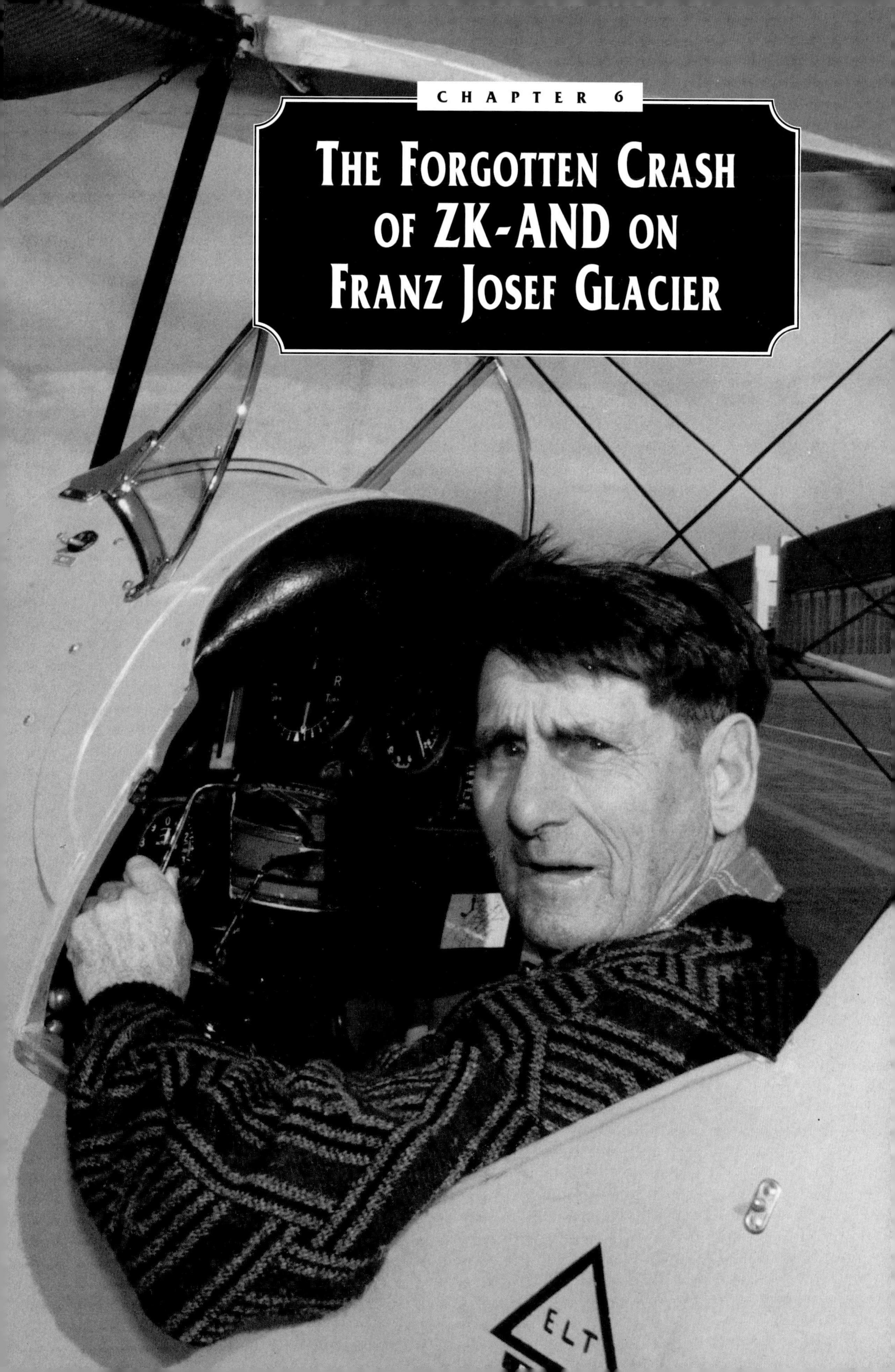

The wheels hit. Then the nose hit. We did three nose-to-tail somersaults, hearing an awful crunch each time a wing was torn off.

Murray Thomas

KEN PATERSON AND Murray Thomas are two unlikely candidates for a life-long friendship. No two people could be more different. Ken is a retired primary school headmaster and the archetypal gentleman. You would expect to meet him at any highbrow classical orchestral performance in the Christchurch Town Hall. Murray is a retired tradesman, not nearly so refined. He could be expected to be found delving into one sort of prank or another — a real hard case. Ken and Murray are veteran pilots. They share a conviction that flying an aeroplane with an extra set of wings — a biplane — attracts a special kind of camaraderie. But their friendship has also been sealed by an almost forgotten, albeit remarkable, tale of search and survival that followed a plane crash on the Franz Josef Glacier nearly half a century ago.

TO START THEIR story, an aeroplane with an extra set of wings had to be found. That was easy. A restored Tiger Moth barnstorming from the former Wigram Air Force Base is a common sight over Christchurch. It is very much like the Tiger Moths Ken and Murray flew on the South Island West Coast, and they needed little persuasion when I suggested we go and have a look. Once installed in the familiar open cockpits, memories of early aero club flying soon came flooding back.

Most vivid were memories of their scenic flights over Franz Josef

Murray Thomas flying ZK-AND over Greymouth on 30 April 1949. The photograph was taken by Margaret Instone, from an aeroplane piloted by Ken Paterson.

Glacier, which ended abruptly on 23 April 1950, when the Tiger Moth ZK-AND Murray Thomas was flying struck an ice pinnacle and cartwheeled into a crevasse. The crash was followed by an extensive air search, which failed to find any trace of the missing aeroplane, and a successful rescue by two glacier guides, Ralph Warburton and Stephen Graham — and Butch, a loveable border collie.

'It's the forgotten crash of Franz Josef,' recalled Ken Paterson. 'Whenever people talk about crashes on the glacier it's never mentioned. We did get on the BBC news, and there were spectacular photographs in the newspapers taken by Ralph Warburton, but these days you would have to do something a bit more spectacular to get noticed — even if a glacier is about the worst place to choose to land on.'

Over a 50-year period three aircraft have crashed near the same spot on Franz Josef. The first, on 29 October 1943, involved Air Travel's Fox Moth ZK-AEK, which today is restored and flying at Wanaka. The Fox Moth was being flown by Orville Darcy 'Aussie' Openshaw. Despite the considerable wreckage, 'Aussie' and his passengers (four women from the WAAF) survived with a few cuts and blood noses. On 25 October 1993 a twin-engined Nomad on charter from Auckland crashed, killing six German tourists and three New Zealand crew. The Fox Moth and Nomad crashes have been well documented. Little is known about the 1950 Tiger Moth crash.

KEN AND MURRAY met on the West Coast and got into flying. Ken, aged 24, was teaching at a Greymouth school. Murray, aged 22, worked in Trumans' general store. Both young men had always dreamed of flying. Ken believes that in 1946, when he obtained his Private Pilot's Licence, he may have been the first person on the West Coast to learn to fly from scratch and get a civil licence after World War II.

'I had always wanted to fly. I was born in England and was only six weeks old when my parents emigrated to New Zealand in 1925. We went to live in Greymouth. As I grew up I used to run down to the airfield whenever I heard an aeroplane fly over, or down to Blaketown where the aeroplanes landed on the beach at low tide.'

With no flying instructor or ground engineer in Greymouth, Ken had to go to Hokitika, catching the 7 am railcar. He then walked across the combined rail and road bridge to the Air Travel NZ Ltd airfield on the south bank of the Hokitika River. Norm Suttie, an Air Travel pilot, was his instructor.

A mountain guide overlooks the Franz Josef Glacier during the search for ZK-AND. A cross marks the spot where the survivors were found.
RALPH WARBURTON

'Norm Suttie was quite a character. I was always a bit rough on the controls until one day he said, "Look Ken, just imagine that that joystick you are holding between your legs is your cock. Be a bit more gentle with it!"'

The Private Pilot's 'A' Licence test involved flying three figure-of-eights between two points about 800 yards apart, and landing within a given distance of an airfield marker. Next, the student pilot took off again, climbed to 2000 feet, closed the throttle and landed with no engine, again within a certain distance from the marker. The examiner watched from the ground. A few questions were asked about aircraft performance and aviation in general, and a licence was issued to fly solo.

An advanced licence endorsement to carry passengers involved 25 hours solo, dual cross-country flights, a solo cross-country flight of more than 50 miles, and three hours of advanced dual instruction that included steep turns, recovery from stalls and cross-wind landings.

Murray Thomas said he enjoyed climbing mountains so he joined an alpine club. When the aero club started he imagined an aeroplane would provide a quicker and much easier way to climb mountains. He met Ken and they both started flying. Those days an hour in the air cost £3 15s, or about a week's wages. To help the flying fund Murray worked as a taxi-dispatch officer at nights. 'Ken and I realised as soon as we met that we were very different people. But we have always been cobbers.'

The West Coast United Aero Club, representing Karamea, Westport, Greymouth and Hokitika, had three Tiger Moths surplus from the war. ZK-AND was special for Ken, being the first aeroplane he flew solo.

Ken and Murray flew south to the glaciers on 22 April 1950. It was a clear Saturday morning and the weather for the weekend looked ideal for the two pilots wanting to earn some cash from scenic flying. Ken was flying ZK-AND, and Murray, ZK-ALP. Ken had already made several glacier flights. Murray, who got his pilot's licence about 18 months later than Ken, was about to make his first flight over the glacier.

'The aero club never really had a proper licence to take passengers on scenic flights. We issued a free ticket and then asked for an appropriate donation,' Ken recalled. 'There was never a shortage of people wanting a joyride. A glacier is really a huge basin of snow that has tumbled over an icefall. It is usually very steep from top to bottom, but Franz Josef is also quite a steep drop from one side to the other.

'On Sunday morning Murray and I made several glacier flights. I flew up the right-hand side (the high side) of the glacier to the Defiance hut at about 6000 feet. From there I throttled back to cruise power and zig-zagged down, turning away from the glacier at each turn. It was very spectacular flying across the crumpled ice.

'At the time I didn't realise that Murray flew up the left side (the lower side) of the glacier and did the flight in reverse. We believed we followed good airmanship, always having an escape route, but we were really flying string bags of aeroplanes that were notoriously underpowered.'

The weekend had been very successful and it certainly boosted the flying fund. After lunch on Sunday the two pilots were refuelling, hand pumping from a 44-gallon drum, preparing to fly back to Greymouth.

'My Tiger Moth was refuelled ready to go and I was busy refuelling ALP when a middle-aged man, a farmer from the North Island, his wife and daughter turned up. The daughter was about our age and looked all right. I think Murray took an instant fancy to her. But it was her father, Norman Marshall from Ngaruawahia, who wanted a flight. I said to Murray, "You might as well take AND and fly the chap over the glacier."'

(The 'daughter' was actually a family friend touring New Zealand with the Marshalls. She was Wendy McNaughton, described by a cousin as a vivacious blonde girl who turned the head of many a young man during her South Island travels. Wendy died in a car crash during the 1980s.)

Twenty minutes later Murray had not returned as he should have done. Ken waited another five minutes and then started to get a little uneasy. He then took off, accompanied by Russell Sutherland, a Greymouth dentist. They flew over the normal route, and saw nothing.

'I alerted Air Traffic Control in Christchurch and our Greymouth Aero Club that an aircraft was possibly missing. I then searched until late in the afternoon. By that time the wind had got up and it was very bumpy.'

HAVING CRASHED ON the glacier, Murray Thomas was attempting to secure his passenger, a much heavier man than the pilot. To do this Murray had to unfasten his passenger's seat strap and haul him up with just one hand, without letting him drop into the gaping crevasse. The Tiger Moth was held by the tail, jammed into the top of an ice pinnacle.

'We had ended up in one of the roughest parts of the glacier. It was all pinnacles and crevasses. To have tried to go anywhere would have been madness. All we could do was stare into the cold blue depths of the crevasse we were suspended over.'

Murray had approached the glacier at about 2000 feet and climbed on a zig-zag course to the Almer hut. With ice above and below, and on each side, judging one's exact position becomes difficult. He turned as usual above a trough of smooth snow, throttled back, and started to descend over the pinnacles.

'The ground rose even though it was further down the glacier. It always looked as if we would touch the pinnacles but we always had plenty of clearance. Not this time. I could see the wheels were going to hit the top of a pinnacle.

'The wheels hit. Then the nose hit. We did three nose-to-tail somersaults, hearing an awful crunch each time a wing was torn off. Apart from the awful shock we were unhurt when everything stopped crashing about us. I ripped out an instrument panel and tried to use it as a reflector. When Ken started the search he was passing so close above I could almost read his air speed indicator, yet he didn't spot us. I even tried to set a seat cushion alight to create some smoke but we were probably lucky I didn't succeed. There was a lot of petrol about.

'Even next day with other aircraft joining the search we weren't seen. For them to find us in that very broken part of the glacier would

Much relieved, Murray Thomas, left, and his erstwhile passenger, Norman Marshall, pose for Ralph Warburton's camera at the glacier crash site on 24 April 1950.
RALPH WARBURTON

Guide Stephen Graham looks over the wreckage of the crashed Tiger Moth.
RALPH WARBURTON

be like a speeding motorcyclist trying to spot something through a picket fence. These days a helicopter could have found us quite easily.'

The night spent on the glacier was very cold. Fortunately they were dressed for open cockpit flying and sheltered in what was left of the plane. But Murray's passenger was in a frightful mental state and did not believe he would be rescued. Murray spent much of the night comforting his passenger and preventing him from sliding down into the crevasse.

ALMOST 24 HOURS after the crash they were found by two experienced alpine guides, Ralph Warburton and Stephen Graham. Ralph Warburton, now living in Wanaka, is also known for his fine alpine photography. Stephen Graham, living close to Christchurch, is remembered for his border collie, Butch, who often accompanied him on the glacier. Butch was the runt of the litter. With two extra feet and claws to use as crampons, glacier trekking was just good fun for Butch. When the going got too steep, Butch simply walked in his master's footsteps.

The rescue is still vivid in the guides' minds. When they spotted the crash early on Monday afternoon and saw the occupants were alive they did not let them know they were almost upon them until they were sure they could be reached.

Later, when I talked to Ralph Warburton, he told me the two men were just clinging to the wrecked aeroplane with absolutely no way of getting off. 'I think Norman Marshall was resigned to the fact that he would die on the glacier.

'We were wearing clinkered boots, and I also had crampons, which I got Norman to put on. I also had a spare pair of socks, which I got

Murray to pull on over his flying boots. That was a trick I had learned from a visiting Swiss guide. It gave Murray the necessary grip on the ice for about two hours, till the socks wore out. They were two very lucky men. Norman had a small graze above one eye. That was all.'

Ralph said he and Stephen had no idea where the aeroplane might have been when they started searching, or if they were on the glacier at all. They might have gone to look at the wild country of the Gallery Valley.

'Stephen and I went up either side of the glacier looking in all the big holes and gullies. It had been perfectly clear when they had been flying on Sunday morning but by the middle of the day a strong easterly wind was pouring down the glacier. There would have been plenty of downdrafts. As we worked our way up we both began to hear weak calls for help, brought down the glacier on the wind. We climbed towards the cries — towards the centre of the glacier. And the weak cries became louder.

'At last we saw a head move about 100 yards away, but the holes between each pinnacle became deeper and deeper. It took 15 minutes to cover the last few yards.'

Stephen had Butch with him. Butch didn't exactly find the missing airmen, although one newspaper reporter wrote an endearing story about the event, claiming he did. The fact was that the border collie was unable to negotiate the treacherous ice pinnacles. But Stephen said Butch knew where the men were once they were within about half a mile. 'He was very good at following a track in the glacier.' Later, Murray said they had heard a dog barking, and that seemed quite strange.

MURRAY RECALLED SEEING his friend Ken coming towards him as he and Norman and the two guides were walking up the track towards the Franz Josef township. 'I started singing, "Baby it's cold out there", which was a popular song at the time.'

Ralph Warburton had recorded the rescue magnificently on film, and one photograph became 'Picture of the Month' in *Time*.

'It was disappointing to see the photograph credited to Green and Hahn Photography and not to me,' recalled Ralph Warburton. 'The caption also said the photograph was taken on a Speed Graphic camera at 100th of a second at f8. I had taken it with my Rolleicord at 250th of a second at f11.'

Soon after the rescue the pilots shifted to Christchurch and settled into married life, with little spare money for flying. The friendship continued, with each being best man at the other's wedding. Ken took up flying again for a short time with the National Airways Corporation Flying Club during the 1970s but found the regulations for private pilots had become much more stringent. Today he leaves all the flying to his son Geoff, an Air New Zealand Boeing 767 captain.

Murray has suffered a stroke, but will still hobble outdoors whenever he hears the Wigram Tiger Moth joyriding over Christchurch.

'It was the Tiger Moth that saved us,' he says, if anyone mentions the incident. 'Those days we were young and inexperienced. Not many people were scenic flying over the glaciers. My wife tells me that we were all just young and silly then.'

Ken can recall the partying that went on at Franz Josef after the rescue. Then the whole thing faded into insignificance. He once mentioned the crash to a helicopter pilot at Franz Josef and he said he'd never heard of it. The young pilot from Mount Cook Airlines who was flying the Wigram Tiger Moth the day we called in September 1995 had not heard of it either. But he was fascinated by the story, and especially Murray's somewhat comical account of the air search led by his friend.

'There we were stuck down a crevasse and listening to those aeroplanes flying over so close to us. I knew Ken would be flying one of them, but he never saw us poor freezing buggers stuck down in the

Starting the long walk down the glacier, Stephen Graham, left, offers encouragement to crash victims, Norman Marshall and Murray Thomas.
RALPH WARBURTON

With extra feet, and claws to use as crampons, glacier trekking was just good fun for Butch, Stephen Graham's border collie.
RALPH WARBURTON

ice. Bloody hopeless, he was. We were hungry as hell when they did finally spot us. They dropped a parcel, and what do you think was in it? Bandages! Bloody bandages, that was all! I tell you, they were all bloody hopeless.'

Ken said they were very well hidden and he only spotted them after the guides found the wreck. 'Murray later told me I had flown directly over him. It was a mile across the glacier and the ice was all crumpled.

'The crash did create quite a stir at the time because private flying was just getting into stride again after the war. The photographs Ralph took really made it into something.

'I flew Murray back to Greymouth on Tuesday. I wanted to get him back into the air as soon as possible. There was no Civil Aviation inquiry into the accident. Air accident investigation had not been set up after the war. The police asked a few questions and agreed with us when we told them a glacier is one of the worst places to land an aeroplane.'

When I talked to Stephen Graham he said, 'I don't think the young pilots realised how quickly the glacier climbs and I think Murray was also caught by a downdraft. Many people since have made the same mistake, but with much greater consequences.'

THE WRECKAGE OF Tiger Moth ZK-AND remains to this day gripped somewhere within the glacier, although it has been claimed that a wheel was recovered, and that for many years it supported a wheelbarrow used in the Franz Josef township. Murray Thomas died on 4 November 1997.

ASSOCIATION

CHAPTER 7

AEROBATICS, PRECISION AND CHALLENGES

Pam Collings, an aviator who has fulfilled many dreams, relaxes at Forest Field, her private North Canterbury airfield. The visiting aeroplane is a Canterbury Aero Club Cherokee 140.
ROY SINCLAIR

I stood wide-eyed and open-mouthed, watching an aeroplane perform manoeuvres I thought were not possible. From that moment my dream was to compete at a World Aerobatic Championships.

Pam Collings

A ROAD LEADS to the West Eyreton farm owned by Ces and Pam Collings. I did not use it to get there. When I asked Pam for directions she breezily brushed aside my request and suggested I get my daughter to fly me out. 'Kirsten will know where to find us at Forest Field,' she said.

It seemed a great way to start a new story. We took off from the grass strip outside the Canterbury Aero Club and, 10 minutes later, were flying up the north bank of the Waimakariri River. To me one paddock from 2500 feet looks the same as the next but Kirsten soon picked up the tell-tale signs of an airfield. She compared what she was seeing beyond the spinning propeller with the Visual Flight Guide open on her lap. Then I spotted the limp white windsock. With no appreciable wind, my pilot had a choice of three grass runways. She applied a notch of flap, adjusted her airspeed and did the usual impres-

Pam Collings enjoys a special moment with a Pitts Special model made for her by Ces shortly before they married. 'Pam grizzled about owning a Pitts Special so I made her one,' says Ces. 'It wasn't good enough but it was the best I could do at the time.' The model sat on their wedding cake.
CHRISTCHURCH STAR

sive flyover — checking it all out — chose runway 18/36, and banked the Cherokee 140 steeply. With another notch of flap applied, landing checks completed, full-flap, we were on finals.

On a clear winter morning, in July 1997, I was on my way to talk to the New Zealand Airwomen's Association president, who is perhaps better known for her aerobatics flying at world championship level. I had somehow expected to see her out on the airfield, frantically waving instructions up to us. But no sign of life was evident as we touched down. We rollicked along the strip and mercifully came to a stop near an open-sided shed that promised shelter for the high-winged aeroplane inside. With the motor idling we looked for a house, and taxied back along the runway. We arrived at the door. Smells from the coffee pot inside suggested a visitor was expected. Pam was busy hanging out the washing. My pilot, pristine in her flying instructor's uniform, was soon back in the aeroplane, leaving me behind to discover an aviator who has had the luck to fulfil many dreams.

Pam Collings was at a World Aerobatic Championships event in France when she saw her first Pitts Special. That was in 1972. She stood wide-eyed and open-mouthed as she watched the aeroplane perform aerobatic manoeuvres she would not have thought possible. Later, flying her own Pitts S-1S, she became the first New Zealand pilot to compete in a World Aerobatic Championships. She has been followed by a MiG jet fighter as she flew across the border between Austria and Hungary, while on her way to Russia. She has owned a succession of small aeroplanes. She now enjoys living beside her own private airfield.

'I THOUGHT I heard someone arriving,' she said in her cheery greeting. Over coffee she talked about the dream of most pilots to have an aeroplane at the back door. She explained how she and Ces had gone one better. Forest Field is much more than a farm cocky's paddock.

'Ten years ago we started to achieve our dream to have our own airfield. We found this piece of land that happened to be the right L shape. In Canterbury you really need to have three runways to cope with the prevailing winds. You've got the north-easterly sea breeze; the nor-wester blowing over the mountains, and then you've got the good old southerly. The three runways fit perfectly into our property.

'It's all been developed quietly over the past eight years. We undid a lot of fences and put them back up in different places. We took out trees and bridged a culvert. The aircraft we had then was a four-seater high-winged Maule. It could fly off a small runway but we wanted something that was suitable for the average private pilot. Aero club aeroplanes can come in here safely. Forest Field is now published on the aeronautical charts.

'Ces is also a pilot as well as the airfield groundsman, mower, or manager — or whatever you like to call him. Although it is a private airfield it is our responsibility to maintain it to the published standards.'

These days Pam does not own an aeroplane but she is looking after a friend's Piper Cub while a homebuilt amphibian is being completed. And she looks forward to friends dropping in, saying she has more visitors from different parts of the country than when she and Ces lived in town.

'We had a couple of Germans here just before last Christmas. They were flying around the world. They had been told about New Zealand being a country where you could stand on a ski field and swim in the ocean, all on the same day. We have heard recently that they crashed in Canada and were both badly burned. When we met them they were people who were achieving a dream.

'We get a lot of visitors from the aero clubs and other flying organisations as well as private aircraft owners. It gives people a different airfield to look at — and we are even discovering that horses can get used to the noise of aeroplanes.'

An immaculate Pitts Special and its proud owner, Pam Collings, at the Canterbury Aero Club hangar in 1976 soon after the aeroplane (still wearing its United States N76NZ registration) arrived in New Zealand.
BILL GAMBLE

Pam Collings with the DM Allan Memorial Cup, for professional pilots aerobatics, which she won at the 1976 Royal New Zealand Aero Club competitions held in Palmerston North. VC BROWNE

WHEN PAM WAS growing up in Christchurch no one in her family flew aeroplanes. 'It's something I had never thought of doing. Then we saw a *Star* newspaper scholarship being offered for flying lessons. Dad said he would enter my brother. I remember thinking, if my brother can enter, why can't I? We both entered but neither of us got anywhere. At least it had started me thinking about flying.

'The following year (1962) Airwork, the local Piper agents, and the Canterbury Aero Club, sponsored a Powder Puff flying scholarship just for girls. I suspect they got the "Powder Puff" from the name of a long-standing women's air race in the United States. It's now called the "All Women's Trans-continental Air Race". Anyway, I won the "Powder Puff" scholarship — even though I never wore much makeup, and still don't — and that got me through my Private Pilot's Licence. At the same time I was doing a BSc degree at the University of Canterbury, and planning a library career.'

AS WE TALK we pause to watch another visitor, in a Piper Tomahawk, touch down on the grass and then take off. Pam is telling me about growing up with two older brothers, an older sister, and veteran MG sports cars — a 1932 J2 and 1937 TA. She was soon learning how to change oil, grind valves, and partaking in the ultimate challenge —

driving them. Flying, she later discovered, was based on coordination and motor skills. She was a student pilot for two years, getting her Private Pilot's Licence in 1965.

'I soon realised I was not the sort of person who got satisfaction from going cross-country — flying from A to B. Rather than go somewhere I enjoyed just going up; me and my aeroplane. I would try and improve my skills, even if I just improved landing accurately to a mark.

During a visit to Blenheim I was taken up in a Tiger Moth and we did a loop. I really enjoyed that.

'I recall having to have the straps done up pretty tight. At the top of the loop there wasn't anything between me and the world out there.'

Learning aerobatics flying was not frightening, Pam tells me. Everything is done to a discipline. And, everything starts at a very safe height, with an instructor. Not too much can happen. Even competition flying is simplified by practising manoeuvres, individually, then stringing them together at a high altitude before quietly bringing them down lower as you gain experience. Aerobatics was just another skill to master.

Putting the Pitts Special through a few aerobatic manoeuvres over Otaki while returning home from the 1976 Palmerston North Royal NZ Aero Club competitions.
CES COLLINGS

Pitts
SPECIAL
N76NZ

'Like anything, there is an element of risk, but you minimise that risk.'

Pam did her basic aerobatic training in a Citabria aeroplane. She progressed through club competitions. Then, in 1972, she travelled overseas. It was the year when the World Aerobatic Championships were held in France.

'I was aged 27, and older than most young people setting out on their obligatory overseas experience. I had earned enough money to go overseas for 10 months without needing to work. I arrived in Kathmandu and went from there to London by bus.

'In Britain I met a couple of girls and we travelled around Europe with a car and a tent. We timed it so we ended up at the World Aerobatic Championships. Fortunately, my companions also enjoyed the aerobatics, and we stayed the whole week. The desire was born there to compete one day at a world championship event.'

Pam met Bill Thomas from the United States team and arranged to visit him in Florida on the way home to New Zealand. He ran a flying school and offered a 10-hour advanced aerobatics course in a two-place Pitts Special.

'Having flown one of Bill Thomas's Pitts, I was really hooked. I knew I wanted to own one. I went home and tried to figure out how it would come about. The Eighth World Aerobatic Championships were to be held in the United States in 1976. I was aiming to be there — flying my own aeroplane.'

Buying an aeroplane manufactured in the United States proved to be an interesting exercise. Pam's family helped by getting the overseas funds. But an alien could not own an aeroplane in the United States. 'We had to form a corporation with an American as a shareholder. A lot of little things didn't make it as simple as it would be today. The Pitts S-1S cost $US20,000 which, in 1975, worked out at $NZ14,000.

'It was the fulfilment of one of my dreams — to buy a Pitts and then spend 10 months in the United States competing in various aerobatics competitions. I guess a lot of parents help their kids to achieve what they want to do. A number of people have said to me, "Oh gee! I always wanted to do something like that." I realised a lot of people have dreams but don't manage to achieve them. I couldn't have done it without the help from my family. Somehow you have to get assistance when it is needed most and pay it back later in life. By the time you save the money through your own efforts you have often passed the stage where you are able to do the thing you had dreamed about.'

THESE DAYS, MANY New Zealanders have seen a Pitts Special biplane in New Zealand skies. That was not the case in the 1970s. 'It's really quite an old biplane design — 1945 — it's as old as I am,' Pam says. 'It's structurally sound, and a great performer because of its high power-to-weight ratio. Short highly stressed wings make it an ideally manoeuvrable aeroplane for aerobatics. It has little in common with a better known biplane, the Tiger Moth, which is much slower and more graceful.'

Early in 1975 Pam drove up to the factory — at 6000 feet, in Afton, Wyoming. Her Pitts was completed but it was without its American N76NZ registration, or any of the requested paint-work.

'They probably imagined that someone from New Zealand might not turn up and they weren't game to put the paint on. As it turned out it was a very distinctive Pitts with a tiki on the tail, and a moko. Such decorations would probably not be politically correct these days. But I had a pride in New Zealand. The Pitts also had the Commonwealth Games symbol. That was a clever logo designed for the 1974 games in Christchurch.'

The Pitts was ferried out to Bill Thomas's flying school in Florida. Because Pam had bought the aeroplane through him, he provided 10 hours' instruction, alternating between a two-place dual-control Pitts and her own single-place aeroplane.

'But I hadn't learned all the manoeuvres I would need to know by the time I left Bill, so I sat down with him and a tape recorder. I then went around the country with my tape recorder learning this manoeuvre and that manoeuvre, working through the levels: Sportsman, Intermediate, and Advanced. Unlimited, the next level, is the World Championships class. I travelled through 26 states during my 10 months of training. The Pitts had very little luggage space. I sent my two suitcases on by Greyhound bus to where I might be in about three weeks' time.'

EVERYTHING LOOKED PROMISING for the World Aerobatic Championships the following year. Pam had her aeroplane, and she was close to the venue. It all looked as if it would be very simple. Then the United States pulled out of hosting the event. Perhaps they didn't get the sponsors. The event was now to be held at Kiev, in Russia.

'Suddenly I was confronted with a great logistics problem. Here I was, in the United States, with an aeroplane. If I wanted to compete I would somehow have to get to Russia. I returned to New Zealand

In her uniform representing New Zealand Pam Collings is about to fly her Pitts Special from Trausdorf, in Austria, to the World Aerobatic Championships in Russia.

Flying in formation, Pam Collings photographed companion Pitts Special aircraft over Illinois in the United States.

and had the Pitts shipped home. Luckily, I got a lot of support from friends at the Canterbury Aero Club. We all got involved in fundraising. Posters were made. Castrol offered sponsorship in return for airshows and promotions.

Eventually she was ready to set off for Kiev to represent New Zealand in her new Pitts, accompanied by an even newer husband: Pam and Ces had been married in February 1976. The difficulties and costs of air freighting an aerobatics aeroplane to the other side of the world and back left them in debt for many years.

'It cost us $20,000 just to get there. Air freight was the killer. With the Pitts partially dismantled, with propeller and rudder off, it fitted on a pallet sitting sideways in a Boeing 747. At one stage air freight charges were calculated by volume, and because an axle stuck out a little, by the time Air New Zealand measured all that extra volume it made about $7000 difference.

'Our engineer got so angry. He said he would saw the axle off! Ces merely asked why I didn't play golf or something instead. I would only have to carry a set of golf clubs round the world.'

Pam Collings trained with the Australian team at Trausdorf, a small Austrian town. She faced problems with the weather, and with red tape — and at one stage wondered if she would get to Kiev after all.

Flying from Austria to Russia was another event fraught with difficulties. 'We had to get permission to fly across the border into Hungary where we were to meet up with the Hungarian team at Budapest. We were instructed to cross the border at 0600 GMT — not a minute before or a minute after — and at 4000 feet.

'This is difficult to achieve when the weather is threatening to dictate otherwise. Unbeknown to me at the time a Russian MiG jet was circling overhead. I was told about this later by the people at the Vienna Airport radar. They said they had been concerned for me because a glider had been shot down not so long ago.

'As it turned out it soon became impossible to maintain 4000 feet over Hungary. Then the conditions got so bad I lost sight of the leader. I knew I could not continue on my own and would have to turn back. Somehow I managed to find my way back across the border to Austria. Later I heard the others had been forced down very low before they reached Kiev.'

Pam made several more attempts to fly into Russia. Eventually, with help from the British team, she arrived in Kiev but was too late to enjoy the opening ceremony. In the ensuing championships she finished about the middle of the field, and twelfth out of thirteen women competitors. The top five women's places went to Russian pilots flying Yak-50s.

'I wasn't last, and I was chuffed by my performance, footing it at a world competition level. A lot of money and time had gone into it. But coming from New Zealand, I was often practising in a vacuum. I didn't even know if I was practising right. We had no aerobatics flying comparable to the Unlimited world championships. Then there was a lot of nervousness. Sometimes you make a mistake in the first sequence and think you've blown it. You then relax a bit and start to fly a lot better.'

The next world championships, in Czechoslovakia, were held in 1978. New Zealand was then in the middle of a fuel crisis. Aviation fuel for private flying was restricted to 50 per cent of what a pilot had used the year before. Pam had spent much of 1977 paying back debt, and did little flying. She had very little fuel credit. Even the flying events at the Air Women's Association rally were cancelled that year.

'No way could I have gone to Czechoslovakia. Even in 1980 my prospects looked doubtful for the championships being held at Oshkosh in Wisconsin. Two months before the event one of the organisers rang me. The Eastern block countries had pulled out, leaving only the United States and France with entries in the Women's contest. They needed three countries for a world contest. If I didn't go, there would be no world championship for women.

'I was suddenly needing to go from nought to world standard in just a couple of months. I did a bit of training here. The Americans were very helpful. They found a pilot willing to loan me an aeroplane.

That was a pretty big thing. A Pitts is a very personal aeroplane. It was a generous gesture to let someone they didn't know fly it.

'The trouble was, when I went to fly it, the borrowed Pitts was a lot heavier than a normal competition aeroplane. It also appeared to have a problem with oil pressure. When I queried the oil pressure I was told it had been like that for a while.

'I flew the aeroplane once. There were a few things about it that caused me some concern. To fly an aeroplane, coming down to 300 feet at that Unlimited level, you've got to be pretty confident. I had to make a difficult decision. How do you tell someone that their pride and joy isn't up to scratch when they've offered to loan it to you? I then thought, well, it's my life at stake.

'My decision was soon justified. A couple of weeks later an engine failure resulted in the aeroplane making a forced landing.'

Pam trained with the United States team, using one of their aeroplanes, and finished eighth out of nine women entrants. The following week she enjoyed a day at the famous Oshkosh air show. That was quite an experience, seeing some of the best aerobatics acts and an incredible number of aeroplanes.

THE PITTS SPECIAL ZK-PAC (as it was registered in New Zealand) was sold in 1981. Owning a single-seater Pitts had disadvantages. Pam and Ces had to take two aeroplanes whenever she was competing. Ces often provided commentaries. Pam had intended to replace the Pitts with a two-seater aerobatic aeroplane, but costs had increased to a stage where that was no longer an option. She was suddenly out of competition aerobatic flying.

'Yes, it was difficult to part with the Pitts. It had been a part of my life for four years or more. It was eventually sold in Australia, which was some comfort. I don't know if I would have wanted to see it flying around here when it wasn't mine. So when it went it really went. It is still flown by a Melbourne aerobatics club.

'Your life goes through cycles, and I had probably achieved what I wanted with straight competition flying. I had also heard about precision flying, involving navigation and landing skills. It was a type of flying that subsequently provided New Zealanders with a more affordable way of competing internationally. It seemed to be a natural progression from the competition flying already undertaken by member clubs of the Royal New Zealand Aero Club.'

AT FOREST FIELD, on an almost balmy winter's morning, international aerobatics competitions seemed somewhat remote. Coffee had given way to lunch — homemade bread and soup. Ces had joined us. Pam went on to talk about her interrupted career as a librarian at the University of Canterbury. Flying gradually turned into a full-time job, instructing at the Canterbury Aero Club.

'That became very rewarding. It was always satisfying seeing people progress, particularly if they had been struggling at a certain point in their training. Everyone has problems at certain stages. It's all too easy to dismiss someone just because they are slow, especially at an early stage.

'I recall one student pilot who really struggled. I wondered if he would ever make it, or if it was the right thing for him. He went on to become a highly qualified instructor. Being a slow learner is not necessarily a bad thing. Everything in flying is experience. You are still building valuable experience while you are going through things slowly. Ideally, student pilots should be soaking up flying, progressing through bit by bit and gaining a wide variety of experiences.'

During her own flying training, Pam had few problems. She enjoyed good coordination and, early on, mastered tail wheel landings in the aero club's Piper Cub trainer.

Friendships and fellowships, in aero clubs and at international aerobatics events, have been as rewarding as the flying. This has also been the case in the New Zealand Airwomen's Association, founded in 1959 by Rhona Fraser.

'Fellowship is still very important. Aviation is still a man's world. It is changing. But it's still a difficult thing to get into. It's nice to be able to talk to other women who fly — who talk the same language — about the patches when flying is going all wrong. Once, if a woman told people in her normal social environment that she flew, people would have looked at her as if she were mad.

'We have women with a great sense of humour — and a lot of achievers. We have airline captains, and a British Aerospace test pilot. We have had members who were among the aviators who made the pioneering flights of the 1930s, through to young student pilots. Airline flying is something women couldn't get into until recently. When I was the right age Air New Zealand were not accepting women. When they were, and I applied, I was told I was too old. I was 34. No one had ever told me I was too old for something at 34!

'These days some people are terrified of a group being all women. I enjoy the company of men, but we also do well as airwomen, and we have a lot of fun. Men still have their rugby clubs. There are

Pam Lock
Flying Kiwi

different satisfactions with different friendships. Some people still think we are a bunch of women who should be baking cakes or something. We did produce a recipe book some years ago, called *Flying in the Kitchen*. It was quite a useful book designed for women who have little time to spend in the kitchen because we would rather be out flying.

'Many of our members run a home, have a family, and some also run businesses. All these activities have to be juggled in with flying. Women seem to be very successful when managing so many things.'

ANOTHER PASSION IS promoting flight safety. Following her full-time aero club instructing, in 1984 Pam joined the Civil Aviation Division (now Civil Aviation authority) as an investigating officer looking into breaches of regulations. In 1989 she became assistant editor of the CAA flight safety magazine.

'This has become very rewarding work with a lot of variety. We also produce videos. Our task is to instil a safety culture into aviation. Most people are trying to do a reasonable job. But financial restraints can

The Pitts Special with its New Zealand ZK-PAC registration.
CES COLLINGS

tempt some to cut corners. And eager younger pilots out there are sometimes ready to walk on broken glass to gain the hours necessary to get a flying job somewhere.

'If one safety-conscious pilot turns down a flight it can be a tough decision because there will always be someone in the wings who is prepared to do it. Ultimately, flying people need to be able to stand up and be counted.

'CAA regulations provide only a minimum checklist. Many aero clubs and airlines will set their own tighter rules. Individual pilots also need to set their own limits.'

WE MIGHT HAVE talked longer about flight safety but Kirsten had landed to take me home and I still wanted to know about the Collings's next venture — the homebuilt amphibian that started life as a 'Seahawk'. It then became a 'Seahawker' and, following several modifications to the design, the 'Glass Goose'. A partner in the venture, Bruce Fraser is a former airline pilot and aircraft engineer.

'Bruce took on the somewhat demoralising task of building the aeroplane. It's all composite fibreglass material. It's almost up to the painting stage. I've said for many years that it will be ready for Christmas. This year, I might be right.

'It will be something different. An amphibian opens up a whole new world of dreams and challenges. Landing on water will be a bit different. It's hard to know what your ideal aeroplane will be. Each type of aeroplane is different and, so too, are the challenges.'

If I had stayed longer I would have liked to hear the stories behind the framed certificates on the wall of Pam's workroom. I was intrigued by the names 'Fédération Aéronautique Internationale' and 'Paul Tissandier Diploma', and one certificate 'For Services to Aeronautics and Airsports 1993'. But the aero club had already phoned, looking for their overdue aeroplane and an errant flying instructor.

I HAVE NEVER liked takeoffs. I could never master them myself. At Wellington, sitting beside Kirsten, I have watched the waves of Lyall Bay approach all too quickly. At Forest Field, lined up on runway 18, she holds the revving aeroplane on its brakes as she prepares for a short-field takeoff. She has applied a notch of flap. We roll and lurch high-speed over the grass. The shed at the other end approaches and slides, unscathed, close underneath. I relax, and even volunteer to attempt the straight-and-level over Eyrewell Forest during the short flight home. Soon we are descending towards the aero club's grass

In 1989 Ces and Pam Collings owned a four-seat Maule, seen here under tow at Forest Field.
PAM COLLINGS

runway. I look down on the sealed runway 20/02 and in my earphones I have a personal Airways commentary of what I am seeing. For the moment I am a part of it. Qantas Flight 42, a B-747 400, is holding; the Mount Cook Airline ATR is cleared to land after the Ansett 146; and Echo Bravo Mike (that's us) is cleared for the grass. From high above, it all looks so appealing — even magical.

'Flying's a bit of a bug,' Pam had casually told me. 'You get a real adrenalin buzz too. But I've always thought of flying as satisfying rather than thrill-seeking. It's all about precision. You get withdrawal symptoms if you don't fly. A lot of pilots say that.'

CHAPTER 8

Flying the Grand Traverse of Mt Cook

Near the summit of Mount Cook, a pair of twin turbo-prop Nomad N24 aircraft encircle New Zealand's tallest mountains during a 'Grand Traverse' flight from Tekapo.
AIR SAFARIS

We talked about our ultimate dream for Air Safaris. It involved building a sealed strip, and a hangar big enough for two Cessna aeroplanes. It all sounded rather grand.

Richard Rayward

IT WILL BE a cliff-hanger, Richard Rayward tells us. One of his Air Safaris Nomad N24 aircraft is flying from the West Coast, over the main divide to Tekapo. At the same time a ground fog from the south-east is persistently advancing towards the airfield. Approaching broadside, the fog will engulf the runway almost in one gulp. I sense Richard's frustration as he predicts the necessary visual landing will be missed by just two minutes. Fourteen tourist passengers and the pilot, Tim Rayward, Richard's son, are in no immediate danger but a diversion to an alternative landing strip, perhaps as far away as Timaru, is on the cards. A quick radio call confirms that ground fog is also advancing towards the closest alternative — Air Safaris' airfield at Glentanner Park in the Tasman Valley.

Tekapo's runway is still partially clear as we hear the first faint sounds of twin turbo props. In clear skies, November Mike Hotel continues flying towards the airfield. Soon, from directly above, the pilot can see his landing strip clearly through low-lying cloud. But visibility is likely to be lost as perspective and light change during his approach on finals. We wait while the fog, swirling, engulfing, and silent, shows no regard for frustrated aviators. The Nomad, having overflown the airfield and turned onto its landing approach, is lost to view beyond the intervening fog bank. Sounds of relaxed engines tell us the Nomad is still descending. Several eerie seconds pass. We hear engines being powered up; the landing has been abandoned. We see the Nomad climb away, looking tantalisingly magnificent in late sunlight. Richard handles several urgent radio communications at once. Is Glentanner still clear? It is, but for how many more minutes? Instructions go to the pilot, then to Glentanner, and back to the pilot. Flying time to Glentanner is about eight minutes.

Then, with a slight directional shift in the gentle air currents, the far end of Tekapo's runway is clearing. Richard is speaking on the radio again. The Nomad returns and lands towards a lowering sun. Embarking passengers are smiling. They have enjoyed a great day visiting the West Coast glaciers, and scenic flying above the Mt Cook and Westland national parks. For the pilot, the little drama at the end of his day merely promised an inconvenient diversion to a distant airfield. Almost nonchalantly, he completes his after-flight checks as low cloud once again closes its grip, this time tightly, on the entire Mackenzie basin, leaving the snow mountains to float, surreal, above a binding sea of whiteness.

'AIR SAFARIS' AND the 'Grand Traverse Flight of Mount Cook' are two appealing names associated with New Zealand tourism. With a fleet of five Nomad N24 and four Cessna 207 aircraft, Air Safaris ranks as one of New Zealand's largest air operators of non-scheduled scenic flights. In recent times the company has won the enviable Air New Zealand Award for Enterprise and, in 1996, the Civil Aviation Director's Award for flight safety. In partnership with Graeme Murray, Richard Rayward had been running the successful aviation venture for about 26 years when I caught up with him in June 1997. I found him living in pleasant comfort close to Lake Tekapo. Comfort had not always been an integral part of his life. Thirty years previously, he spent his early married life flying, and living off the land, in remote south Westland valleys. But I had first met him some time before that, during the mid-1960s, when we worked for the National Film Unit in Wellington. We shared a keen interest in photography. Richard was a motion picture cameraman. I was a processing laboratory technician. And while I spent much of my spare time photographing aircraft, Richard was learning to fly a Victa trainer from Wellington's airport.

Offering some of the best views in New Zealand, a Cessna Stationair 8 flies beside Mount Cook (3754m). AIR SAFARIS

Over time, I watched as a passion for photography was overtaken by a passion for flying.

'I WAS ALWAYS keen on flying,' he said. 'From an early age, growing up in New Plymouth, I read flying magazines, and books about the adventures of such heroes as Biggles and Douglas Bader till they were running out of my ears. Then one day, during a visit to the optician, all my dreams for flying went into a fatal tailspin. He asked me the usual question: what did I want to do when I grew up?

'"I want to be a pilot. I want to join the Air Force," I replied, feeling somewhat pleased with myself. To that, he merely said, "Well, with your eyesight, you might as well forget all about that!"

'It's strange how a chance comment can affect your life. I assumed I would never get a pilot's licence. Exactly what he found wrong with my eyes I will never know. I am aged 55 now, and I still don't wear glasses.'

Richard went off to university in Christchurch and started a science degree. All the while he was dreaming about his other great interest — photography. He left his degree unfinished when he joined the National Film Unit. Being New Zealand's only significant film studio, jobs in the government-owned National Film Unit were sought after. A cameraman was a position to be envied.

'I had bought myself an 8 mm cine camera and proceeded to impress the great Film Unit directors like Oxley Hughan with the films I had made. I expect he soon got sick of seeing my amateur film-making efforts and, probably to avoid having to see any more, he gave me a job.'

That was in 1964. Richard filmed a lot for television, working with presenters such as Ian Johnstone. He filmed the Deep Cove project involving the construction of the tail race through Fiordland's mountains from the Lake Manapouri hydro station, and climbers reaching the top of Mt Aspiring. Dragging 35 mm Arriflex film cameras, he climbed to the top of Aspiring with senior cameraman Grant Foster.

'I did not have a great head for heights those days. I was roped to Grant. He was so enthusiastic about the shots we were getting. I was sure we were both going to fall off.'

While Richard was not filming he was flying, gradually building up the hours and experience for his Private Pilot's Licence. It all started one day when three Film Unit cameramen, rushing into the city, spotted a sign at the Wellington Aero Club.

'It was one of those spur-of-the-moment things. The aero club was advertising flying scholarships. You had a trial flight and then spent so much to fly as far as solo. I went in and signed up with the other two. I was committed to take flying lessons, but I knew it was going to be a pointless exercise. Once I required the medical to fly solo I would be thrown out because of my poor eyesight. When the dreaded day finally arrived I passed my medical without comment.

'"But what about my eyes?" I asked. To that the examining doctor replied, "What about your eyes? They meet the standard." Suddenly, I became enthusiastic about my flying. I put everything into it.'

Looking back, Richard says learning to fly was just as he had dreamed it would be. The images he had once formed while reading all those books exactly fitted the reality. The aero club had just got the Victa aircraft. It turned out to be a very good training aeroplane for Wellington. It could handle the wind. But it was greeted with some scepticism.

'We had an instructor who was an experienced older chap. When they had told him the aero club was going to buy an aircraft made in Australia by the Victa Lawn Mower Company, he wondered what the world was coming to. When they told him the Victa would be put together with pop rivets, he really thought the world had come to an end.'

Richard said learning to fly at Wellington was different, rather than difficult. Robby Henson, another older instructor, was incredibly patient. This was despite one of Richard's Film Unit colleagues, Wayne Williams, having trouble staying on the runway. One day Wayne

Richard Rayward in the cockpit of an Air Safaris Nomad N24 aircraft.
ROY SINCLAIR

started to veer from the great wide sealed strip towards the grass, and threatened to run over the VASI boxes concealing the approach lights.

'Robby, in just the slightest of raised voices, was still reassuring as he said, "Wayne, you are really supposed to stay on the runway." For my part, I had a lot of trouble with landings. I would always get a mental block when I should have been just holding the aeroplane off before putting it onto the ground.

'We went to Paraparaumu to do our first solo and solo consolidation flying before returning to Wellington. I had done about 15 hours at Wellington when I went out one night and made a complete botch of my circuits. It was a beautiful calm night, but every time I came in I was far too high. My instructor was furious. "You are supposed to know how to fly by now," he bellowed.

'I did about three more terrible circuits and suddenly realised it was the first time I had tried to land at Wellington without a 30 to 40-knot head wind.

'One student pilot used to make us laugh. During a flying test, as he did his climb out from Wellington, the testing officer smugly pulled the throttle closed to simulate an engine failure on takeoff. The irate student promptly pushed the throttle back to full power and said, "What the hell did you do that for?"'

RICHARD RAYWARD WAS aged 24 when he got his Private Pilot's Licence. 'On today's standards I was a real oldie. I was a late starter because of my earlier eyesight diagnosis.' In the meantime he met and married Rosslyne, an Australian city girl from Adelaide. Working for the Film Unit meant he was away from home about 70 per cent of most weeks.

'It was not a good situation for two newly married people so we started to think of ways we could spend more time together. Also, I wanted to get the flying hours necessary for a Commercial Pilot's Licence and knew that would not be easy on the salary being paid at the Film Unit.

'About that time I was sent away again, to the South Island to work on a national parks film. I was to try and film deer and chamois, using a long lens on the 35 mm Arriflex camera. Accompanied by Bruce Jenkinson, a well-known mountaineer, we spent several days camped on top of mountain ranges overlooking the Landsborough. The head of a valley down on the West Coast side was almost totally enclosed apart from one outlet. To me, it looked like a little slice of heaven. Bruce and I sat, looking down, and we fantasised about building an airstrip down there. I imagined living in that idyllic valley with Ros. I could build her a little cabin. The more I fantasised, the more it became my dream. We could be together. It would be our paradise.'

Later, Richard took a week off from the Film Unit and, with Bruce Jenkinson, walked across the mountains from Lake Ohau to the Landsborough and found his valley at the head of Clark Valley. With ice axes they formed a short and very rough airstrip. They used their backpacks to carry shingle to fill in the worst of the holes. Worried that hunters might spot their airstrip, they cleverly marked it with randomly planted tussock. Another pilot would have to know how to line up the tussock to spot the airstrip. It had been an arduous week. By the time he walked back to Lake Ohau the heels had gone from his boots.

'I was almost crippled. Arriving back at Wellington I was unable to walk forwards down the steps from the NAC Viscount. I had to turn around and go down backwards. Ros and I committed ourselves to the south Westland venture. We put all our savings into buying a

Graeme Murray, Richard Rayward's partner in Air Safaris, has a Private Pilot's Licence but spends his time running an administration and sales office in Tekapo township. 'It's my job to fill the seats on Richard's aeroplanes — but Richard keeps buying more aeroplanes with more seats to fill,' he says.
ROY SINCLAIR

Newly married and living in 'blissful' isolation, Ros Rayward starts her day refuelling ZK-BDE . . .
RICHARD RAYWARD

. . . and reading a letter from home while camping in the Landsborough.
RICHARD RAYWARD

former topdressing Cessna 180, ZK-BDE, and I gave my notice at the Film Unit.

'I then went through a time of total despair as I wondered if I would ever get to fly the Cessna properly. Most pilots have to learn to fly twice, starting with a modern aeroplane with a tricycle undercarriage. When the main wheels hit the runway the weight of the engine flops the aeroplane onto its nose wheel. The nose wheel then stays on the runway. Flying an old-style tail dragger is a different kettle of fish. When a tail-wheel aircraft touches the ground it tends to start bouncing, especially when the undercarriage is already springy, as is the case with the 180. You end up with a fairly wide arc situation. Most pilots have a lot of fun, and anguish, learning to land a tail-wheeler.

'I then had to learn how to land on short strips if I was to land safely in our paradise valley. About this time Ros and I packed up and flew to Timaru where my brother's wife's family had a farm nearby. I practised landing in their paddocks, starting with the biggest and gradually working down to the shortest until I figured I was getting reasonably proficient.

'Then one day Bruce and I headed off to have a go at landing on our improvised strip. From above I somehow knew I would never be able to fly in. The strip we had built was on Marks Flat. It looked just too small. A narrow gorge tumbles the creek from the flat and out towards the Landsborough. My tiny valley was completely surrounded by big mountains. We had built the strip to only about 150 metres with the idea that I would fly in with some tools to complete the job. Dejected, we flew back to the Landsborough where we knew there was a longer strip.

'One problem was not knowing what the direction or strength of the wind was on the ground. Knowing what the wind was doing was critical for such a short strip. And I had only about 60 hours' flying, mostly off Wellington airport. The type of flying I was now embarking on required some very different skills. Bruce walked over the top of the mountains and I waited and flew over again next day. He had a fire going. I watched the smoke as I circled and, once again, went through the process of convincing myself that it was not really possible. But how was I going to get our dream under way if I couldn't even land there?

'So I lined up and, with full flap, came in as slowly as I could. The Cessna flopped onto the end of the strip and I managed to stop just before running off the other end. Bruce and I danced around congratulating ourselves on having got this far. My hand had been gripping the control column so tightly that it took half an hour before I could uncurl it properly. In the meantime we had walked back along the runway and retrieved the boots, stores, and other gear that had flown out as I landed. This became a regular practice. Even when the improvised runway was made longer — to about 350 metres — and smoother, the Cessna's doors continued to fly open on touchdown.'

Those days, people going into the wilds applied for a hunting permit. No one talked too much about building an airstrip; they just did it. Nowadays, much of the Landsborough is classified as wilderness and controlled by strict environmental regulations.

Ros WAS STRAIGHT from the city. A pharmacist. She knew all about preparing prescriptions — and makeup. She enjoyed wearing shoes with high heels. If she was to survive in the wilderness she had a lot to learn.

'About the time we bought the aeroplane I told Ros I would have to buy her a pair of strong leather boots. She took one look at these boots and bluntly told me she would not be seen dead in them. Within a week she was living in the boots.

'We camped in several different huts. One, in our chosen valley, was made of branches and plastic. Another was frequently in danger of

Supply-dropping to hunters camped in isolated mountain areas was part of Air Safaris' work in the early days. The Cessna 185, ZK-DJM, was the first new aeroplane purchased for Air Safaris. RICHARD RAYWARD

Preparing to film the Southern Alps, Richard Rayward, right, helps National Film Unit cameraman Grant Foster mount a 35 mm Arriflex camera on the Cessna 185.

being washed away whenever the Pyke River flooded. One night we hurriedly had to abandon the hut and our possessions, as water was about to pour through. We climbed a tree and wedged ourselves in a fork above the flood. Ros never complained. She made herself as comfortable as possible and went to sleep. I often tell people that in just a short time Ros went from the comforts of an Australian city to the fork of a tree in south Westland.

'Whenever the weather blew up at night we would be worried about the aeroplane. One night, in April 1968, we spent the first half of the night worrying about the aeroplane. Then we forgot about the aeroplane and worried about the hut. It was snowing and blowing a gale. Only much later (we had no radio) we realised we had been on the fringe of the storm that had wrecked the inter-island ferry, Wahine, at the entrance to Wellington harbour. Fifty-one people had been drowned.

'Life was simple. Our only priorities were our next meal and whether we would have a dry bed that night. We were quite poor and had to scratch and save. I found some old gloves and a balaclava for Ros to wear. Sometimes we were trapped on the wrong side of a river without food. We resorted to making soup by boiling our potato peelings. And we found a deer caught in a tree and drowned as the river quickly flooded, so we had venison.

'Yet the two years we spent in our secluded valley were probably among the happiest in our lives. While such an experience might have caused most fledgling marriages to fall apart, I believe ours was strengthened. We had to work together to survive in that sort of environment. We built quite a foundation of companionship, which was to survive much more difficult times, many years later. In the end we had to drag ourselves away.

'We were lucky not to have had any disasters. We could have. I had set out with only the minimum flying experience. I had to learn to fly safely in mountains. The flying was very challenging, and satisfying. Many people pre-

dicted we would end up having a nasty prang, as others before us had done. I was always very careful but I would be the first to say we had our fair share of luck.

'Ros was very trusting. Frequently I left her alone in a remote valley while I flew out deer I had shot. Somehow she knew I would always come back to get her. I had to come back. I was the only person, anywhere, who knew where she was. My mind boggles whenever I think about it these days.'

And they had some tremendous adventures. They were earning an

The Swiss-made Pilatus Porter introduced turbo-prop power to scenic flying in 1978. 'We were told we would run ourselves broke flying the Pilatus Porter,' says Richard Rayward.
AIR SAFARIS

enviable reputation as rebels, especially with the commercial pilots of Southern Scenic who were flying hunters and tourists into the same remote valleys. On one occasion Richard and Ros were camped beside a small landing strip at the head of the Arawata River when they heard Southern Scenic fly over.

'We knew they would probably be landing hunters further up the valley and would soon be back. That morning I had shot a stag and had just managed to get it across the river. It was a very big animal and I was trying to drag it up to the aircraft. By the time Southern Scenic flew over the second time I had Ros harnessed in the pack frame with the straps tied to the deer. She was straining to drag the deer along and I was walking behind waving a big stick. The aeroplane came down very low. We often sat in our paradise and laughed together as we thought of the stories that might have circulated back in so-called civilisation.'

On another occasion they were able to help prevent a near disaster when a hapless deershooter was attempting to get a jet boat into Lake McKerrow. Richard and Ros had met him down at Martins Bay. To get the jet boat into the Hollyford River and Lake McKerrow (a simple matter these days with helicopters), it had to be taken out to the open sea from Milford Sound, north along the coast, and driven over the treacherous Hollyford bar.

'I saw him again later when he was heading off, towing the jet boat from Te Anau to Milford Sound,' Richard recalled. 'I asked if he had a

life jacket and when he said he didn't I lent him one we had in the Cessna. We had to carry it whenever we flew across Cook Strait. It had never been out of the packet. I arranged to fly down to Martins Bay and meet him as he crossed from the ocean into the river.

'As it turned out he was tossed out, and he lost his boat. Fortunately he had been wearing the life jacket, or he might also have lost his life. As it was, he was pretty battered when he washed up on the rocks — and he had swallowed a lot of water.

'We brought him to the airstrip and I prepared to fly him out to the doctor at Te Anau. Ros was to wait at Martins Bay, on her own. Soon after we took off, the Cessna's cabin suddenly filled with smoke. I'll never forget the look on the jet-boater's face. He had just survived drowning, and now he was about to be burned to death in an aeroplane!'

Luckily an alternative landing strip lay straight ahead. Richard landed quickly and skidded to a halt. The generator had seized on takeoff and a rubber belt had continued to spin against the jammed pulley. Once the offending belt was removed the aeroplane was flown to Te Anau.

'I arrived back at Martins Bay just on dark and to my horror a ground fog had formed over the strip. At that time of day there was nowhere else for me to go. I was committed to landing despite a possibly perilous outcome. Ros, on the ground, had been worrying herself sick as the light faded. Knowing of the danger, in her desperation, she

Fitted with skis, the 'Porter' takes off from Mount Gerald in 1980.
AIR SAFARIS

A passenger's view from a Nomad N24, heading up the Godley River beyond Lake Tekapo.
ROY SINCLAIR

ran up and down the landing strip singing the Lord's Prayer. As she did so the fog parted to each side, and I landed.

'Ros still maintains it was her singing that momentarily cleared the fog. I suspect it had more to do with the low run I had made over where I thought the strip should have been. The slipstream was enough to scatter the fog.'

RICHARD AND ROS returned to a comparatively dull suburban existence after two years in south Westland. 'We couldn't live in the wilds forever,' Richard told me, and I detected a little sadness in the admission. He sat for a time, in silence, thinking perhaps about an idyllic shared life when the world was almost perfect. In any event, the decision to leave the wilds was forced by the Cessna requiring a

Certificate of Airworthiness. They flew to Timaru and lived in a house by a railway line.

'For several weeks I jumped out of bed every time a train went past during the night. Any roaring sound was something to be dreaded. It meant the river was flooding. Our camp was about to be washed away.'

CERTIFICATE OF AIRWORTHINESS requirements meant a lot of work had to be done on the Cessna 180. Engineers at Timaru's Aerotech Ltd let Richard Rayward work on the aeroplane himself. They then found him a job as an aircraft tradesman and he stayed on, doing aircraft engineering work for more than two years. All the while he and Ros were planning their next adventure — among some of New Zealand's lavish alpine environments, close to the Mount Cook National Park.

'For some time I had known Graeme Murray. Graeme was a friend of Laurie Prouting and his father, Malcolm, of Mesopotamia Station in the Rangitata Valley. We all got together and, in 1970, formed a partnership to fly hunters and fishermen to normally inaccessible spots. We called our new venture "Air Safaris". The Cessna 180 ZK-BDE became the first Air Safaris aeroplane.'

The upper Rangitata is not as remote as South Westland; but more remote were some of the air strips they built — one took 10 days to get a bulldozer in. I recall visiting Richard and Ros at Mesopotamia and enjoying a cup of tea. They had been there for about three years and had two children, Tim and Bridget. Their new home was about an hour's drive on a shingle road from Peel Forest. In somewhat basic farm workers' accommodation they were living comfortably, and Richard was still doing quite a bit of camera work for the National Film Unit and Television New Zealand. Special wing-mounted cameras enabled spectacular motion picture footage in the mountains, including one awesome shot taken as the Cessna flew between the striking twin peaks of the Two Thumbs range. Watching his latest films on 16 mm, in a blacked-out back-country room, was almost like old times when we shared a passion for photography and cinema at the National Film Unit studios in Wellington.

But I was not the only visitor of any importance to drop in for a cup of tea with the Raywards or their business partners.

During the 1974 Royal Tour, Prince Charles and Princess Anne were staying at Mt Peel. They had arrived in atrocious weather. The young Royals, disappointed, soon became bored. Finally, someone rang the Proutings and asked if the weather was any better up their way. It was.

'"Could we bring the prince and princess up and boil the billy in a musterers' hut?" was the next question. We were told we did not have to do anything. We just had to fly in and be there to greet the Royals.

'We had time to clean up the appointed hut as much as possible, removing the worst of the graffiti from its walls. Eventually the Royals and their escorts arrived in three RNZAF Iroquois helicopters. The prince and princess were really good to talk to. They expressed a genuine interest in the high country and, of course, the musterers' smoky billy tea they had been told about. All went well as we put the billy on to boil. Only then was it discovered that the tea had been left behind! "Do you have any?" they asked me, and I said there was sure to be tea, somewhere, in a musterers' hut.

'I found some out the back but, to my horror, it was covered in mouse droppings. I scraped them off as best I could before presenting the tin to the officials. At least the Royals got to drink their billy tea.'

WORKING UNDER THE restrictive rules of the old Air Services Licensing regime, Air Safaris managed to get a licence to pick up from

A 'Grand Traverse' flight on the West Coast side of the Main Divide . . .
ROY SINCLAIR

Christchurch and other airports and fly tourists around Mt Cook. Business was difficult. 'Over summer I would also land at small strips near the Peel Forest and Lake Clearwater camping grounds. I knocked on tents trying to sell $5 joyrides.

'The hunting and fishing were great. Laurie Prouting was a keen pilot too. We would camp in a back-country hut with our clients. We always felt responsible for hunters and fishermen until we flew them out again.

'I already had quite a lot of mountain flying experience but a commercial operation required even more care. One prerequisite for flying in mountains is always to have a 100 per cent safe alternative way out should something go wrong. That is still the case today in Air Safaris. Flying up a valley, or across a pass, we always have a course of action. A pilot must be able to turn in a valley, knowing it is possible to fly back. You give yourself a lot of margin. Sometimes, margins can be reduced as judgement improves.

'From my own experience, and those who fly with Air Safaris today, the longer you fly in the mountains, the bigger the clearances you tend to give between the aircraft and the mountains or passes. You realise you don't have to fly close to a big mountain to give your passengers a thrill. They are every bit as impressed when they are a

. . . and beside Mount Tasman (3496m), New Zealand's second highest mountain, a precipitous mass of ice and rock.
ROY SINCLAIR

kilometre or so away from big mountains like Mt Tasman or Mt Cook. The mountains will always look close but we could often turn in the space between the aircraft and the mountain. Apart from the obvious safety aspect, the slightly greater separation is better for passengers framing up their photographs.

'I will always remember when I was starting out to fly on the West Coast. I asked the advice of Tex Smith, a very experienced bush pilot who flew out of Queenstown. He said, "Remember, it's not the mountains that are dangerous. It's only the pilots who are dangerous. And don't ever let financial considerations affect your operational decisions."'

Mesopotamia, and the Prouting family, offered a great lifestyle but Air Safaris was never going to become a good business. There were also problems in associating a high country sheep station with tourism.

'We were dealing with wild animals at a time when conservation interests were applying pressure to get rid of the last Himalayan thar. It was not seen as appropriate to maintain supposedly environmentally harmful animals (deer and thar) for tourism. Things have since changed. There are probably more thar now than there were in the 1970s. They are now regarded as a rare Asian mountain species, surviving in New Zealand's Southern Alps.

'We were also accused of restricting areas to the Kiwi hunter. Because we were dealing with people aged in their sixties and seventies who could not compete with the Kiwi hunter in terms of chasing animals around, we did have to keep some areas quiet so animals were not too wary. As soon as you do that everyone thinks you have hordes of great trophy animals hidden away. That was certainly not the case.

'From a business point of view, living at Mesopotamia meant the aeroplane would sit for days at a time without use. That was uneconomical. During 1973 Ros and I had started flying over to a grass strip at Lake Tekapo and, with help from Laurie Prouting, we flew scenic flights around Mt Cook. Then, the next year, we reluctantly agreed to wind up our financial ties with Mesopotamia. Ros and I shifted to Tekapo, and Graeme Murray and I bought out the two Prouting shareholders. By that time we had gone from having one of the oldest Cessna 180s to having one of the first Cessna 185s in New Zealand. ZK-DJM was brand spanking new.'

The new Air Safaris involved enormous flying hours. Richard did most of the flying although he was often assisted by an experienced top-dressing pilot from Timaru. A lot of tours arrived in Tekapo at about 3 pm and left by 10 am the next day. Most people wanted to fly around Mt Cook. During busy weeks, the Cessna 185 flew more than 50 hours. On one occasion Richard flew all 43 people from one camping tour, plus the cook, around Mt Cook. It took nine flights.

About that time a Dr Dick, who had a holiday home at Tekapo, phoned asking if his son and family, just out from England, could be taken for a scenic flight around the mountains.

'Initially I said no. The weather was a bit rough and I didn't think they would enjoy it. I told the old doctor that I had just knocked flying on the head for the day. He replied that he didn't think his son and family would mind if it was a little rough. He was quite insistent.

'They came out and did a flight, and it was not too bad. They quite enjoyed it. The doctor's son sat next to me and he showed a lot of interest in the aeroplane. I pointed out the altimeter and showed him how it worked; then the airspeed indicator and the slip-and-turn indicator. I even showed him how to use the ailerons and how to assist a turn with the rudder. He struck me as being a super-modest and unassuming sort of chap.

'When we got back he even helped me tie down the aeroplane. Those days we didn't have a hangar. Because he appeared to have a genuine interest in aviation I showed him how the elevators and rudder on the tail section operated. Then something he said made me a little suspicious. I asked, "You don't fly yourself by any chance do you?"

'"Just a little bit," he said.

'"With an aero club or flying school?"

'"No, not really."

'"Well, who do you fly with?"

'And he said, "Oh — the RAF."

"Big aircraft or small?" I asked.

"Just small ones."

'It turned out that he was Wing Commander Ian Dick, the leader of the Red Arrows aerobatic team. I had walked right into it. It was the classic personification of an old saying in aviation: "Those who have done the most usually say the least, and those who have done the least say the most."'

RICHARD RAYWARD CAN recall a day when he and Graeme talked about their ultimate dream for Air Safaris. The dream involved having their own sealed airstrip at Tekapo and a hangar big enough to hold two Cessna aeroplanes. It all sounded rather grand at the time but it was not long before the dream was a reality, and Air Safaris still had a long way to go.

'By 1975 we had built our own airstrip and the hangar. It was the first time we had built a hangar. We had not built anything in our lives so it was quite a challenge. We also bought a new Cessna 206, and another new 206 the following year. We had three aeroplanes, each able to carry five passengers. We had three pilots.

'Ron Small was the first pilot we employed. Later he went off to fly helicopters and earned himself an MBE for plucking climbers from the top of Mt Cook. Gavin Craig, our second pilot, is now flying with the Helicopter Line.'

Frustration came with the larger Air Safaris. June and July proved to be the absolute doldrums. Very few people were about to go scenic flying, and the weather was often perfect. Mountains always look their best on a clear winter's day.

'We have the same frustration, even today,' Richard said. 'Back then we knew a lot of people were up at the Tekapo ski field enjoying magnificent weather. We figured that if they wouldn't come to us then we would go to them. So we ordered our first set of aircraft skis, even though we knew we were likely to come into conflict with Mount Cook Airline.

'Harry Wigley, the airline's founder, had pioneered ski-plane landings on the Tasman and West Coast glaciers. Over the years he had built up ski-plane flights into an extremely successful tourist venture, which Mount Cook Airline, understandably, believed was their exclusive domain. Knowing there was considerable mystique associated with ski-plane operations, we ordered our skis secretly. The story goes that, not long after we ordered our skis, one of the Mount Cook Airline managers was in the United States visiting the same ski manufacturer. He tripped over a box and when he looked down he saw it was addressed to Air Safaris Air Services, Tekapo, New Zealand!

'As it turned out we had a lot of fun flying our ski-plane from the Tekapo ski field, and it did bring us a little bit more business through June and July. Although we were starting to become a competitor for Mount Cook Airline's ski-plane operation, and we were to have several battles with them to get what we wanted through the Air Services Licensing system, we always enjoyed a good relationship with their chief pilots and operations managers.

'They let us use their facilities, including their private strip at Mt

Cook, whenever we needed to fly hunters into their patch. Looking back, I do sympathise with the Mount Cook Airline's very protective attitude. I guess we were starting to chip away at their business. We became a wee thorn in the bigger company's side. As time went on we became a much larger thorn. For all that we did have our moments, and we did have plenty of laughs.'

Air Safaris' core business was, and still is, 'The Grand Traverse of Mount Cook', a 50-minute flight from Tekapo that encircles Mt Tasman and Mt Cook, and overflies Franz Josef Glacier and Fox Glacier. Without having to land on a glacier, Air Safaris could offer greater departure reliability. Glacier landings, although they offer an enviable experience for tourists, are frequently jeopardised by wind, low cloud, and lighting conditions.

'Mount Cook Airline had a magnificent publicity machine. The idea of landing on a glacier became a good incentive for an overseas visitor to come to New Zealand. We had to convince tourists that our flight was as good. Tour companies and coach drivers had been brainwashed into thinking a scenic flight involving a ski-plane glacier landing was the only flight worth doing.

'We were selling a much longer flight for less money. We could also offer a lot of contrast. Our flights offered views of Lake Tekapo, with its aqua-blue water caused by glacier silt suspended in the lake, and high country stations with their famous merino sheep, as we worked our way up the Godley Valley and into the bigger mountains. The highlight was flying along all the main divide peaks from Ellie de Beaumont to Mt Sefton. The name of our flight was appropriate. The "Grand Traverse" is also the name of the climb along the long summit ridge of Mt Cook with its three high peaks.

'We worked out an informative commentary. Tourists were always fascinated by the colour of Lake Tekapo. But, sometimes, as the day's flying wore on, our commentaries suffered. I would be talking to my passengers and suddenly realise I had just told them about merino sheep being suspended in the lake — and about glacial silt grazing the tops of mountains!'

ADDING A TURBO prop high-winged Pilatus Porter, able to carry 10 passengers, brought a new image to Air Safaris in 1978. As business increased, the Air Safaris partners saw little sense in adding small aeroplanes to the fleet and having them all follow one another around Mt Cook. Another consideration was the added noise created by aircraft flying over a national park. Richard recalls numerous people saying that he and Graeme were completely mad if they were serious about a Pilatus Porter.

'We would run ourselves broke, we were told. Mount Cook Airline had assessed the Pilatus Porter and decided it was not suitable, although they did fly them later. For us, it was a great milestone. With its unusual appearance distinguished by a large square tail, the Pilatus Porter became almost synonymous with Air Safaris. Wherever Ros and I went, people would ask about the "Porter" and I would always get into this great discussion. It used to drive Ros mad.

'Economically it stacked up very well against the smaller Cessnas. It was very easy to fly, and made a great ski-plane. It was also quieter flying around mountains.'

The new aeroplane with a reversible turbo prop was ideal for dropping off and picking up skiers from the more remote ski slopes. Air Safaris landed in places where winter snow covered river flats, or in old river terraces high up in the mountains. Improvised airstrips often finished at steep bluffs, or creeks. With a ski-equipped Cessna 185 it was edge-of-the-seat stuff taking off from such places. But a 'Porter' when fully loaded would get off easily, even with a 15- or 20-knot tail wind.

'With a conventional aircraft the only braking on snow was the drag of the skis. If we didn't like the look of things during a takeoff run we could put the "Porter" in full reverse prop — and stop. It was a great aeroplane for confined spaces.

'By comparison, if you look down on the ski-plane marks on the Tasman Glacier you can see that Mount Cook Cessna 185s sometimes require a very long run — even a kilometre or more — to get airborne from soft snow. We seldom had that much room to operate in. But eventually, the type of flying the "Porter" was ideal for was done more and more by helicopters.

'We had also bought a Cessna 207, taking seven passengers, and the Pilatus Porter became less of a feature of Air Safaris.'

The next really big financial commitment came with the Nomad N22 in 1980. Built by the Australian Government primarily for use as a light military transport, the Nomad became the stylish high-wing twin turbo prop aeroplane seen in the Australian *Flying Doctors* television series. Three of the present Air Safaris fleet of stretched Nomad N24s have flown for the real-life Flying Doctors. Carrying 15 passengers and flown by a single pilot, the Nomad soon proved to be ideal for New Zealand's scenic flying. Other attributes included very short takeoff and landing capabilities, and reverse pitch propellers.

'The Nomad would even give the Pilatus Porter a fright as a short-field aircraft. The N24s we fly now will stop within 200 metres with a full load of passengers. The legal length of the strips we use are, of course, considerably longer than that. The Nomad has a unique flap system fully across the wing enabling a slow stalling speed. With full flap the Nomad will fly very slowly (about 65 knots) comfortably. Operating costs are comparatively low for an aeroplane of its size, and it is quiet. For Air Safaris the Nomad is close to being the perfect aeroplane.'

Acquiring a fleet of Nomads from various operators also involved Air Safaris' pilots in some interesting oceanic flying. Three were flown to New Zealand from Australia, island-hopping via Lord Howe and Norfolk. One was dismantled and shipped from the United States. Two were flown from Western Samoa.

Knowing that most delivery flight problems were associated with the use of additional ferry fuel tanks, Richard Rayward flew the Nomads with their standard tanks, giving the aircraft slightly less than six hours in the air. The flight from Western Samoa when Air Safaris purchased an N22 and a stretched N24 from Polynesian Airlines was particularly ambitious.

'We figured we could island-hop to Wallis Island, Fiji, Vanuata, New Caledonia, and Norfolk. Shell arranged fuel at all the islands except Wallis, which was to remain a mystery until we got there. Tom Middleton, who now manages Biplane Adventures at Wanaka Airport (he is also a display pilot and training officer for Wanaka's Alpine Fighter Collection), flew the Nomad N22 and I flew the N24. Keith Mitchell, a friend who was also a pilot and engineer, came along to take care of engineering, navigation, and tea making.

Air Safaris' N24 Nomad ZK-NME caught in an air-to-air photograph by Japanese photographer J Yokokura.

'Keith and I left Tom in Samoa waiting for the final preparations on his Nomad to be completed while we flew the first 278 nautical-mile leg to check out the fuel supply at Wallis. The Wallis stop was also complicated by it being a French-speaking island. We were, therefore, somewhat relieved when our first communication with Wallis Tower attracted a reply in English. But our confidence was soon dashed as we realised the controller's English was limited to standard aviation calls only, which he recited parrot-fashion. Anything we said that was not strictly aeronautical phraseology was met with a stony silence. We didn't speak any French.

'We had the island on radar for quite some time before the obligatory coral reef, and then the island itself came into view. A pretty sight. The airfield appeared where we expected to see it — a large runway basking in the sun and dominating the island.

'A beat-up Jeep came belting towards us as we taxied. It was driven by a guy in old scruffies. He looked like someone who might have just arrived from Algeria but he seemed friendly enough despite our complete inability to understand one another. Our New Zealand registered aircraft on a French island added to the mounting confusion.

'We somehow managed to establish how many US dollars (in $100 notes) would buy so much fuel and, mercifully, the refuelling started. We then had to convey that another aircraft looking much the same, in identical colours, would be arriving in two hours and we also wanted to leave money for that aeroplane's fuel.

'This explanation, again, proved to be difficult. They got the impression that we were telling them there were two aircraft when there was really only one. Were Keith and I seeing double? We then found a small, well-organised met station and, lo and behold, the non-English-speaking officer had two dossiers on the weather waiting for us. Clearly he was expecting two aeroplanes. Again, where was the other one? Again we tried to explain. We were, however, able to call Tom on the HF (long-range) radio and confirm he was on his way to Wallis. He sounded lonely and somewhat forlorn, but otherwise he was OK.

'We reluctantly took off, a little worried about not waiting for old Tom, and headed for Nandi. At least we had paved the way at Wallis and he shouldn't be held up too long refuelling. But as we climbed away to 10,000 feet we realised the refueller had probably underestimated the amount of fuel he had put into our aeroplane. Would Tom get the same amount of fuel for the equivalent US dollars we had left behind? He would definitely need all the fuel for the long 461 nautical mile leg to Nandi. Flying time was just over three hours.

'Fortunately, we were able to talk to Tom on our company line-of-sight VHF frequency. We briefed him and suggested he have some plan of action should the refueller, having realised he had undercharged us, get nasty, and refuse Tom his required fuel.

'We listened on the radio as he landed. Then we waited anxiously — and the miles between us speedily ticked away — until we finally heard the tower give Tom his clearance for takeoff from Wallis. With considerable relief we heard him talking to Nandi on the HF as he filed his flight-plan details.

'Throughout the flight to New Zealand we were amazed by the uncanny accuracy of the Omega navigation in our Nomad. It was accurate in terms of track, and distance to run. Oceanic flights are really no big deal but they do have their difficulties for an operation like Air Safaris that is more familiar with mountain flying. A flight of an international nature requires extensive organisation involving fuel cards, radio and navigation equipment, charts, life raft and other survival gear, and customs. Ironically, if we fly to Australia, a three-day flight via Norfolk and Lord Howe, the longest leg is from Tekapo to Auckland.'

THESE DAYS THE Air Safaris Nomad fleet comprises five stretched N24s. Yet despite its considerable success in New Zealand, Richard Rayward admits the Nomad has become a much-maligned aeroplane in Australia where it originated.

'All our pilots are very enthusiastic about the Nomad. They love flying the aeroplane. But the Nomad received some very bad publicity in Australia following severe crashes while it was being used by the military. As with any aeroplane, the Nomad has areas that need to be looked after very carefully. It has huge tail feathers — rudder and full-flying tailplane. We have always fastened the control locks as soon as a Nomad is parked on the ground. That way a gust of wind, or a helicopter landing close by, will not force the rudder or elevators to bang against their stops. We try not to bring the engines up to full power, giving the back end a lot of work, while the aeroplane is at a standstill.

'Other areas also require care, and that very likely explains why we have had such a good run over many years while flying a comparatively large fleet of Nomads. One of the big frustrations has been spending an awful lot of money to comply with ADs (service bulletins) to do work because of things that have happened overseas. We are 99 per cent certain that problems with the Nomad have nothing to do with the flight modes. They have a lot to do with what has been happening on the ground, especially a lack of care in certain critical areas.'

If the Nomad does have a failing it could be that the military priority was excessive when the aeroplane was developed during the 1970s by Melbourne's Government Aircraft Factories. Richard Rayward believes the Nomad would have enjoyed greater success had civilian pilots been involved at the development stage. As it was, the Nomad, in its stretched N24 configuration, was soon discovered to have civilian uses in commuter airline flying, as well as for the Flying Doctors.

'The basic structure is good. It's a very strong aeroplane, but more effort could have gone into passenger areas that get extensive use. The weak points, although they have no implications for safety, can become very annoying.'

The Air Safari Nomads and Cessna fleet can provide a capacity of 100 seats, enabling the company to cope with the pressure of 1990s tourism. Asian groups, especially, travel on very tight timetables. Everyone wants to fly. No one has time to stop for long. Four or more tour buses may turn up all at once, requiring an operator to have a large capacity for a short time.

'When we started, 90 per cent of our passengers were Australians. Now, we would be lucky if we fly 5 per cent Australians. Instead we have a real mix of people, and a lot of backpackers. We have pilots who speak German or Dutch. I know enough Japanese to cope with at least some difficult situations. *Chotto matte kudasai* (just wait a little please) will stop Japanese tourists in their tracks if they are running towards a turning propeller.

'It is always important to be involved with people. Almost always, everyone says they enjoyed the flight. They have had a real buzz flying so close to the big mountains. You feel you have really done something for them.'

Tekapo has proved to be the ideal location for Air Safaris, being far enough from the main divide to miss the worst of the weather. Air Safaris is often able to fly, and get above the weather, when the ski-planes are grounded in the Tasman Valley. Often, Air Safaris can modify the flight to suit weather conditions.

'A regular scenario for us is calculating rates for shorter flights. One day when the weather was not so good I went to a lot of trouble to explain an alternative flight to a German escort. He then left, and his tour party waved to me from their coach. A little disappointed I went into the office only to discover my German-speaking pilot doubled up with laughter.

'"What's the joke," I asked.

'"Do you know what he told all those people after you spent all that time telling them what they could do?"

'Of course I had no idea, so I said, "Well, what did he say?"

'My pilot said, "He told them, this guy's trying to rip us off!"'

Other amusing incidents occur when people are flying in a small aeroplane for the first time. 'They are used to big jets, where they are completely unaware of what happens as the engines start up. Sitting in the Nomad they look out as we start one engine. They see the propeller is turning and then point frantically at the other wing and the engine that is still idle. They don't realise we start one engine at a time.'

Air sickness is not the problem it once was. Different nationalities are more prone to being sick than others, and flights are planned accordingly. Every flight is different and it has almost become a sport for Air Safaris pilots to predict flying conditions and attempt to provide a smooth ride.

'Most days some aspect of the weather in the mountains can be challenging. Many winds, particularly the prevailing nor-westerly, are predictable and you know where to fly to get smoother up-flowing

Richard and Ros Rayward at home, beside an idyllic Lake Tekapo. ROY SINCLAIR

air. That in itself can be frustrating. You warn people that the flight might be a bit bumpy and then try like hell to miss all the bumps. Then you get back after giving them a smooth flight only to hear them mutter, "He wouldn't know what turbulence was!" Sometimes you wonder if you should have given them a few good bumps!'

While scenic flying, it is often easy to decide when not to fly. That was not the case during the early days of Air Safaris when deer-stalkers were going in to a back-country strip.

'They didn't want to be left behind just because it was a bit rough,' Richard recalls. 'I had to fly these guys in during a screaming nor-westerly. It was a pretty rough afternoon with heavy rain around the main divide. I was landing down the strip into the wind and concentrating pretty hard as we came in over the last of the matagouri.

'Just as I was about to flare over the threshold the chap behind me threw up. He put his hands over his mouth as everything exploded. That had the effect of firing it all over the dashboard and windscreen, and completely showering me. With my concentration shattered, I overshot and went around to make another approach. The worst of it was while I was trying to climb out — all the bits of mangled carrot and other stuff were dripping from the sun visor onto my face. And that was not the first time I had been hit from behind. A rather attractive lass, a youth hosteller, had downed a milkshake before we took off for Fox Glacier one day. The milkshake didn't quite make it; I was hit from the back seat.'

SCENIC FLYING OVER New Zealand's national parks has attracted its share of criticism in recent years. Trampers and mountaineers seeking solitude say aeroplanes flying low around mountains destroy the sense of quiet wilderness that attracted them to the mountains in the first place. Richard Rayward says he can sometimes be torn between different philosophies relating to mountains. He has a long-time personal passion for the outdoors, and he can recall times of solitude when he and Ros lived in remote South Island valleys. He also has a vested interest in tourism.

'Aviators have a responsibility to be considerate and appreciate the value of national parks to other users,' he says. Scenic flying enables a large number of people to see the beauty of the Mt Cook and Westland national parks without leaving any trace. Most of the people we fly would not be able, or have the time, to tramp or climb into the national parks we fly over. We try and fly around mountains with low RPM settings to minimise noise, and maintain safe distances.

'If you nail people down to what their real complaint is about aircraft it's almost always related to their flying ridiculously low or close. We can all learn to live together in mountains if aircraft keep a good distance from climbers.

'I would be very much against trying to restrict or close off airspace in the mountains. I don't think that would fix problems of disturbance on the ground. It would certainly jeopardise flight safety around Mt Cook and Westland national parks. You need to have the ability to take routes that suit the weather of the day.'

HAVING CLOCKED UP about 12,000 flying hours, Richard Rayward has never had any ambition to join an airline. Some pilots who have done just that have returned to fly with Air Safaris. 'It's great to have a stable work force, but it's not so good for all the keen young pilots who knock on our door looking for a job,' he said.

In a real sense, what he has achieved at Air Safaris is a logical conclusion to his South Island aviation beginnings in the Landsborough. Yet he is not one to be carried away with his own success. He is humble. And he will put others before himself. He was like that when I first met him at the National Film Unit. Happily, he has not changed. With his business partner, Graeme Murray, he will plan a future for Air Safaris that will cope with the increasing demands of modern tourism. Flight safety will always be a priority.

'I have always looked forward to going to work. My work has always been my hobby,' he told me as I was leaving. 'I can see a day, perhaps not too many years away, when I will no longer be flying and an aeroplane will no longer be part of our life. Perhaps I will then return to photography. The world has so many remote and beautiful places — like those Ros and I discovered all those years ago. Always, there will be those fascinating and unusual subjects to photograph.'

CHAPTER 9

Veteran Champion of Flight Training

Ken Fenwick, still instructing at the Waikato Aero Club in 1996. His Flying Training Manual *is written in a clear, friendly style.*
Roy Sinclair

You have got to be patient if you are going to get someone off the street, teach them to fly, and get them to the stage where they can go off on their own. That's really worth something.

Ken Fenwick

FLYING INSTRUCTOR AND author of the legendary *Flying Training Manual* used in aero clubs throughout New Zealand, Ken Fenwick would not tell me his age when I called on him in September 1996. 'A lot of people have asked me that,' he said ruefully, 'and I only tell them the year I was born; that was 1917. You can work the rest out for yourself.'

He was still instructing at the Hamilton Aero Club and without a doubt would have been New Zealand's longest-serving flying instructor with an instructor's 'A' Cat rating. He has probably initiated the flying training of more Air New Zealand pilots than anyone else. His own flying hours recorded in 23 logbooks total over 25,500, considerably more than your average Boeing 747 pilot. His two sons fly with airlines. Ewan is an Air New Zealand 747-400 captain. Lindsay flies DC-9s for the American North West Airline. In the 1995 Queen's Honours Ken Fenwick was awarded an MBE for his services to aviation.

Ken's wife, Wilma, appears to have no interest in flying in light aircraft, although for many years she was in charge of the Waikato Aero Club office — and she can reel off a string of names of Air New Zealand pilots her husband trained as far as their Private Pilot's Licence.

'Up to six hours a day of dual instruction over two years was darned hard work in a Tiger Moth's open cockpit. And it was damn cold down there in those Christchurch winters.'
LORIE LUCAS

Yet, despite such credentials — and an apparent inability to became the archetypal grandfather — Ken does not readily admit to having any great enthusiasm for his obvious achievements, or his long commitment to a high standard of pilot training. Most people, he told me, have had a bellyful of instructing after two or three years at the most.

Instructing can be boring. You rarely touch the controls. You let the student pilot sitting beside you in the left-hand seat fly the aeroplane. The student is all cockeyed and cross-controlled. He or she is learning, and you understand why the aeroplane is being flown the way it is. But you (the instructor) are just sitting there observing, when you know you learned to fly in order to enjoy yourself — and you're not flying at all!

'For young pilots, instructing can be a means to an end. It's a stepping stone for an airline career. The young pilots are filling up their logbooks and making some money to get by on until they reach the 1500 hours or so (with multi-engine instrument ratings) required by the airlines, where there is big money to be earned.'

In hindsight, Ken admitted the airlines would have been the way for him to go. When he started there was very little difference in pay scale between an aero club chief flying instructor and an airline job. Over the years the gap has widened remarkably, and instructing has as many disappointments as rewards.

'You can take an interest in people so long as they start flying and keep going. You can put a heck of a lot of work into an individual and get them half way to a Private Pilot's Licence and then they toss it away. That doesn't help your frame of mind, and it happens quite a lot. It is surprising how many give it away when they initially had ideas of using their pilot's licence as the beginning of a career.

'On such occasions you, the instructor, are left with the old saying: "You can teach a monkey to fly. It's just a matter of who runs out of patience first — the instructor or the monkey!"'

Despite the lack of enthusiasm I detected a suppressed pride, which promised to become as obvious as the friendly twinkle in Ken's eye. He was definitely not dour. He laughed a lot as he talked about flying, but he kept a tight rein on his modesty.

The Fenwick *Flying Training Manual* is written in a clear friendly style. Although it is basically a textbook, it invites reader participation. It reflects the real Ken Fenwick.

He laughed when I asked, 'What makes a good instructor?' We had been discussing problems that can be caused by bad instructors who are merely using the position to gain flying hours for an airline job.

'It's a bit like that ad on the TV that asks, "What makes a good farmer?" I would say, "A lot of hard work." Flying instructors certainly need to have the right temperament. A good instructor is one who can sort out the different personalities. It's no use getting mad with a student. Sometimes you have got to bully a little bit, but some students go to pieces if you start to bully, and the flying lesson becomes a waste of time. You have got to be patient if you are going to get someone off the street, teach them to fly, and get them to the stage where they can go off on their own. That's really worth something.'

KEN FENWICK'S OWN interest in aviation began when he was about 17 and living in the southern Wairarapa. A pilot turned up in an Avion offering joyrides. Ken went up, and hung onto about everything but the propeller. 'I wasn't very happy at all.'

Then the war broke out. 'I wasn't keen to be a soldier, and I was not a good enough swimmer to join the Navy, so that left the Air Force. I applied for that. I was living in the country so they sent out assignments to see if I was good enough. I was subsequently sent for my initial training to Levin in February 1942. I was then shifted to Rotorua and then to Harewood for flying training on Tiger Moths.'

The Airspeed Oxford became the popular twin-engined trainer of the Second World War. 'Once you were up and away the Oxford was a very nice aeroplane to fly.'

I asked if he remembered his first solo — a rather daft question to ask of an aviator — and Ken almost jumped from his seat. 'Too right. You remember your first solo. Everybody remembers their first solo. It's a momentous occasion that no student pilot will ever forget.'

Another 80 or so flying hours followed on Tiger Moths and he was sent the short distance from Harewood to Wigram for twin-engine training with Airspeed Oxfords, Nevil Shute's last aeroplane. (Author Nevil Shute Norway, best known for *No Highway*, *A Town Like Alice* and several other novels that convey a passion for aviation, founded Airspeed Limited in 1931. The Airspeed Oxford — thousands were

built after Airspeed had been taken over by de Havilland in 1940 — became the popular twin-engine trainer used in British Commonwealth countries throughout the Second World War.)

'The Airspeed Oxford was a very good design and it also looked good. But it did not have constant speed propellers, and that, combined with fixed propeller pitch, meant there was quite a long run to get off the ground. Once you were up and away the Oxford was a very nice aeroplane to fly.

'A couple of them crashed while I was at Wigram. One was during the latter part of 1943 while on a night flying exercise. One of our fellows, for some reason, never bothered strapping himself in. He was

The Catalina was one of Ken Fenwick's operational wartime aeroplanes. He did not like them, or the type of flying. These days a Catalina flying is a rare sight. ZK-PBY, an amphibious Catalina, takes off from the Wanaka strip during the 1996 Warbirds Over Wanaka air show. The Canadian-built Catalina, owned by a New Zealand group, featured in a 1988 BBC documentary, The Last African Flying Boat.

Roy Sinclair

just a casual sort of guy. On this occasion he came in to land and made a mess of it so he decided to go round again.

'Instead of lifting his undercarriage as he intended to do, he raised the flaps and, of course, the Oxford didn't perform very well unless everything was going right. Raising the flaps on his go-around meant the Oxford just sunk in. It crashed into the ground and caught fire.

'The rescue team went out and we all thought that was the end of old Bill. But because Bill wasn't strapped in he was catapulted through the Perspex and they picked him up about a chain away, a bit dazed but he was OK. He subsequently went off on the next flying course.'

Ken Fenwick was posted to an instructors' course at Tauranga before returning to Harewood, this time to instruct on Tiger Moths.

'Up to six hours of dual instruction each day over the next two years was darned hard work. And it was damn cold down there in those Christchurch winters.'

By way of contrast he was sent to do a navigation course at New Plymouth before being posted to Lauthala Bay in Fiji where he flew Catalina flying boats on long reconnaissance flights.

'I didn't really like them, especially getting soaked in the sea while tying up at the buoy — our Catalinas were not amphibians — or even the type of flying. But they were good for what they were made for. They could fly 24 hours on standard tanks or 28 with additional tanks.'

Ken was then a Flying Officer and was soon promoted to Flight Lieutenant. While continuing to serve in active reserve after the war he became a Squadron Leader.

When he left the Air Force he took up agricultural contracting, away from flying. He was busy chaffcutting, haybaling, working threshing mills, and involved in any sort of harvesting. Then he started a bit of flying at the Wairarapa Aero Club. In 1949 he took a job instructing at Wanganui and finally moved to Hamilton where he spent 27 years as the aero club's chief flying instructor.

A special interest has been aerobatics. To do them precisely takes hours and hours of practice. 'Anybody can get around haphazardly doing stall turns and barrel rolls but to do them properly is another matter. Well-performed precise aerobatics, that's one thing I really like watching. Most of us have been limited by the aeroplane. These days we have special aeroplanes for aerobatics. An aeroplane of the Pitts calibre, for example, will demonstrate to a pilot with ability the way an aeroplane can be flown.'

Training good pilots in New Zealand has not changed too much since the Tiger Moth days. High standards are achieved and it's a lot easier in modern trainers — Piper Tomahawks and Cessna 152s that will fly well with very little rudder movement. If you didn't know how to use your feet on the rudder pedals in a Tiger Moth, you didn't go anywhere.

'Hamilton is in Cessna Country but the Tomahawks that are popular in Canterbury are also very good. They have roomy cabins with a good view all around. They hug the ground a bit till they decide to fly, and you've got to use your feet on the rudder pedals a little more than other trainers. Landing is what most people have trouble with — putting the thing on the ground. Modern tricycle undercarriages have made it so much easier.'

THE FENWICK *FLYING Training Manual* evolved along with increased requirements for student pilots to study. Prior to about 1955 the amount of study for a Private Pilot's Licence was almost negligible. A testing officer came around the airfield and asked a few questions and that was all there was to the theory aspect of flying.

'As the requirements for written examinations became more stringent I realised that those who were brought up in the country, as I had been, needed a book that was related to New Zealand flying conditions. These days there are other training manuals, and some are imported, but at one stage we were selling 2000 or so a year. Now we sell about 1200 a year. Our policy has been to sell them at a reasonable rate to ensure they are available to all pilots, aero clubs and flying schools.'

The most recent edition is dated 1994. The big problem is to keep a manual up to date as rules and regulations constantly change.

'Pilots of the old school need to keep up with the information in the manual. What they were taught about Visual Flight Rules might contravene what is taught these days about flying within the minimum limits of a controlled air space. Pilots can get pulled up and face hefty fines.'

The Fenwick boys, Ewan and Lindsay, predictably got their interest in flying from their father. Ken said there was nothing much else for them at weekends while he was working out at the airfield. Ewan had a one-track mind when it came to flying, but Lindsay did have other interests.

'I taught them both as far as solo. I gave them each £25 to get started and told them, "That's all you're going to get." If £25 was paid in advance you got an extra 5 per cent credit. The boys cooked meals for people, cleaned aeroplanes, and took jobs in freezing works and as builder's labourers. Sometimes they got cheap instruction by going with an instructor to an outlying airfield, at Te Kuiti or Te Aroha, and hung around all day to get another lesson on the way home. People think they got their flying for nothing. They did not.

Teaching older people to fly has a special satisfaction. 'It's a real challenge for them. They might take longer to go solo but once they get everything set up they retain the skills better. More women than ever before are learning, too, as aeroplanes become easier to fly. I don't think a young woman will retain the knowledge as well as a male unless she keeps at it — although in competition flying they are well up with the guys. And we have a lot of very dedicated women instructors about now. Once they really get interested they will be very methodical in what they do, and particularly good with their ground briefings.'

Ken did not go along with an often-expressed belief that an instructor is someone for the student pilot to kill. 'No, I've never thought that. People say, "By Joves, I'd never have your job. It must be scary." It's not like that. I've never thought instructing was the slightest bit scary. Most times you know what the student is going to do before they do it. There's nothing new for them to do; someone's done it before them.'

He brushed aside most of my questions about his MBE honour, saying it was supposedly for services to aviation. 'It doesn't mean a lot really. I think they put the names in a hat and stick a pin through to see who they spear. I think I was just able to hang around long enough.'

Ewan and Lindsay are an obvious source of pride. He said it was a big job to have, taking those huge jets off the ground in all sorts of weather.

'It's such a challenging job knowing how to use all that modern equipment. It amazes me the number of checks airline pilots have got to have, and the simulator checks, to keep them up to speed. We only hear about pilots when they reportedly go to sleep at 30,000 feet while flying with the autopilot.'

He is amused at the prospect of a pilot going to sleep. 'They might go to sleep occasionally, I don't really know.'

There are no real regrets about not being an airline pilot himself. If he had been, he would have retired many years ago. He plans to keep flying until his next medical and, perhaps, his next.

'I've just had one. That gives me another six months at least. As long as I'm fit and well and enjoy what I'm doing, instructing will keep me out of my wife's hair. I am only doing about 15 hours' flying a month, not a great number of hours. That's about right for me. I don't know what I would do without my flying.'

WE VISITED THE Hamilton Aero Club and, once among his aeroplanes, Ken talked about some of the finer points of flying an aeroplane and, especially, how to make that perfect landing. As he talked, his hands moved constantly to demonstrate the ever-changing attitude of the perfectly controlled aeroplane. Finally, with some reverence, he talked once more about those airline pilots whose experiences he had chosen not to share.

'When you apply power to a Boeing 747-400, that is the most powerful machine, apart from nuclear power, that we can control,' he said.

IN 1997 KEN Fenwick received a Director of Civil Aviation award for his contribution to flight safety. The award almost coincided with his 80th birthday when he announced his plans to retire from flying — when his pilot's licence expired later in the year.

A young professionally trained Canterbury Aero Club pilot prepares for a flight home from Wellington.
ROY SINCLAIR

CHAPTER 10

Skies of Solitude and Friendship

Going for the record. Isobell Storey, with her Paracommander parachute, comes close to earth after jumping from 18,500 feet, breaking the Australasian women's altitude record. The year is 1968.

The ultimate in flying is being on your own — just you, the aeroplane and the elements.

Isobell Storey

DOWN THE STREET, Isobell Storey is someone who appears unremarkable. Just one of the crowd. A neatly dressed mature woman who recently retired from a long nursing career; the woman who is seen doing voluntary work at a Hamilton suburban police station. She speaks quietly, almost apologetically. But what she says can pack a punch. I met her the day after her 67th birthday. 'I must be getting towards being the grandmother of active New Zealand aviators,' she said in greeting.

Since 1968 she has held an Australasian altitude record for women's parachuting and, in July 1997, she was still flying as a private pilot. She had not long been back in the air, having had her medical renewed following a serious operation for cancer. To celebrate her birthday she bought an airline ticket and spent a weekend in Christchurch catching up with friends from the New Zealand Airwomen's Association.

The social weekend, although very enjoyable on this occasion, was not her usual style. She is more often on her own, picking June or July to fly south with one of the Waikato Aero Club planes. 'I just love winter flying in the South Island. The weather is often settled. The snow and sheer beauty of everything are just wonderful. I have always been a bit of a loner. Most of my friends want to fly to Christchurch to see the sights and do the restaurants. That's not my scene at all. I like to land at the isolated back-country places — Erewhon, Mesopotamia or Glenorchy — and visit the people there, rather than the cities or larger towns.

'I do not mind being on my own while I fly. By the time I have spent 15 or 20 hours flying south, my aeroplane has become a friend. I talk to it. When I get home I say, "You did well."

'There's something very special about flying, and only pilots know what it is.'

I sensed a little regret when she said the 1997 winter was going to be the first in a long while when she has not made her South Island safari. (She was saving for a trip to Argentina to visit her son and his family.) Still, she was enjoying a weekend among friends. And she was not too concerned about her age so long as she was able to add to the remarkable number of flying hours — about 1200 — already recorded in her Pilot Logbook.

'I really haven't done anything exciting with my flying,' she told me. 'I've just done a lot of it.'

FOR AS LONG as she can remember, Isobell Storey desperately wanted to become a pilot. 'I always used to rush out and watch aeroplanes go over — I still do. Flying was just something I always wanted to do.'

But during the 1960s, a mother of three children and living near Morrinsville, she could not afford flying lessons. Instead, she joined the Waikato Parachute Club, thinking she could afford at least a one-way ride in an aeroplane. In 1964 she became the first New Zealand married woman with children to take up parachuting. She was parachuting for seven years. She became the first New Zealand woman to do a water jump — into Lake Karapiro on the Waikato River. Then, on 9 May 1968, a jump from 18,500 feet became an Australasian women's parachuting altitude record. Almost 30 years on, the record has not been broken.

'I remember the day I decided to take up parachuting. I went out to the club and said, "I'm 34; do you think I'm too old?" Then I quickly added, "I'm a very young 34!" They took me on and I enjoyed it. I became an instructor — and I was involved with aeroplanes.'

Isobell's first parachute jump was not as scary as the subsequent third, fourth, or fifth. 'When you have never done something like parachuting before, you don't know what to expect,' she says.

'You've gone up there wanting to jump, so you are not particularly scared — just very excited. And you trust implicitly the people who

Isobell Storey. 'I must be getting towards being the grandmother of active New Zealand aviators.'
ROY SINCLAIR

have trained you. You put your whole faith in them. You are tapped on the shoulder — and you jump. And it's marvellous, and you do another one. Only then do you start to think, what if? If something happens, am I experienced enough to cope with it?

'So by the fourth or fifth jump you are starting to think about it. You realise you are getting into something that is potentially pretty hazardous stuff. Gradually, you sort of overcome that, but you always treat parachuting with respect. Any sport, but particularly parachuting, has to be played by the rules. You believe that if you do all the right things then you probably won't hurt yourself. If you start being a cowboy, it bites. And when it bites, it bites!'

In seven years Isobell Storey experienced only one serious equipment malfunction, caused by her Paracommander parachute not opening properly. She says the one thing that saved her life on that occasion was an article she had read in a magazine, just a few days before her 100th jump.

'I had read about a woman whose parachute failed to open properly when she jumped from an aeroplane during a demonstration over Sydney's Bondi Beach. If you get slightly head down when you jump, as the parachute deploys out, the lines can get wrapped round your feet. That's exactly what happened. I was hanging with my head down and feet up — and the parachute was only partially open.

'The woman I had read about had been doing exactly what I was doing — trying to unwind the lines. She had fallen and died on Bondi while still trying to free her foot.

'You can kick yourself around a bit up there. There's your foot stuck up in the air with these lines wrapped round and you know that if you get this much off, the parachute will blossom. You lose awareness of falling at 120 mph towards the earth.

'Then, it suddenly came back to me. I'm doing exactly the same as the woman I had read about. I am struggling to free *my* foot, and if I do this I will die! I stopped struggling and threw out my reserve parachute, which tangled up with the main chute as well. Then it puffed out to one side. The main then deflated and fell, enveloping me completely. I couldn't see where I was going. All I knew was that I was coming down nice and gently. You get that feeling of suspension, and no noise of air rushing past. You know you are not hurtling down. I landed in a paddock some distance from the airfield.

'I didn't at any stage feel particularly upset. At first I thought I would untangle my foot and I'd be right. Even after I realised I would die, without doubt, I just concentrated on getting to the ground without hurting myself. People over at the club, about half a mile away, started tearing over in cars to where I was going to land, not quite sure what they would find. But I was fine. It was one way to remember my 100th jump.'

An especially memorable event, on 29 January 1966, was when she was part of a display jump for the opening of Auckland's International Airport at Mangere. 'We took off from Ardmore and did a mass drop onto a small strip of runway close to buildings, a tremendous number of aeroplanes, and the beach and harbour. One or two people did end up in the water but I managed not to do that.'

For her 200th jump, two years later, she wanted to jump from 20,000 feet over Rukuhia and claim the Australasian Women's altitude record. She asked Denny Main, a foundation club instructor, to be her jump mate. They had jumped a lot together.

'We had to hire a twin-engine Aerocommander from the Rotorua Aero Club. It was piloted by Rotorua's Chief Flying Instructor, Ian Palmer. A long-time friend, Mike Cuming, supplied us with oxygen, which sustained us above 7500 feet. We got up to 18,500 feet when an oil line froze in one engine. It was that cold. Ian Palmer said we would have to jump. He couldn't go any higher with one engine.

'Those days you flew across where you hoped to land, and threw out drift markers made from rolled-up crêpe paper. As they fell they would unravel, and from the wind drift you estimated your exit point. With the parachutes used today you can fly them almost like an aeroplane. Ours, being round with slots, were not so manoeuvrable.

'At 18,500 feet we threw out the drift markers, but from that height a couple of ribbons are soon lost to view. We then just threw off our oxygen masks and jumped. The air was pretty thin during the 80 seconds of free fall to the opening height at 2500 feet. By that stage we knew we had miscalculated and got it all wrong. We ended up in the churchyard, a mile away from the airfield. A couple of horses bolted through the paddocks as they got spooked by these things coming out of the sky. Ice caked our goggles and my fingers were close to being frost-bitten. They remained very white for several days. It had been minus 26 degrees Fahrenheit at our exit point.

'It didn't matter where I landed as long as I got out at the right height. I didn't achieve the 20,000 feet I had hoped for but I was confident it had been an Australasian women's record. There had been nothing much above about 12,000 feet.'

Isobell carried a sealed barograph (an aneroid barometer) to record the height. The equipment was subsequently sent to the New

These days, modern parachutes can be controlled almost like an aeroplane. This is demonstrated in a display jump at a Warbirds Over Wanaka air show.
ROY SINCLAIR

Another memorable event was making a test jump, accompanied by Denny Main, from a New Zealand-made Fletcher FU-24, ZK-CVW, on 19 July 1968.
WAIKATO TIMES

Zealand Federation of Parachute Clubs to be checked, and the record ratified.

She became involved in what is known as 'relative work', when several parachutists link up and work together during the free fall. 'We could do all sorts of manoeuvres — flip and roll, barrel roll, or a loop. We could do almost anything an aeroplane could do, except go back up.'

As an instructor during the late 1960s she helped to train Malcolm Campbell, who later founded Eagle Airlines. 'I chucked Malcolm out on his first jump.'

Another memorable event was on 19 July 1968. Isobell Storey and Denny Main did a test jump from a New Zealand-made Fletcher top-dressing aeroplane, ZK-CVW, flown by agricultural pilot Doug MacElwain. The jump was recorded in an air-to-air photograph by a *Waikato Times* photographer.

Landings, standing up, were often hard and fast. Sometimes club members would break an ankle or a leg. On one occasion Isobell dislocated an elbow when a wind gust caught her while landing. She hated night jumps. Her last jump on 3 April 1971 was at night, just to get her D licence. (The D licence is the parachutists' top grade.)

'Jumping from 5500 feet, I have to say I was scared. I couldn't see a thing and our equipment was not very good by today's standards. You had to carry a torch to try and see where you were going. I missed the airfield that time too. But I landed unscathed. At night you didn't know what was under you — trees, houses, or powerlines.

By that time Isobell had made more than 300 jumps. She had also started nursing and was earning enough money to fly.

'Flying was much more satisfying. Parachuting was a means to an end — a one-way ride on an aeroplane. That's all it was. I couldn't afford two ways, so one way did. But there was certainly satisfaction in parachuting as you started to get up higher, doing more intricate stuff, and being entirely reliant on your ability.

'Parachuting was also changing. Different people, sometimes the wrong people, were getting involved. We called them "pub jumpers" — guys who just wanted to do the one big jump and brag about it in the pub afterwards.

'It was all part of marketing parachuting. You paid $90 into someone's back pocket and did your first parachute jump after a couple of hours' training. When money came into it like that, I didn't like it. Parachuting became a bravado sort of act. Parachuting requires people who are level-headed and disciplined. We trained people for about a month before their first jump. We strapped them up in hangars spreadeagled out, and all that. When they made that first jump we made sure the wind was not above about eight knots.

'We told them, as they do on Air New Zealand, what to do "in the unlikely event of" a malfunction. You never know when a malfunction is going to happen. I had one after more than 90 jumps. It could have happened during that first jump. And you don't know how you are going to handle stress till it happens. If I hadn't browsed through a particular magazine and read about another woman's fatal accident when I did, I wouldn't be sitting here talking to you.'

A GOOD BIT of self-discipline learned while parachuting went into Isobell's flying. She sold her parachuting gear and started flying at the Waikato Aero Club in 1971. Ken Fenwick was her flying instructor.

'Even in those days women were not *totally* accepted into this man's domain of flying. The attitude was, OK, we'll teach you but you're a woman, you shouldn't really be doing this. Ken Fenwick never said anything like that to me. But it had been said that he thought a woman should not be within 100 feet of an aeroplane!

'Anyway, he taught me, and he taught me to fly well. He was an excellent instructor. He never got a student pilot tense or uptight. He never screamed or yelled. He would always say, "We will go through this together" and he would talk you through it. Once you got to know a little about what you were doing he would just sit there with his arms folded looking out his side window and I would be thinking, perhaps I am doing all right? He must have had very wide vision because he knew exactly what was happening on the panel — whether you were in balance, or out of it.

'I stuck with Ken till I went solo. Every student pilot's right is to have one instructor they can relate to, at least until they go solo. After that it's probably not a bad idea to fly with a few other instructors with different ideas, and get their feedback. Some are better than others. There's nothing worse than an instructor who is sitting there ready to grab the controls. I believe Ken could have unwrapped his arms in a flash if he had had to. That's how he was. He made me feel confident.

'Having spent most weekends over seven years in aeroplanes while parachuting I had gained experience that helped me with balance and gauging descent while flying the Cessna 150s. But I was 40 when I started flying. At that age you tend to set very high standards and goals. Apart from Ken Fenwick, all the instructors were a whole lot younger than I was. If I couldn't achieve something I got quite frustrated. Landings were very difficult. While attempting to get it just right, I would usually flare too high and drop onto the ground.'

With 20 hours in the air and still 'very green and wet behind the ears', Isobell Storey set off on a map-reading course from Hamilton to Ngaruawahia, then to Pirongia and Cambridge, and back to Hamilton. The weather was getting bad and the cloud base was lowering. To fly to Cambridge on the last leg of the flight she had to cross the extended centre line of Hamilton's south runway.

'I didn't tell the controller I was going to cross. I just went across and, right in front of me, a Fokker Friendship just popped out of the clouds. I was so close to it. I could see all the rivets on the fuselage — and all the people sitting up in their seats. I then went under, behind the Fokker's wing. Fortunately, the captain didn't see me but the controller called up the aero club when I got back and asked me to come up for a wee chat.

'He was really good. He realised I was aggrieved about it. He said he didn't think there would be an incident report because the captain was unaware of me being there. "I'm not going to tell anyone either," he said. The airliner came out of cloud on instruments. By the time the controller picked me up with his glasses it was too late for him to do anything. He chose to say nothing and hoped like hell we didn't hit each other.

'I can still see that Fokker Friendship very clearly, even after all those years. I think I might have said an involuntary SHIT as it flew past.'

The day Isobell was scheduled to do her Private Pilot's Licence flying test was another horrible day. On such occasions it is the student pilot's choice whether or not to go on with the test.

'Ken said, "It doesn't look too good out there." He then said, "But you don't want to be a fair-weather pilot all your life, do you?"

'And I said, "I suppose not," and went off to become a qualified private pilot.'

'Several people said I should do my commercial licence but I could not see any point. Those days, a woman couldn't even work in a control tower, let alone fly an aeroplane for an airline. A lot of money would be spent getting a licence, and no one would employ me. If I were young again I would make flying a career. It wasn't an option when I learned to fly. You accepted it because that was the way it was. Then, women became more assertive and thought, well, is there any reason why we can't? One of the first things women objected to strongly — and it got struck out of the medical requirements — was the question, "When was your last menstruation?" That had nothing to do with flying aeroplanes.

'I can clearly remember flying on a cross-country from Rotorua when I called up the tower and got this woman's voice in my headset. That was quite amazing — the first woman I had struck on the airways.

'These days a lot of women are learning to fly. Many become excellent instructors. On the airways we hear women calling up from Air New Zealand and Ansett. I believe women approach things more

Isobell Storey gives instructions to pilot Brian Harvey before making a parachute jump over Waikato.
PRESS PHOTO SERVICE

cautiously. Fewer women are involved in road crashes than men. Aviation is a very acceptable career for a woman.'

DESPITE AN OBVIOUS gender discrimination during the 1970s, Isobell Storey is no raving paragon of women's rights. Far from it. She has a great respect for her flying instructor, Ken Fenwick. Another aviator she talks of is Fred Ladd, whom she met while parachuting.

'I once jumped out at 6000 feet from an aeroplane flown by Fred Ladd. He was a lovely, happy, cheerful man who is best known for his Wigeon amphibian float planes and his often compassionate services, through the 1950s and 1960s, to the people inhabiting Great Barrier and 40 or more other isolated islands of the Hauraki Gulf. Fred was famous for his little verses such as "A Shower of Spray and We're Away", which became the title of his biography. He wrote in my parachuting logbook, "This Storey dropped to Glory." It was his first experience as a drop pilot and also, he said, the first time he had "taken off full and returned empty".'

Isobell got to know him a little better later. He had volunteered his pilot's licence in, following a dizzy spell while driving his car around Lake Taupo near where he lived. When he had pulled himself together he thought that if that had happened on short final, it wouldn't be good. Fred never had another problem, and tried for a long time, in vain, to get his licence back. He swam a lot in the lake and climbed Ngauruhoe. He competed in harbour swims at Tauranga. Many people believe the authorities never had any intention of giving Fred Ladd's pilot's licence back.

'About that time I also lost my licence, temporarily, as a result of a slightly irregular ECG test. I visited Fred Ladd several times to see what he was doing about his. I did not want to lose mine just because of a slight blip on the ECG. I called quite a few times in 1981 while I was fighting to get my PPL back. His wife, Mabel, told me at one stage — when Fred went out to make a cup of tea — that she had been told, "He will never get it back. All his correspondence to the department has been unopened."

'It had been said they had been gunning for him because he was a bit of a naughty boy in his time. In 1967 he flew a Wigeon under the Auckland harbour bridge — on his last day with his Tourist Air Travel — and a few other things. He took up a bit of gliding, but that didn't give him the same satisfaction. He died a couple of years after I got my licence back, a very disappointed man.

'I think Fred Ladd was an extremely able pilot regardless of what the department thought about his antics. He went to the assistance of many people in the Hauraki Gulf. They got to know that Tourist Air Travel's Wigeon amphibian offered a shortcut to the doctor or hospital. Fred's little verse for medical emergencies was, "Those in pain take to the air, To quickly get the doctor's care —"

'He was flying back to Rotorua from Taupo one day when an oil line burst and sprayed oil all over the window. He couldn't see anything. Somehow he managed to get his aeroplane, full of passengers, down onto some rough country and remained substantially intact. Nobody got hurt. Fred never took any credit for that. He just said it was "the hand of God".'

Isobell laughs as she tells the next part of the story: 'Fred was quite a religious man. I'm a bit of a sceptic, and I do not think God had a lot to do with it, quite frankly. I think it was sheer skill on Fred's part that all those people walked out of that. After I got my licence back I felt too embarrassed to visit Fred and Mabel. They were a really nice couple.'

FLYING, AND MEETING people in the South Island are among other cherished memories. Isobell met Richard Rayward at Air Safaris when Air Safaris was very small, with just two aeroplanes. 'I phoned Richard from Blenheim to check on the weather down in the mountains at Lake Tekapo. He told me about his strip being narrow and sloping. I would need a fair bit of control while landing if I were not to go off the straight and narrow. He and his wife, Ros, invited me to stay with them and we have been friends ever since.'

On another occasion, at the Greymouth Aero Club, Isobell met Cherie Marshall, who would later fly Mount Cook Airline's ski-planes and, in 1996, Jean Batten's Percival Gull G-ADPR. It was the aeroplane Jean Batten flew from England to South America in 1935, and from England to New Zealand the following year.

'She was only a teenager, about 18, when she approached me and said "hello" while I was tying down. She carried on talking as I finished putting in my pickets. Seeing my AA Book, she asked where I was staying. When I said I didn't know yet, she invited me home for a cup of tea and I ended up staying the night. Cherie was then a student pilot. Her father, Peter Hodgkinson, was also an excellent pilot and an unassuming West Coaster through and through. He flew Cessna 180s and 185s. When he got to 20,000 hours as a private pilot he stopped putting entries in his Pilot Logbook.

'I met Cherie many times later when she was living at the Mt Cook village. I went on several ski-plane flights and I was once asked if I had a commercial licence. When I said no, the reply was, "Pity, we would have been interested in you."

'It was the one time I regretted not having a commercial licence. I was about 50 then, with a fair bit of experience flying in mountains.'

On another occasion, when she took a Cherokee Six, 'a reasonably decent sort of aeroplane', on one of her South Island safaris, she was asked if she was a doctor. 'No,' was her reply, 'just a nurse.'

She called at places like Haast, Wanaka, and Cromwell when they were quite small. Flying took her to the outdoor places she enjoyed so much. In Canterbury she called in at Mt Potts station, and she met the Urquharts at Erewhon Station near the confluence of the Rangitata, Clyde, and Havelock Rivers. 'They were very welcoming. We ended up enjoying a bush barbecue up the Clyde River.'

She met David Miller at Paradise. In 1996 he was suffering from kidney failure and was undergoing dialysis. 'He was wanting to give his 183-hectare property, beyond the head of Lake Wakatipu, away to a charitable trust. It was worth about $3 million and he wanted it to revert to its natural state and be of use to disabled and disadvantaged people. He bred dogs. He had about 25 border collie working dogs. Some had appeared on television's *Country Calendar*.

'I became totally fascinated by this man. I went up and knocked on his door just to say "hello". I was invited in by the district nurse, who was also calling. Another woman, from Germany, was visiting New Zealand especially to catalogue his amazing art collection.

'David had left the big rambling family home to live in a cottage. His wife had left him some time ago. She probably couldn't stand the isolation. David had lived at Paradise since he was 15. He had been a mountain guide and a hunter. He knew every peak — they are mostly named after Greek gods. Arcadia is the name of the next property. With his health deteriorating, he wanted to give everything away, rather than sell it.

'They're the sort of places I want to fly to. They're the sort of people I like to meet,' says Isobell Storey.

BRUCE KERR, CHIEF flying instructor at Queenstown, started her mountain flying training and took her to Milford Sound. She was also taught by Russell Baker, chief pilot for Air Fiordland, who is 'an absolute ace in mountains'. From Phil Keane, Southern Air's chief pilot, she got a special rating and became approved to fly into Milford.

She talks with great passion of lunching at Milford and flying the Milford Track — up the Arthur Valley, past the Sutherland Falls. From high above Mackinnon Pass she looks down on Lake Quill, feeding the huge falls. She will also look down on the Quintin airstrip, but will choose not to land. She flies down the Clinton canyon, down the lake to Te Anau, and across to Lake Wakatipu. Instead of going on to Queenstown, she flies up the lake and lands on a small strip at Glenorchy. Nearby is a little tavern where she stays the night. 'No, you are never lonely,' she tells me. 'You're just busy looking at everything, and monitoring your radio, all the time.

'I have had lots of flights into, and from, Milford and I just thoroughly enjoy them. Nevertheless, before each visit I will get an update on briefings from a local operator. Mountain flying, especially, demands discipline. If you do it right you'll be OK. In bad weather, when you are feeling uneasy and starting to wonder about going on, there's always another day tomorrow. There's an old aviation saying, "The sun has shone on many a wreck." Even if you get to where you are going in bad weather, you have only proved you have been a bit lucky.'

Yet, for all her care, she knows that any pilot can be caught out. She had been flying for 22 years, believing she had the instincts of an old outhouse rat, when she was caught in cloud. It happened while she was flying to the South Island in 1994. The weather from Hamilton was CAVOK (cloud and visibility OK) apart from a heavy band of showers moving east from about 20 miles north of Wanganui to Taihape. The weather was fine at Wanganui and cloudless further along the coast to Paraparaumu, and all the way to Christchurch.

'About eight miles south of Raetihi I contacted Ohakea for a clearance through their zone at 4000 feet, and to proceed down the beach bound for Omaka. This clearance was given. I could see clearly right through to Wanganui where the weather was obviously fine, with patches of sun on the buildings. But I had misjudged how rapidly the heavy showers were moving towards my flight path — until it became obvious I would have to change my heading.

'I advised Ohakea and began a left-hand turn to avoid cloud. Next thing I was in cloud, experiencing just how snugly cloud fits around the viewing bay of an aeroplane. For a non-instrument-rated VFR (Visual Flight Rules) pilot this situation quickly produces incredible feelings of inadequacy and isolation. Such conditions, more often than not, have a fatal outcome. You become so totally disorientated you are unable to fly the aeroplane.'

Isobell says two things saved her that day. One was a changed attitude towards pilots who get into difficulties. There was a time when such an admission promised some sort of persecution from aviation authorities. It was better to keep quiet, even if you might soon be dead. These days, the emphasis is on assistance.

The second factor was the Airways Corporation's sophisticated radar system, which had been running for about two years. A special feature is the secondary surveillance radar component that draws information directly from a transponder in the aircraft. Once the pilot

Fred Ladd, an exuberant Wigeon float-plane pilot of the 1950s and 1960s, won Isobell Storey's admiration.
NZ HERALD

gives a requested SQUAWK code the air traffic controller, looking at a radar screen, can identify the aircraft, its call sign, height, ground speed, and other details.

'I realised that help was just a radio transmission away. The new Airways Corporation technology, combined with the calm assistance from the Ohakea controller, undoubtedly saved me from a fatal outcome.

'His instructions were for me to concentrate on keeping my wings level, assuring me I had ample terrain clearance, and that my ground speed was good. He just kept on talking as he monitored my progress on his screen. He kept telling me to keep the wings level and not to worry about terrain clearance. He would take care of that. It was just as if I was learning instrument flying with an instructor sitting beside me. As I lost the feeling of being alone, I could concentrate on the job in hand.

'The controller was then telling me my heading was good and soon I would be seeing Wanganui, which was 15 miles away. And as quickly as I had entered the cloud, I burst out into clear skies.'

When she landed at Omaka, a message from the nearby Woodbourne airport was waiting, asking Isobell to phone Ohakea. She did, and was thanked for requesting Air Traffic Control assistance when it was required.

IN SEPTEMBER 1996 Isobell Storey had a bowel cancer diagnosed and removed. The operation was successful, but it was not so easy getting her medical reinstated, subject to regular checks by her surgeon. Escalating costs of medical assessments by the Civil Aviation Authority ($135 an hour) is going to get rid of many general aviation pilots, she says. Some assessments apparently take several hours. In the meantime, she is making the most of her pilot's licence. She had clocked up 50 hours since being authorised to fly again.

'Now that I am not working I am free to fly any time. People often want me to fly them somewhere. A real estate agent and aero club member, who is no longer flying himself, will get me to fly him to a seminar somewhere. It turns out to be an economical travel option when you can get to where you are going and back again the same day.'

Another friend, Terry Pidduck, living on Great Barrier, commutes to his business in Cambridge. He and his wife, Bev, also own a Cherokee, which Isobell often flies. During one flight to Great Barrier she was forced down by low cloud around the Firth of

Thames, and had to follow the coastline of the Coromandel Peninsula around the top of Cape Barrier. She was hit by a sudden turbulence, so strong that the aeroplane was tipped up on one side. The door, on the up side, was sprung open and the first aid kit and everything else broke out.

'I hit my head so hard on the roof it was still sore a week later. I can't say I was frightened. I have never got to the stage where I was scared of being killed. It is just something one deals with. Reaction is all instinctive. You work the rudder and ailerons until you're on the right kilter again. As I turned a corner and approached my landing I could not see the airstrip because of this enormous rainbow. It was so bright, just where I was trying to look. Perhaps I am the only pilot whose vision has been obscured by a rainbow.'

Sometimes, on flights to and from Great Barrier, she is accompanied by the Pidducks and their old English sheepdog, Miss Paddington, who sits on the back seat and almost goes berserk once the aeroplane is over Colville Channel and close to home.

'When we have Miss Paddington on board I will call up the tower and say, 'Three POB (People on Board) and one dog. Should we ever disappear into the sea I would like to think they were searching for Miss Paddington as well.'

ISOBELL FLICKS THROUGH a small album of photographs recalling highlights of her parachuting and flying. She stops at one photograph of a fellow parachutist, Ron Flynn. He is waving, during his free fall, as if he is saying goodbye. A few minutes later he was drowned — trapped and tangled in his parachute in Lake Rotorua. Looking at another photograph, she talks about formation flying.

'A group of three of us called ourselves "Waikato Formation". We competed in three national events. We were third in one. Altogether we did more than 40 hours of formation flying. We were a really good team. It is inherently dangerous to fly so close to another aeroplane. Taking off and landing in formation requires a great deal of confidence and trust in each other. You know that if you clip wings you're going to kill yourselves. We formed a close bond of friendship.'

Finally, she holds the album open at a photograph taken about the time of her parachute altitude record. She looks up and smiles. 'You know,' she says, 'I was once quite beautiful.'

And I know I will sometimes pass a woman in the street who will remind me of Isobell Storey. She will no longer be just one of the crowd. I will be thinking, has she ever jumped out of an aeroplane at

6000 feet? Is the local aero club her second home? Does she spend her winters flying through the Southern Alps? Has she ever touched down on some isolated strip and met someone willing to give away a $3 million paradise? Would she smile if I mentioned the name Fred Ladd? If I spoke to her, would she offer to take me flying?

No, such a person will always be a potential aviator. The word 'unremarkable' no longer fits.

A winter scene on the Milford Track, looking towards the Sutherland Falls and Lake Quill, from an aircraft flying in the Arthur River valley.
KIRSTEN SINCLAIR

PDL
AIR RACE

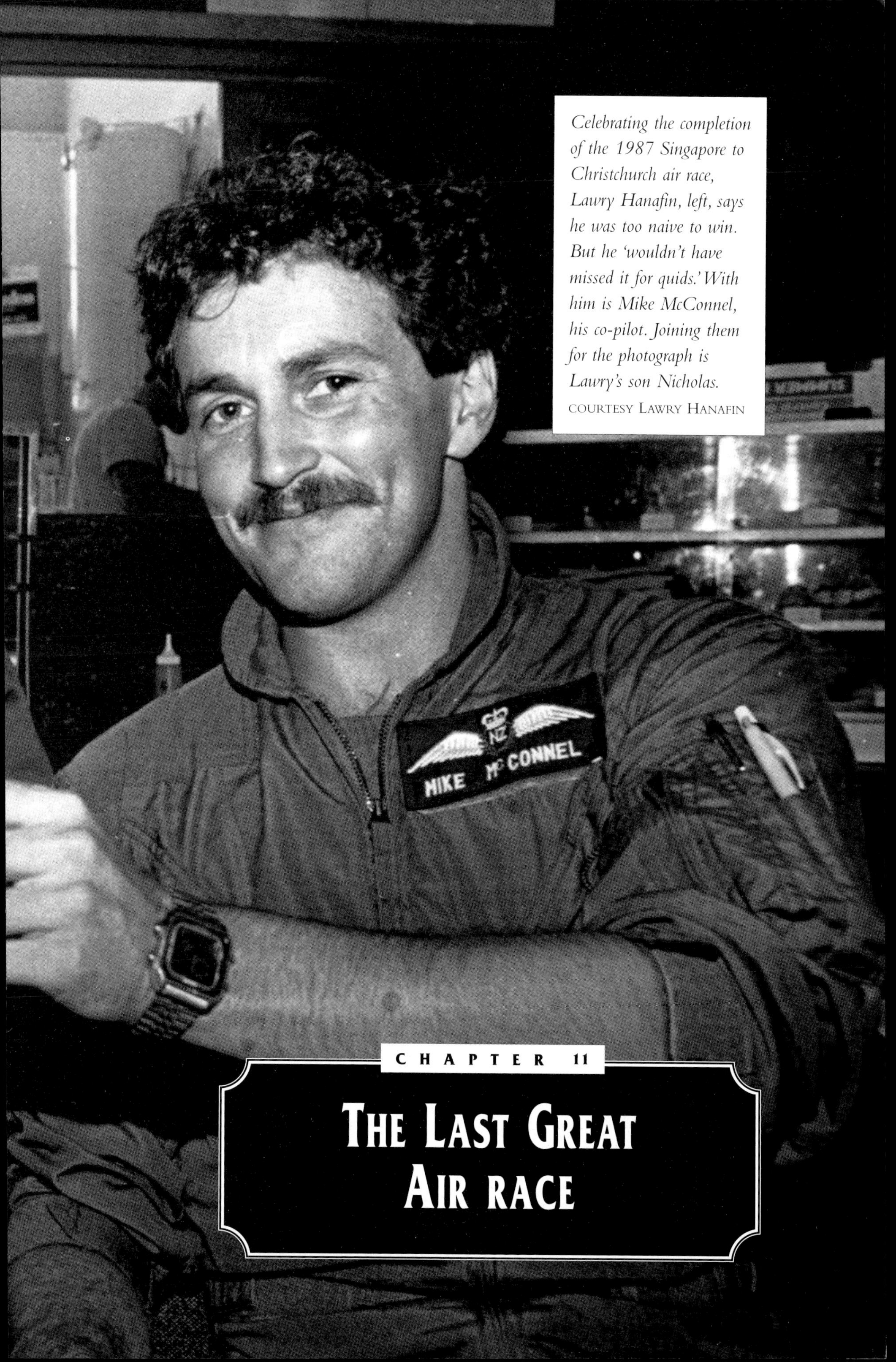

Celebrating the completion of the 1987 Singapore to Christchurch air race, Lawry Hanafin, left, says he was too naive to win. But he 'wouldn't have missed it for quids.' With him is Mike McConnel, his co-pilot. Joining them for the photograph is Lawry's son Nicholas.
COURTESY LAWRY HANAFIN

CHAPTER 11

THE LAST GREAT AIR RACE

I definitely went into the race to win. I wanted to win the Tiger Moth prize. But I spent more on the race than it would have cost to buy a Tiger Moth.

Lawry Hanafin

HIS FRIENDS WERE amused. His wife and four young children were not. Why should a 37-year-old family man take on a daring flight of more than 8000 km in a 22-year-old single-engine aeroplane? Lawry Hanafin says it was because he was desperate to win a vintage Tiger Moth, the handicap prize for the 1987 International Air Race from Singapore to Christchurch.

As it turned out he did not win. He was inexperienced, naive, and perhaps even too honest. To win the race, staged to commemorate the 50th anniversary of Christchurch International Airport, required more than flying skills and good planning. It also demanded an artful interpretation of race rules to secure a favourable handicap. A year of legal action followed the event as disgruntled people tried to use the courts to enforce what they thought was fair. And getting to Singapore with his command pilot, Mike McConnel, was almost as momentous as the race itself. Lawry says the story has never really been told.

THESE DAYS LAWRY Hanafin runs the successful chain of Hanafin Photo Stores. Flying is something that belongs to his past. His Piper Cherokee, Delta Bravo Charlie, has been sold. His Private Pilot's Licence lapsed some years ago. But when I visited him in December

Lawry Hanafin's Cherokee Six, ZK-DBC, at Singapore's Seletar airport.
LAWRY HANAFIN

1997 I found him surrounded with aeronautical charts, newspaper clippings, copies of *New Zealand Wings* magazine, and even the headsets he had used during the 1987 air race.

'I have really been having a great time going through all these bits and pieces,' he told me in greeting. 'The minute I heard about the air race I thought, that's for me. I want to have a go at this. Singapore to Christchurch!'

Looking up from an unfolded chart spread across a generous dining table, Lawry was clearly enjoying the reminiscing.

'It's hard to imagine how different technology was then, compared with now. Today anyone doing this sort of thing has GPS (Global Positioning System) navigation. You know exactly where you are at any point of the flight. Ten years ago you could not buy, for a reasonable sum of money, any navigational device that would tell you where you were — apart from celestial navigation, which you couldn't use in an enclosed Cherokee cockpit. I guess that was the challenge. We could use only a compass and fly a direct reckoning course hour after hour.

'At no stage of the flight, once we were beyond the range of land-based radio beacons (NDBs), were we able to predict accurately where we were. Across oceans, the featureless Australian hinterland, and often flying at night, there were no visual indications to confirm we were going in the right direction. We just hoped we were. We did no calculations for wind drift.

'We had our HF radio. We could talk to people. That was all right down towards Australia and New Zealand. But in Indonesia and Singapore people just seemed to go to bed. No one was there to talk to. When we tried to get some advice or help, there was no one there who wanted to know you.'

The timing of the air race was fortuitous. Two years previously Lawry Hanafin had pranged his aeroplane. It had been completely rebuilt, courtesy of the insurance company.

'In 1987 my Cherokee Six was an old plane with 6000 hours in the air. But it was straight out of an overhaul an aeroplane of that age would not normally have got. The wings, everything, had been completely stripped. I had every bit of confidence in the plane.'

PERHAPS THE BEST remembered international air races are the famous MacRobertson race from Mildenhall (England) to Melbourne in 1934, and the London to Christchurch race of 1953. The former, won by Scott and Campbell-Black flying a twin-engine de Havilland Comet, has been the subject of books and a dramatic television miniseries. Competitors included some of the great pioneers of flight: Amy Johnson, Jim Mollison, and a New Zealander who later became known as Captain HC Walker, flying Vickers Viscounts for National Airways Corporation.

The October 1953 race, although not so well documented, is remembered for being the first flight from Heathrow, London to New Zealand in less than 24 hours. It was won by Flight Lieutenant Monty Burton in an RAF Canberra. Burton's elapsed time of 23 hours 53 minutes won him and his crew the famed Harewood Gold Cup. The race, coinciding with the 50th anniversary of powered flight, involved eight aircraft (military and civil) from four countries.

In 1987, the Singapore to Christchurch race (sponsored by Sir Robertson Stewart and his PDL Industries) was a bigger event, attracting 39 entrants from New Zealand, Australia, Singapore, and Britain. Class A was for light aircraft competing for a first prize of $20,000. Class B was for civil and military aircraft competing for the Jubilee Gold Trophy. The handicap prize, a $60,000 vintage Tiger Moth, could be won by an entrant in either class. The Tiger Moth is what Lawry Hanafin was determined to win. He spent an entire year in preparation.

'FINDING A COMMAND pilot with the necessary instrument ratings to lodge an International Flight Plan was the biggest task,' says Lawry. 'I didn't have those ratings. I soon discovered there were not all that many pilots who wanted to sit in the front seat of a single-engine aeroplane for hours on end, going to Singapore and back, for no remuneration.

'Flight Lieutenant Mike McConnel was winding up his Air Force career, having just landed a job with Ansett New Zealand. He was technically the command pilot. He flew the right-hand seat and I flew the left. I flew the aeroplane.'

The next objective was to nominate a route. Once the route was nominated the pilots had to stick to it. Most entrants flew an official route from Singapore to Bali, then Darwin, and across Australia to Mt Isa and Brisbane. Single-engine aeroplanes would then island-hop the Tasman, landing at Lord Howe and Norfolk.

'We thought we had an ace card in our nominated southern route, flying from Bali to Port Hedland, across Australia to Ceduna, Hobart, and trans-Tasman to Christchurch. We did a lot of research, using Air Force information and paying particular attention to prevailing west-to-east winds.

'Once you had nominated your route you then nominated your cruise speed. Rules stipulated how that cruise speed was to be arrived at from the aeroplane's operating manual. The race organisers calculated the miles, took your nominated cruise speed and divided that speed into your flight plan distance. They made the appropriate allowances for each landing and gave you a start time in Singapore.

'The theory was that all the aircraft, whether they be single-engine or Boeing 747s, should arrive in Christchurch about the same time, or at least by 4 pm on Friday 28 March. Everyone would be in Christchurch for an air show planned for the weekend.

'As it turned out our chosen route worked for us to a certain extent. We actually beat our handicap time of 24 hours 30 minutes. We would have got caned had we taken that northern route as most other entrants did. With our handicap speed, we would have come last by a country mile.

'Boyd Munro, an Australian who won the race with a flying time of 22 hours 51 minutes, flew the same route as we did but he did it better. From Singapore he flew straight down to Christmas Island, which did not have an official airfield. He had flown in fuel before the race. He then refuelled at Perth and Hobart.'

Several rules had to be adhered to. An entrant could not fly more than 24 hours without a 12-hour stop. Time on the ground had to

Despite the apparent proliferation of instruments, the Cherokee Six had nothing that would guarantee accurate navigation over oceans and other featureless landscapes. 'That was the challenge,' says Lawry Hanafin. LAWRY HANAFIN

be a minimum of 30 minutes but any time over an hour was wasted. An hour was allowed for letting down, approach, refuelling, taking off and climbing back to altitude again.

'The rules were quite clear on what survival gear we had to carry. It included a fishing knife, length of line, fishhook, emergency rations, life jacket, life raft, and quite a list of other things.

'All our survival gear was strapped on top of two 44-gallon ferry fuel tanks behind our seats. We started off wearing our life jackets. Had we had an engine failure it would have been a struggle getting into a life jacket while descending towards the ocean. But we became so uncomfortably hot we soon discarded the life jackets.

'A lot of the flying was over ocean. With a single-engine aeroplane you almost become paranoid. Every time you moved your head, and the headphone moved, you thought you heard something. "Hear that?" one of us would say.

'"Hear what?" the other would reply.

'"The bloody engine's missing."

'We were equipped reasonably well. The big issue was, how well could you ditch an aeroplane at sea?'

LAWRY HANAFIN SAYS preparations for the flight to Singapore were difficult. Civil Aviation did not want to encourage an international race where half the entrants were flying single-engine aeroplanes.

'When we phoned to ask about the requirements for flying an aeroplane offshore we were answered with, "Oh, it's in the regulations" or "See regulation such and such". They were no help at all.

Lawry and Jacquie Hanafin and their four children reunited at the end of the air race.
LAWRY HANAFIN

'At that time New Zealand-registered light aircraft didn't have to have the ZK prefix as part of the registration. We were also allowed slightly smaller lettering than international convention. Once you flew offshore you had to have the full international registration. Civil Aviation people waited until the aircraft were flying into Auckland, on the way out, then swooped in, saying the aircraft didn't comply for this or that reason.

'We were held up in Christchurch with other problems. We heard about what was going on in Auckland and were able to make last-minute modifications. It became more of a race to get to Singapore. We made it to the pilots' pre-race briefing with only 12 hours to spare.'

The distance to Singapore — flying into prevailing winds — turned out to be almost twice as long as the air race. Lawry and his co-pilot wanted to check out all the airports they were to land at along their nominated route. But single-engine aeroplanes were not permitted to fly the Tasman to Australia direct, although this is what Lawry and Mike did during the race. So they had to island-hop from Auckland to Coffs Harbour in New South Wales, landing on the way at Norfolk and Lord Howe.

'We thought it was important to make contact with the people and suss out the refuelling facilities. We particularly wanted to go to Hobart, normally a relatively easy exercise. But we had to fly many, many extra hours to achieve that 1200-mile gap.

'Even then, we had planned to fly direct to Sydney from Lord Howe. We had lodged the flight plan and were about to take off when they cancelled the flight plan on us. We had to go to Coffs Harbour.'

With the rush to get away and frustrations involving regulations, the reality of the flight did not hit until they left the Northland coast for Norfolk Island on 15 March. The Cherokee Six was heavy with extra fuel and equipment. It was a long haul of an hour or more to get to the maximum altitude of 10,000 feet. And at 10,000 feet they discovered the limitations of traditional radios.

Lawry's wife, Jacquie, was flying to Singapore with Singapore Airlines and returning to Christchurch on Singapore's Boeing 747-312 race entry.

'When I had announced my interest in the air race, Jacquie had told me that if I went ahead and went into the race, then that was it. "What responsible husband with wife and four young children, and a business in a lot of debt, would go off and do something as stupid as this?" she kept telling me. I had agreed with her as I kept on with my planning. In the end it was a friend, Adrienne Stewart, who encouraged Jacquie to join her and fly to Singapore. It was comforting to know that Jacquie would be waiting for me.'

A FUEL LEAK in the ferry tank system that was never found meant the cockpit constantly smelled of avgas. Those days Lawry was a cigarette smoker but with the smell and all the extra fuel in the cabin, he could not smoke while he was flying. At each landing he would dash away and heave on a fag, leaving Mike to chat with the refuellers and file the flight plan. At Ceduna, in South Australia, the pilots also had a chance to grab a dubious pie before the long eight-hour hop to Denpasar in Bali.

By mid-afternoon they were an hour into the flight. It was so hot the pilots had placed their charts around the windows to keep the sun out. They couldn't see a thing as they just flew a compass heading. Lawry glanced at Mike. He was pale and sweating. He didn't look too well. Lawry takes up the story:

'"You all right there?" I said to Mike.

'He said, "I think I have to take a crap!"

'I said, "Mike, we talked about this before we started. The deal was that we controlled our bowels. We have nothing to crap into."

'He then said, "I've got to take a crap or I'll —"

'And I said, "How are you going to do that?"

'Mike pulled a sick bag out of the door pocket and said he would shit into that. I told him, "No you won't, mate. Well, not in the front of the aeroplane with me!"

'Mike had to somehow get himself down the back by climbing over the fuel tanks. With all our survival gear nicely taped to the top, that was not an easy thing to do. I'm bigger than Mike and I wouldn't have made it. Mike did, though.

'Next thing I was overpowered by this stench. It was revolting. I had my head at the small storm flap, gasping for fresh air. Then Mike's telling me he's feeling really good as he hands me this warm sick bag, telling me to get rid of it. As Mike gets back over the fuel tanks I'm trying not to throw up as I try to push this thing out the tiny window.

'The pie didn't affect me at all, but there was no stopping Mike. After that he was fine. It was the only mishap of that kind during the entire flight. We normally just ate a little chocolate and sipped water.'

A drama of a different kind was experienced at the next landing. Before departing New Zealand, Lawry Hanafin had been advised to contact an agent in Bali and pay $US200. The agent would then arrange for a clearance to land in transit to Singapore and again during the race. Believing the clearance fee to be no more than a scam, and knowing that a permit to land cost only $US10, he approached the Bali consulate in New Zealand. What followed was a document trail telling him it would be no problem landing at Bali so long as he had the proper authority. This never arrived. Landing at Denpasar they were greeted by policemen with guns drawn.

'They clearly wanted to arrest us and lock us up. I showed them all the letters and documents. That was not good enough. We had been flying almost eight hours and they wouldn't even let us go to the toilet or buy food. Strangely, they allowed us to refuel the aeroplane.

'Refuelling was still going on while they were discussing whether to arrest us or not. When they finally said we could go — "But don't come back without appropriate approvals" — we did a quick walk around the aeroplane in preparation for the flight to Singapore. The temperature was about 32 degrees.

'Normally when we took on fuel and calculated reserves we would slip a bit more on and go to about 400 lb over our maximum gross weight. We actually had approval to go 200 lbs over our gross weight. During our discussion with the Bali authorities, the guys had just kept pumping the gas till all the holes were full. We were 650 lbs overweight for takeoff. The prospect was a little frightening.

'I said to Mike, "I think we are going to be a little heavy on takeoff."

'Mike said, "I think we need to take some out."

First home in the 1987 Singapore to Christchurch air race is Singapore Airline's Boeing 747 entry. Singapore's Captain Freddie Koh discusses the flight with the sponsor, PDL chairman, Sir Robertson Stewart. THE PRESS

'I said, "Are you going to turn around and argue with these people and ask them to take some gas out of the aeroplane?"

'"No," he said, so we hopped in the plane and fired it up. The way the fuel system worked, we drew off the ferry tanks first till they were empty, then we drew off the wing tanks. We had no way of dumping fuel from the ferry tanks. What we could do was transfer fuel from the ferry tanks to the wing tanks, which we did immediately we fired up. Taxiing as slowly as we could, we allowed the wing tank overflow valves to dribble gas onto the ground. In that temperature the fuel was vaporising as soon as it was coming out of the tanks — at a rate of a litre or two a minute.

'What followed was a very wishy-washy takeoff from Bali. Luckily the runway was long. We used it all. It took us an hour to pass through 1000 feet. The first 300 feet was just nailbiting as the Cherokee wallowed between a stall and gaining altitude. We were heading into the night.'

LANDING AT SINGAPORE'S Seletar military airport also became an exciting arrival. ZK-DBC was being cleared to land downwind on runway 11 while Jacquie, surrounded by armed soldiers, was attempting to get some information about her husband's arrival. She had been assured by the flight controller of the ETA, but local authorities told her there had been no word from Delta Bravo Charlie. There was certainly no mention of the aeroplane on the arrivals board. Jacquie made them phone the control tower. They knew nothing.

'We had reported overhead, having been cleared from Changi to fly to Seletar. A sing-song Chinese voice in the Seletar tower cleared us to join downwind. We reported downwind, and turned on final approach. Then we heard, "Negative Delta Bravo Charlie. You are not on final." We then overshot.

'Soon we were cleared a second time to join downwind. Again, when we were on finals, we were refused permission to land.

'On the ground Jacquie was becoming more and more determined as the argument continued with the armed authorities. It was late on Friday night. Jacquie was insisting, "I know that my husband's aeroplane is very close and it's due here now." And the authorities were just as adamant that Delta Bravo Charlie was not scheduled that night.

'Then Jacquie heard the Cherokee overhead. "That's my husband's plane now!" She was getting quite distraught as we were joining downwind for the third time.

'In the air, we turned on finals only to be told yet again we were not cleared to land. I called back and told the tower, "Delta Bravo Charlie, we are on finals for Runway 11 and we are landing."

'The Chinese voice quickly replied, "Affirmative Delta Bravo Charlie."

'The arrival building was quite frightening. Big signs showed a person with a camera, and someone else shooting the person. It was that sort of place. And my wife was still arguing with these armed military people telling them it was definitely her husband's aeroplane.

'It was not a very big building. The arrival room was split by a wall of glass. On one side was a scanning machine. Suddenly Jacquie saw Mike and me standing on the other side of the glass wall. She just burst into tears and flew past this fellow with a gun who was trying to stop her coming through. She grasped hold and no way was she going to let me go. It had taken us five days to get to Singapore.

'Jacquie and I had a lot of fun in Singapore. We had a reception with the New Zealand High Commissioner. Sir Robertson and Lady Stewart were doing a lot to promote their PDL business interests in Singapore to capitalise on their involvement with the air race.

'It was also an intense time. There was an element of spice — being with someone you love and being intensely aware of the race ahead. We were able to savour every moment.'

I ASK LAWRY where he finished in the race. Almost in a whisper he tells me, 'Eighteenth.' The truth is it was a very uneven race with handicap times calculated almost solely on information given by the pilot entrants. In his case he had given a flight plan speed of 138 knots. The information was taken out of the 1965 manual for ZK-DBC.

'It had been printed in days when Americans told lies about the performance of their aeroplanes. Delta Bravo Charlie had never done 138 knots in a straight line. It would only do it downhill!

'I was definitely naive. I didn't read the rules quite as carefully as some of the other people. Only later did I realise that the rules did not require the book speed. They only required a speed you could substantiate. At 75 per cent power, and at an optimum altitude of about 6000 feet, my aeroplane would do around 130 knots.'

The handicap winner, Boyd Munro, flying a twin-engine turbocharged Navajo PA31 Pantha, had based his speed on an altitude of 7000 feet. He had a non-pressurised aeroplane, which in theory cannot fly over 10,000 feet.

'The reality was that he put oxygen on board and climbed to over

20,000 feet. At that height he was motoring along at about 220 knots.

'Many of those who flew high had stripped their planes of every item of excess weight, including heaters. When the pilots arrived in Christchurch they damn near had to be eased out of their aeroplanes and defrosted. Even with all their thermal gear on, it was still minus 40 degrees at 25,000 feet.

'Then you had people like Brent Ferguson who had the quickest plane in the race, a PA46-310P Malibu. He had lodged a flight plan speed of 205 knots and he struggled to achieve that. He finished twentieth. You won the handicap race by how much faster you were than your theoretical speed.

'Tim Wallis, representing his Alpine Deer Group, put in a great performance. He came in fifth, flying a Cessna 210N.'

At the pilots' briefing in Singapore, when all the handicap information was released for the first time, it was realised to what extent the race would be uneven. Lawry says people started jumping up and down in protest. He compared his 138 knots, on which his handicap time was based, with a turbo-charged retractable undercarriage version of his Cherokee Six, with a flight plan speed of only 128.

'I saw the race organisers the same day and said, "This makes no sense." They said it was too late. The calculations had all been made on the information supplied.

'Some pilots, like Mike and me, were naive. Some were more calculating.'

Boyd Munro was, perhaps, more calculating than his competitors. But he also had a lot of experience, having won a Paris to New York air race in 1981. In 1987 he had 4000 hours in his Pilot Logbook. A computer programmer, he took three months off and flew part of his planned route twice. He was so sure of winning that he even got a Tiger Moth rating before he started. He was also the first plane home, winning the outright prize of $20,000.

Lawry Hanafin says that despite his own misgivings about the integrity of the handicapping he did not agree with those who sought court action following the race.

'Boyd Munro won the race and that is that. He alone had the time and money to invest in the race. I met him and we got on very well. He was quite entertaining, and a showman — a nice guy. He knew how to win races. His Navajo Panther was magnificently turned out with shark's teeth painted under the nose.

The Tiger Moth prize for winning the handicap section is chased by Boyd Munro's Piper Navajo Panther.
THE PRESS

'He also knew how to bluff. Before the start of the Paris to New York race he had turned up with two aeroplanes, equipped with air-to-air refuelling. That was somewhat off-putting for the other competitors but there was nothing in the rules about air-to-air refuelling. Boyd was the only one who knew his refuelling experiments hadn't really worked!'

KNOWING THEY WERE not going to win did not lessen the excitement when Lawry and Mike took off from Singapore just after 11 pm on 25 March. If that was not excitement enough, they ran into a great bank of CBs (cumulo-nimbus clouds) about 2 am next morning.

'We spent quite a long time trying to find a way round them. It didn't look as if we could go under. We definitely couldn't go over them in our plane. They were towering more than 10,000 feet above us.

'Finally Mike said, "Fly through them."

'I said, "No. No. That would be foolish."

'Mike said, "They're weak this time of the morning. We've had to fly through CBs in the Air Force."

'And I said, "CBs rip wings off aeroplanes."

'Mike told me to turn the cockpit lights on high. "Just concentrate on the instruments and fly." I was frightened as hell during the first 10 minutes. But when the wings didn't come off I started to think it was not too bad. And we weren't too dazzled by the lightning flashing all around the aeroplane.

'We flew a compass course as well as we could. We experienced huge vertical variations of 2000, 3000 and 4000 feet, in seconds. The vertical speed indicator was at the stops. All I was trying to do was to keep a steady air speed and maintain a compass heading, which was

The nominated Hanafin Singapore to Christchurch route through South Australia and Hobart. Most aircraft flew the official northern route.

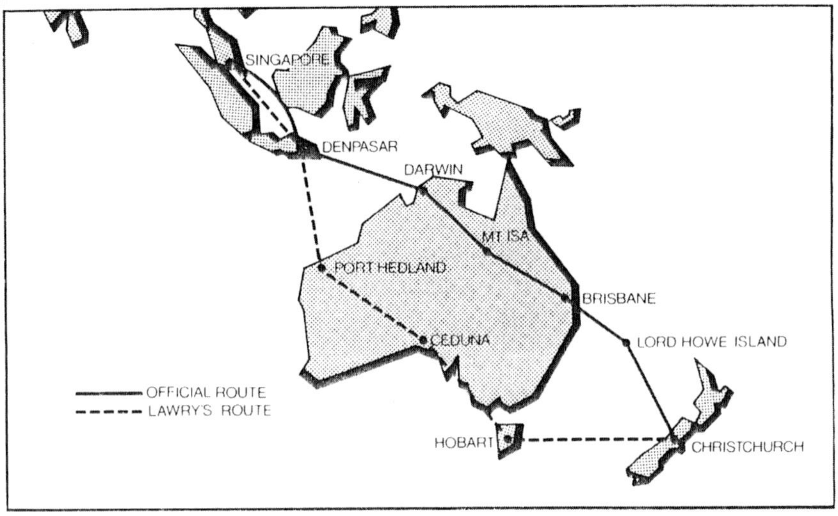

hard to do. I was using full control deflections to maintain a steady state of flight.

'Mike was complaining he could not plot a course with our heading swinging 30 degrees each side of track. In retrospect it was fun. But had I been able to eat during the previous 36 hours I probably would have needed a spare pair of pants. I had been tensed up for weeks. I lost about 15 kg in weight over the weeks leading up to the race. As it turned out, that was fortunate. Very fortunate.'

Storm conditions and head winds lost them an hour on the first leg to Bali. They landed after 7 hours and 45 minutes. The ground crew reception was very different to what they had experienced just a few days previously.

'We were greeted by a "Follow Me" truck. A British Airways 747 had reported an ETA of 10 minutes. It was put on hold so we could take off on time. Once they were on side, the Bali people were very enthusiastic. They placed a great importance on the success of the air race.'

Lawry says there weren't many great moments during the flight to Christchurch. They experienced long periods of boredom. The cockpit, being a noisy place, meant that communication between the two pilots was always difficult.

'We did have a slight emergency during the flight of almost six hours between Bali and Port Hedland. Mike, being an Air Force type, was not good at staying awake. He requested to sleep, as he was entitled to. We had gone for some days without having much sleep, and we had been quite tensed up.

'As Mike nodded off I made a mental note that the fuel tanks had to be changed after about another 20 minutes. Then I unintentionally went to sleep. I awoke to dead silence. The silence must have awoken me. The tank had run dry. We had gone from 10,000 feet to 8000 feet, and our heading had changed drastically.

'The prop was still spinning as I selected a tank with gas in it. Then there was that cough-cough, and vroooooom. It was a lovely sound. I then noticed how absolutely beautiful the Indian Ocean was. Mike didn't wake up.'

A REMAINING SNAG was getting a clearance to fly the Hobart to Christchurch leg direct. 'We had tried to contact the right people on our way up to Singapore. Finally, at Ceduna, on the return flight, I met someone who asked if I was any relation to James Hanafin — my cousin. This fellow had learnt to fly with James in Auckland. Suddenly the official wheels were oiled and nothing was a problem. Right up to then we might just as well have been facing a stone wall.

'We told the Australian CAA that the RNZAF had an Orion over the Tasman for search and rescue duties. Yes, they did, but the Orion was also in the race and it wasn't stopping for anyone. They believed the story.

'The main advantage of flying trans-Tasman from Hobart was the predictable tail wind. The higher we got, the greater the wind. The maximum recommended altitude for a light aircraft without oxygen is 10,000 feet. We got to 13,500 feet at one stage and remained at that height for a couple of hours.

'We were at the tops of the clouds. They were absolutely dead flat. Every now and again we encountered a small cliff of cloud. We made quite a game of sitting just in the top of the cloud experiencing the sensation as we hit one of these little walls. Wham!

'I suspect we were possibly a little high on lack of oxygen. We were also tired, and excited. The adrenalin was pumping.'

LAWRY SHOWED ME the flight plan path on the charts. It was a line marked with intermittent crosses. He told me the crosses were the reporting points.

'It was really only a theoretical track drawn up before we left. As we flew, the next reporting point was the next cross on the chart. We calculated our flying time and reported when we were at each cross, presuming our calculations were right. In fact, there was no way of really knowing if we were at that position.

'As it turned out, as we approached the South Island we got an NDB fix from Hokitika. It confirmed we were 25 miles south of our track. Not bad after six hours of flying by dead reckoning.'

I ASKED LAWRY if he was disappointed when he knew he couldn't win. He said, 'No. Winning was the goal. That's what motivated me. Our flight time (elapsed time) was 59 hours 12 minutes. That included two 12-hour stops. Our handicap time was 24 hours 30 minutes. We were 161 minutes under our handicap time. We flew the route faster than we theoretically should have.

'We carried a lot of fuel and flew conservatively. Boyd Munro arrived with almost dry tanks. We could cope with bigger inaccuracies.

'I would not have missed the race for quids.'

FOR THE RECORD, the Class B section for military and civil aircraft was won by the RNZAF Orion. The captain was Wing Commander Tony Medcalf of No 5 Squadron, assisted by Flight Lieutenant Merton McNally, who navigated. The Orion crew was awarded the special Jubilee Gold Trophy. The flight time was 10 hours 39 minutes, only slightly longer than the time allowed today for a Boeing 747-400 to cover the same route.

As Lawry Hanafin had said, the Orion was 'not stopping for anyone'.

Not long after the race Lawry flew to Waimate and back to visit inlaws. It was his first flying after finishing the race, which he ended

The Cherokee Six turned in a faultless performance flying from Christchurch to Singapore and back. A week after the flight the starter motor seized and overheated.
LAWRY HANAFIN

with an exhilarating low pass over the Canterbury Aero Club where he had learned to fly.

'When I returned from Waimate I was taxiing towards the aero club when I saw someone outside a hangar suddenly give me the cut-off signal. I stopped and a mechanic said he could hear a bloody awful noise coming from my aeroplane.

'Getting down on the tarmac, I could smell the heat under the bonnet. Something had got very hot. It turned out that the starter motor hadn't released from the fly wheel after the engine was started at Waimate. The starter motor had been howling away at 2500 revs during the 40-minute flight.

'I wondered what would have become of us had it happened during the previous flight with Bravo Delta Charlie. We might have been an hour or so out over the Tasman. A sudden fire at 10,000 feet would not have been a pleasant experience.'

These days Mike McConnel is flying for Cathay Pacific. Lawry told me he had met him recently in Hong Kong and they had reminisced about the Singapore to Christchurch air race. Mike is apparently still very choosy about the pies he takes on board prior to a long flight, even on a Boeing 747.

IN 1989 ONE of the Hanafin photo stores caught fire with devastating results. It was time to convert surplus assets into cash, and Delta Bravo Charlie went. Business required more effort, and any thoughts of flying were parked away in some remote and imaginary hangar.

'Things change,' says a philosophical Lawry Hanafin. 'The kids have grown up. When we had four under five it was easy to load them in an aeroplane and fly off somewhere. I work a lot harder now and that shows in an expanding chain of photo stores. But flying is not quite forgotten.

'Every New Year's Eve I tell Jacquie, "This year I will get my pilot's licence back, and buy another aeroplane."

'Jacquie says, "Yes dear. When I get my Porsche."

'Well, Jacquie still hasn't got the Porsche. And I haven't got my aeroplane!'

CHAPTER 12

INNOVATOR, RISK-TAKER, DREAMER

The Alpine Fighter Collection's stylish Russian Yak-3M about to partake in an orchestrated dogfight over Wanaka.
ROY SINCLAIR

Flying a Spitfire is the nearest thing to having wings of your own.

Tim Wallis

IN A REAL sense my meeting with Sir Tim Wallis was both too late, and too soon. I should have met him almost two years earlier, before he crashed his Mk.XIV Spitfire while taking off from Wanaka airfield on 2 January 1996. On that day he arrived in a Dunedin hospital with only a slim chance of regaining consciousness, or even surviving at all. Yet, despite horrendous head injuries, he did recover — to an extent where, just a few short months later, he attended his famed (fifth) Warbirds Over Wanaka air show. His recovery continues. Had I waited another year to meet him I expect his speech might have improved so much more, and conversation would have become so much easier. Nevertheless my two hour-long meetings with Tim and his wife, Prue, proved to be as inspirational as they were difficult.

In greeting, Tim asked after my daughter, Kirsten. Long before he crashed his Spitfire, I had sent him a newspaper story I had written about Kirsten and other teenage pilots who had taken their somewhat nervous parents flying. Tim had remembered. And he was genuinely interested in Kirsten's progress. Later, when talking about his own progress, he said, 'My future is to make sure I have a good life with my family. I do not want to take any more risks. That's in my past.'

FEW NEW ZEALANDERS of the 1990s would be able to say they have never heard the name 'Tim Wallis'. They would likely associate his name with the biannual Easter Warbirds Over Wanaka air show. In 1993 Tim Wallis was knighted for his services to export and to the community. He also established the Alpine Fighter Collection, which

Sir Tim Wallis; regaining health and planning a new future after a dramatic Spitfire crash on 2 January 1996.
PRUE WALLIS

Another Russian, the dumpy Polikarpov I-16, is one of the most recent of the Alpine Fighter Collection's restoration projects. The I-16 was among the star attractions of the 1998 Warbirds Over Wanaka air show.

forms the nucleus of the New Zealand Fighter Pilots' Museum at Wanaka's airport.

The air show began in 1988 as a community event that first attracted 15,000 people to Wanaka's small airfield. Strict conditions (still enforced) banned commercial operators, leaving the fundraising opportunities for Wanaka people. These days Warbirds Over Wanaka is expected to attract more than 60,000 spectators along with display pilots from New Zealand and around the world.

In an alpine setting, spectators are treated to a procession of stunning displays of aerobatics, formation flying, bungee parachute jumping, and aerial dog fights. Who would have thought, when the Second World War ended, that more than half a century later a German Messerschmitt Bf-109G.10, in mock battle, would take on a British Mk.XVI Spitfire, and a Russian Yak-3, over New Zealand skies? Or that the Japanese Nakajima Ki-43, which once provided a nasty fright for Allied forces fighting the Pacific War, would become a welcome sight on a New Zealand back-country airfield?

A special moment at the 1996 Warbirds Over Wanaka was when I was photographing Ray Hanna, from England, arguably the world's finest display pilot. He was waving from a P51-D Mustang's opened cockpit as he reenacted a flying scene he performed for the film

Empire of the Sun. But while enjoying the flying displays I was aware that, in a tent on the hillside overlooking the airfield, Tim Wallis was also enjoying the show. Having regained consciousness only a few weeks previously, he was on his way to recovery.

SHOULD ANYONE SUGGEST Warbirds Over Wanaka is the world's number one air show, Tim Wallis will quickly disagree. He has been to the great air shows in England and the United States. Those countries have some huge fighter collections.

'No, we do not have the best air show, but Warbirds Over Wanaka is held in a great alpine environment. For us, Wanaka is beautiful. It's natural, and we have some wonderful New Zealand pilots.'

Tim Wallis was born in 1938. As a teenager at Christ's College during the 1950s he would often look up and see the Harvards and Mustangs that had been supplied to the RNZAF following the war. He says he left school to become a doctor. 'I thought that was the thing I wanted to do.' But after less than a year at university he went to work for his father, sawmilling on the West Coast.

'Flying was always a bit of a dream. I needed to earn money to pay for flying lessons. I worked for my dad at Haupiri near Reefton, then down in the Haast. While working with timber I started shooting deer. Then my father became sick with cancer. He died in 1963 when I was still quite young.'

Tim left timber for deer shooting, and learned something about flying from the helicopter pilots he hired to hunt deer. At the Canterbury Aero Club he took up fixed-wing flying and got his Private Pilot's Licence. He bought a Cessna 180 and was taught to fly it by Keith Wakeman, one of New Zealand's pioneer topdressing pilots. Later he was taught to fly helicopters by John Reid of Helicopters New Zealand. Helicopters satisfied his passion for flying, while providing an efficient means of shooting and recovering deer.

'We were working in the heart of the deer country — Haast, Wanaka and Te Anau. We stuck at it and we did well.'

Tim flew the Bell 47G4 and Hiller 12E helicopters. He never thought helicopter flying was dangerous, but successful deer recovery was a matter of margins. Pilots with wide safety margins never recovered great numbers of deer.

As managing director of his Luggate Game Packers Ltd, near Wanaka, he bought the 158 tons gross MV *Ranginui*, which had previously served from the port of Kaiapoi in North Canterbury. Commercial deer hunting using helicopters flying from a ship

Former bush pilot Bill Black recalls 28 rewarding years working with Tim Wallis.
PRUE WALLIS

anchored in the sounds around Fiordland became a reality by the end of 1967. The ship could store 500 carcasses in its chiller hold.

In the meantime, Tim had also bought another much larger ship, the MV *Hotonui*. The intention was to have a freezer mother ship, registered as a venison factory.

The *Ranginui* was sold in 1972. An American syndicate claiming that it wanted to establish a suspect 'sea city' republic on Minerva Reef, in the Tongan group of islands, became the new owner. But Tonga made it clear the reef was their country and the ship would not survive. *Ranginui* never left Lyttelton. Late in 1976 it returned to Luggate Game Packers' ownership.

Mystery still shrouded the ship when it slipped its moorings at Lyttelton late one night and was spotted a few days later in Doubtful Sound, where it was again being fitted out as a floating helicopter base, replacing *Hotonui*, which was subsequently chartered as a fishing support vessel.

When a reporter asked about the *Ranginui*'s new role, Tim Wallis spun an unlikely yarn about massages, saunas, and bored fishermen. The story, embellished in local newspapers, was even picked up by the Australian press. Establishing the world's southernmost massage parlour was not, however, on the Tim Wallis agenda.

FROM THE BEGINNING Tim had employed Bill Black, who now has his own company, South West Helicopters, at Te Anau, and is one of

New Zealand's best-known helicopter pilots. Bill had started his flying career as a bush pilot, flying Cessna 180s and 185s. Part of his work was to recover deer carcasses. For a fledgling deer industry fixed-wing aircraft were much cheaper to operate than helicopters, Bill remembers. 'But the Fiordland strips were short, about 300 yards, and the Cessnas were loaded to the hilt with venison.'

Recalling 28 rewarding years he worked for Tim Wallis, he says he and Tim worked as flying colleagues rather than employer and employee. 'Tim paid my wages, but he was never a boss to me. We spoke our minds and I would tell Tim off if I had to.

'Tim was a big man in those days. He wore a revolver for survival following a helicopter accident in 1968, in which he broke his back and was partially disabled. He could shoot birds and animals if he went down somewhere. Fiordland is a big area to go down in. We had no radio beacons. If you did go down you would never know how long you would be there.

'To me Tim, with his revolver, looked like a modern-day cowboy. He always had a smile that made him look as if he had just been a naughty boy and was about to be found out. And he bent a few aeroplanes.'

Launching a Royal NZ Aero Club Young Eagles flying programme in November 1994, Tim Wallis discusses flying plans with James Woodlock and Emma McKay at West Melton airfield, near Christchurch. JULIANNE MYERS-POULSEN/THE PRESS

TIM WALLIS HAD two serious helicopter accidents. Ironically, when he broke his back he was not shooting deer, but helping a Queenstown friend spread hay to snowbound sheep. He is philosophical about his flying accidents. 'All they proved is that I couldn't fly very well. I hadn't proved there was no deer industry. I did not let the accidents put me off flying. I enjoyed flying too much for that and, besides, I owed a lot of money!'

But there was more to the deer industry than using a helicopter as a shooter's platform. Tim Wallis became one of New Zealand's top business earners, and that required considerable entrepreneurial skill. From the early days when the government saw deer only as a noxious pest, Tim Wallis believed deer could become a viable industry. He instigated shooting deer for their venison and velvet. He initiated a by-product industry. Then, he saw sense in deer farming. That led to live deer recovery, again using helicopters.

Prue Wallis can recall a time when the idea of catching noxious animals and putting them to graze behind high fences was considered very strange.

'First, he had to work out ways of capturing deer. He started with Colin Murdoch's company Paxarm's tranquilliser darts, but with his company, Alpine Helicopters Ltd, he eventually developed a very successful skid-mounted net gun, which enabled a net to be shot over a deer.'

Bill Black says that before they were perfected, many of the methods used to capture deer also caught a few helicopters and brought them down. 'We were firing darts and that could become hazardous if they caught the helicopter blades, although that did not happen to any of Alpine's helicopters.'

One stun gun, Bill says, involved firing two darts on steel lines fed from a type of fishing reel. 'When the needles hit the deer, the pilot was able to immobilise the animal with an electric current applied through the lines.'

Says Prue, 'Tim was always able to focus 100 per cent on a particular problem or idea. Nothing else was allowed to interfere, day or night, until he had followed his ideas through. He always believed in what he was doing.'

ALL THE WHILE Tim Wallis was dreaming about owning some of the Second World War fighter planes he had seen flying over Christchurch when he was a teenager. An even greater dream was to fly a Spitfire, one of the most famous fighter aircraft of World War II. Designed in 1934, more than 20,000 Spitfires had been built by the time production ceased in February 1948.

'To me a Spitfire is very special,' Tim tells me. 'I could own a Mustang, and I did buy one from North America in 1984. But a Spitfire is British, and I am a New Zealander.'

The rebuilt P51-D Mustang began the Alpine Fighter Collection, which was established as a subsidiary of Alpine Deer Group Ltd. Tim sold the Mustang to the New Zealand Historic Aircraft Trust to finance his first Spitfire.

From Stephen Grey, Britain's famed fighter plane collector, he bought FU-P in 1987. In New Zealand the Spitfire, a Mk.XVI, was repainted in the wartime colours it wore while flying in the Royal Australian Air Force No 453 Squadron. FU-P also displays the British Supermarine Number TB863.

Powered by a 1690 hp 12-cylinder Rolls-Royce Packard-built Merlin engine, FU-P had been built late in 1944 and went into operations over the English Channel with 453 Squadron in 1945. In more recent years the aeroplane had a role in the film *The Battle of Britain*.

Sitting at a table, Tim describes the layout of a single-place Spitfire cockpit. 'The throttle is left, undercarriage right, instruments there, and the gun is fired from the control stick. It has a handbrake, and the rudder bar is at your feet.'

I have seen Tim fly FU-P twice. He asks me where, and I tell him at the 1994 Hokitika air show held to celebrate the 60th anniversary of Captain JC (Bert) Mercer establishing New Zealand's first civil airline on the South Island West Coast; and at Wanaka. The latter was in early January 1995.

We had been visiting the Fighter Pilots' Museum when we saw FU-P being rolled out. Tim Wallis climbed into the cockpit and was soon performing a stunning flying display for his own pleasure, and for a small but privileged number of people who just happened to be there on that morning. After he landed, I watched as Tim Wallis climbed out of his Spitfire's cockpit. His limping as he walked from the plane — a legacy from his 1968 helicopter mishap — was in stark contrast to the flawless flying display I had just seen.

Tim remembered that particular day and seemed pleased that I had been there.

He flew a Spitfire for the first time at Whenuapai in 1989. Prue says that when Tim came down he said it was 'the nearest thing to having wings of your own'.

Tim Wallis has since logged 210 hours in FU-P. He has special memories of flying the Spitfire over Mt Aspiring, a mountain that always looks beautiful from above.

'Flying a Spitfire is very free. You can be flying at 200 knots, and then zip it up to 400,' he says.

When I ask if he will buy another to replace the Mk.XIV he crashed, Tim laughs and tells me, 'Spitfires are now too expensive, and a Mk.XIV is too powerful for me!'

The Mk.XIV was particularly powerful, with a propeller that goes in the opposite direction to the Mk.XVI.

THE FULFILMENT OF Tim Wallis's dream to fly and own a Spitfire has resulted in a New Zealand collection of rare frontline fighter aircraft from most of the world's powers. Many of the aircraft have been restored to flying condition at Wanaka. He has also collected some historic biplanes, including the Fox Moth ZK-AEK, which had once flown with Captain Mercer's Air Travel (New Zealand) Ltd. The aeroplane was restored by the Croydon Aircraft Company near Gore (see Chapter 2).

Over the years the Spitfire fighters have been joined by the Hawker Hurricane from England (being restored by Air New Zealand in Christchurch), the Avenger, Corsair and P51-D Mustang from the United States, the Nakajima Ki-43 and Zero replica from Japan, and the Polikarpov I-16s and I-153s, and the Yak-3 from Russia.

One more recent addition is the 1930s Polikarpov I-16, a short dumpy Russian fighter powered by a nine-cylinder Radial ASH 62 1000 hp engine.

'The I-16 looks a bit like a bumble bee but it's also nuggety, and very powerful,' Tim tells me. He first saw one while visiting a St Petersburg museum about 10 years ago. A challenge was to get one 'Down Under', and in flying condition. Four years of hard work and often difficult negotiations with the Russians followed. Then, on 11 October 1997, an I-16 flew from the Wanaka airstrip. It was the first time a Russian I-16 had flown outside the former Soviet Union in 50 years. The New Zealand pilot, Keith Skilling, said it was 'a beautiful aeroplane, very light, very predictable, but old'.

Tim Wallis shows an obvious passion for the Russian aircraft in his Alpine Fighter Collection. I ask why.

'Simple,' he replies. 'They're different. Without Russian fighters in a World War II collection you have a big gap.'

Tim then surprises me by talking about another reason for the Russian component in the Alpine Fighter Collection.

'More than 13 million members of the Russian armed forces were dead or missing after World War II. And 7.7 million civilians were dead or missing. Not many people here know the extent Russia suffered.'

I am learning that, in collecting World War II fighter aircraft, Tim Wallis is also building a memorial to the pilots who flew them. His real heroes are not just people like Douglas Bader, but the New Zealanders: Wing Commander Johnny Checketts, Air Commodore Alan Deere, Group Captain Colin Gray, Group Captain Desmond Scott, and many others.

'They were keen, honest, and good people. They showed the world how good they were,' Tim says. 'New Zealanders are very fine

Re-enacting his brilliant Empire of the Sun *flying display, Ray Hanna waves from a P51-D Mustang's opened cockpit during the 1996 Warbirds Over Wanaka air show.*
ROY SINCLAIR

people who have had to learn to be independent. At the time of the war New Zealand was a small country on its own at the end of the world. New Zealanders were still pioneers, breaking in the country.'

Johnny Johnson, a former Air Vice Marshal and Ace fighter pilot of the RAF, visited the 1994 Warbirds Over Wanaka air show. There, he talked about a survey of top-scoring fighter pilots, which was conducted after the war. The Aces almost all shared good hunting skills and exceptional eyesight. They were also very well coordinated, and very good at ball games.

Interestingly, Tim Wallis grew up with all those attributes. He especially had a passion for hunting, and he played representative rugby for Westland and South Canterbury. Later, a real joy in life was being able to get into an aeroplane and fly himself to wherever he wanted to go.

And for many years he would take off with one of his children ear-muffed and strapped in beside him. So far, two of the boys have gone on to become pilots. One, Toby, is flying helicopters for Alpine Adventures at Fox Glacier.

Tim's knighthood award, he says, was embarrassing, although he now believes it is a worthy acknowledgement to the people who have worked beside him to establish a viable deer industry and the Wanaka air show.

'Some people know when a knighthood is coming,' Prue Wallis recalls. 'But with Tim, it was just a total shock. He came home for lunch one day and opened this official-looking letter. When he read it he just said, "Not me, not me." He dropped it on the table and ran.'

I HAVE TO ask Prue what it is like having a husband who flies aeroplanes that can bite hard whenever flying them gets out of hand. Is it a worry?

'I wouldn't swap him for anything else,' she says. 'As for worrying? If I had worried about Tim flying I would have been in a state of permanent anxiety.'

Prue Wallis had a considerable involvement in Tim's recovery from his Spitfire accident in January 1996. During the eight weeks Tim slept, Prue and their four sons read and talked to him every day as the

Tim Wallis flying his Mk.XVI Supermarine Spitfire, FU-P, off Wanaka airfield in January 1995. The takeoff was followed by an impromptu, and flawless, flying display.
ROY SINCLAIR

letters of condolence poured in from around New Zealand and from overseas. While he was still barely conscious, she had him taken to their home in Wanaka, believing he would respond more readily in a familiar environment. Doubting medical experts reluctantly agreed that anything was worth a try.

'Helping Tim with his recovery has involved learning more about the business. As for the fighter planes, I love them. It was marvellous when Tim was able to become involved with them after so many years of working with deer, although deer will always remain a passion for Tim.

'The Fighter Pilots' Museum, especially, has contributed a great deal to a lot of people. And the Warbirds Over Wanaka air show was a big consequence of Tim's Warbirds involvement. It's a huge community event for Wanaka. It's the standard fundraiser opportunity for local people. It's all been a fascinating part of our lives.'

BEFORE THE SPITFIRE crash, Tim Wallis and his Alpine Deer Group were starting out on an ambitious project that involved buying the 54,000-acre Minaret Station at the head of Lake Wanaka. Previously, Tim Wallis had been spending a lot of time travelling overseas. In Russia he was fortunate in being able to develop a deer farm in Siberia's Altai region, which is famous for its Maral deer velvet.

While travelling in Russia he discovered a country with many wrecked fighter aircraft that had never been seen in the West. That discovery had led to the ambitious I-16 restoration project.

The Minaret property was purchased with the realisation that he may not always have the flexibility, or desire, to travel extensively. By January 1996 Tim had just appointed a manager, bought a barge for lake transport, and seen the beginning of a huge deer-fencing project across the property. Tim Wallis was returning to the deer industry.

'This is Tim's new passion,' says Prue. 'He has really turned full circle. But Tim has also spent two years concentrating on getting better.'

The Minaret project has been fortuitous. Tim Wallis may not fly again on his own. By his own admission he has been damaged quite a bit and his emphasis has had to change, although he is not willing to say what may be possible in the future. 'I have 14,500 hours' flying, and that is a lot of experience. I'm not going to give it away yet.'

Either way, he will still take an interest in the Alpine Fighter Collection and he has plans to develop his Russian I-16 project into an income earner. Without a doubt, Tim Wallis is looking forward to an active and exciting future.

Near Mount Aspiring, in the heart of South Island deer country, Tim Wallis hovers a Hiller 12E helicopter, as Joe Cave hooks on another animal. Helicopters, during the 1960s, satisfied Tim's passion for flying while providing an efficient means of shooting and recovering deer. ROBERT WILSON

AS MY MEETING with Tim and Prue Wallis comes to an end I am a little confused about one thing. What sort of person is Tim Wallis?

On television I had seen daring scenes of deer hunting from low-flying helicopters. And Bill Black had spoken of 'bulldogging' when they flew close to wild deer and jumped onto their backs while capturing animals for deer farms. These impressions had left me with a belief that Tim Wallis was decidedly a macho, cowboy type.

Yet, even in the letters he had written to me, I had suspected him as also being quite a different type — unassuming, generous perhaps, and definitely interested in those, especially younger people, who share his passion for flying.

'He's all those things,' Prue Wallis assures me. 'He's also a very sensitive man and he's larger than life. You don't achieve what Tim has achieved without being larger than life.'

I suggest that Tim's insisting he does not want to take any more risks must be comforting. But Prue Wallis just smiles and says, 'I don't believe it. Tim is a risk taker. That's all there is to it. He's also a survivor.'

The most famous of Luftwaffe fighters, and a star at the 1996 Warbirds Over Wanaka air show, was this visiting Messerschmitt Bf-109G.10. Powered by a Daimler Benz engine, the aeroplane had been restored by its German owner Hans Dittes. ROY SINCLAIR

CHAPTER 13

On Short Finals

CBY

When the girls asked, 'What's the new CO like?' I said, 'Oh he's just a funny little man with a big nose.'

Lorie Lucas

'ONE THING I'LL never do is marry an Air Force officer,' an attractive wartime nurse and transport driver had once promised herself. That was more than 50 years ago. Her name was Loraine Flansburgh-Washbourne and she knew only too well that pilots with fancy ranks could be a bit stuck-up.

'That's just something you discovered at the dances and other social events you went to during those war years. I also did not want to marry a little fellow, one I could have carried under my arm. No, that would not have suited me a bit. He would have to be at least two inches taller than me; he would have to be at least six foot.'

As it turned out, in April 1943, she did marry an Air Force officer; none other than Wing Commander FJ (Popeye) Lucas, her commanding officer and one of New Zealand's celebrated pilots of the Second World War. Fred Lucas had grown up on an Otago farm. He had little interest in education. Instead, he scraped up enough money to join the Otago Aero Club, at Taieri, and work towards his Pilot's 'A' Licence.

Wing Commander FJ (Popeye) Lucas, right, enjoys a conversation with Squadron Leader Bill Tacon. In March 1943 Lucas and Tacon flew (unofficially) the first Douglas C-47 (DC-3) aircraft to arrive in New Zealand. LORIE LUCAS

Having been rejected by the RNZAF prior to the war, he travelled to England, where he was taken on by the RAF. The latter admitted they were taking a gamble but said there was something endearing about Lucas's spirit. He had told his selectors he did not know what 'algebra' was. When asked, 'Do you drink?' he was equally honest with, 'Yes, I have a pint now and again!' Lucas noticed one RAF officer suppressing a grin behind an impressive moustache.

In 1939 he volunteered to transfer to the RNZAF and became part of the New Zealand Flight, later No 75 (NZ) Squadron, flying Wellington bombers. He was awarded with the Distinguished Flying Cross on two occasions — in 1940 and again in 1942. Having completed two bombing tours over Germany (he was promoted to squadron leader before his second tour) he returned to New Zealand. By that time his first wife had died, leaving him with a two-year-old daughter, Wendy, to care for. In New Zealand he commanded No 1 Hudson Anti-submarine Squadron at Whenuapai, formed and commanded No 40 Transport Squadron, and married his second wife, Loraine (Lorie). He then returned to England, where he joined No 487 (NZ) Squadron, flying Mosquito fighter-bombers.

I HAD NOT met the man who is remembered simply as 'Popeye' Lucas, so named after the famous cartoon character. Having read his book *Popeye Lucas Queenstown*, I knew he had pioneered scenic flying from Queenstown after the war. He was also known as one of aviation's great larrikins and I had heard it facetiously said, 'Popeye was everything the RAF would not have wanted.' But Popeye had a special charisma. He also inspired aviation legend. He died on 4 October 1993.

To find out something about Popeye I ventured to a small farmhouse in the back-blocks beyond Motueka, where I spent an enjoyable day talking to Lorie Lucas. It was the day New Zealand yachtsmen, in *Black Magic*, were competing in their second race towards winning the Americas Cup. I promised Lorie I would not arrive until the race was over and, hopefully, won.

Over the first cup of coffee I quickly realised Lorie had a tremendous affection and respect for her late husband. She was painstakingly researching a book, *Popeye's War*, which has since been published. But she had not needed to lean on him for her own considerable successes in life. Lorie Lucas was very much her own woman.

'Popeye was a very decent person. Our marriage was an enjoyable partnership. That is something I could never regret,' she told me.

Lorie Lucas, at home on West Bank Farm.

BUT IT WAS not Popeye who introduced Lorie to aviation. Her uncle was chief flying instructor at the Stratford Aero Club. 'He took me up in a Tiger Moth. We were away up there when I thought he said, "Are you enjoying the flying?" and I said, "Yes."

'He had actually said, "Do you want to loop the loop?"

Next thing the ground was up above and there was I, wondering if I was going to fall out. I was aged 14. From then on I wanted to fly.'

It was the mid-1930s, the time of early intercontinental flying. Lorie was fascinated by New Zealand's Jean Batten.

'Oh yes, I remember her particularly when she was back in New Zealand, not long after her 1936 Percival Gull flight from England. Friends I was staying with at Rotorua took me to afternoon tea with their next-door neighbour. They wanted me to meet a special visitor. And who should turn up but Jean Batten. We sat there and talked. When she went to go home, she couldn't start her car.

'The problem turned out to be spuds stuck up the exhaust pipe. The culprits were local Maori kids. We could hear them behind the bushes, giggling at the to-do. Jean Batten was not amused and got quite shirty about it. I was a little disappointed she couldn't see the fun in it. I think she would have liked to give the kids a good hiding.'

It was Jean Batten's daring deeds that made Lorie determined to fly. She joined the Mangere Aero Club and in 1938 went solo. Then, with war pending, the aeroplanes were taken over by the military.

'Looking back, I should have done more flying. As it was, I kept my Pilot Logbook when, in 1941, I became a WAAF at Whenuapai. With my job in transport I got to know many of the flying blokes and I would occasionally sneak a ride. They sometimes let me take the controls and do straight-and-level. I would put the time in my logbook. Of course, they would have been court-martialled if they had been found out.

'I had wanted to go overseas and join the RAF ambulance service. I had a brother in Canada training to be an air gunner. But because I was also a training nurse, I was not allowed to leave Auckland. At the time, that was a disappointment, especially when we heard that some of the girls had got away. Some even got to fly and ferry aeroplanes in England.

'Then Popeye Lucas arrived at Whenuapai and everyone was saying the new CO was round the twist. He had done so many bombing ops over Germany. He had lost his nerve. "He even carries a gun," was one story I heard.

Jean Batten at Sydney's Mascot airport in 1935. Her daring deeds in aeroplanes were an inspiration to Lorie Lucas who flew to solo at the Mangere Aero Club in 1939. But Jean Batten's impoverished sense of humour was disappointing.
THE PRESS

'I met him when I had to go along to No 3 hangar and pick up the CO's car for a service. As soon as I saw his car I got an idea of what sort he might be. A silver tankard from the officers' mess was lying on the floor. On a seat was a bedraggled corsage. A station dance had been held the night before. Putting two and two together I knew he must have had a little park-up with someone.

'When I went in to ask permission to take the car, someone said, "Come in." And there he was, with his feet up on the desk, leaning back on his chair. I was very much the junior. I didn't even have a rank.

'"Please sir, can I have your car for a DI?" I asked as confidently as I could.

'"Oh, what's a DI?" he replied, looking amused.

'"It's a Daily Inspection, sir," I replied, feeling a little foolish.

'When I got back to the section the girls asked, "What's the new CO like?" And I said, "Oh he's just a funny little man with a big nose."

'Next time I met him he had just had an accident. The steering went on his car. He rammed a stationary tram at the terminus. I had to pick him up from somewhere in the ambulance and take him to hospital.'

One night, several weeks later, Lorie heard that a Hudson was going up to exercise over Auckland with the Army. The exercise involved dodging searchlights. Japanese submarines around the coast

No 40 Squadron Douglas C-47 (DC-3), and Hudson aircraft lined up at Whenuapai in 1944.
LORIE LUCAS/RNZAF

had given Aucklanders a few scares. Popeye, being the most experienced pilot, flew the aeroplane. But it was a gunnery officer who asked if Lorie 'would like to have a flip tonight'.

'I said I would love to and he said, "Well, you get someone to take over your ambulance," which I did. The transport sergeant turned a blind eye as I was given a parachute and prepared for the flight. The way I was dressed, and it being dark, it was not easy to recognise me as a woman. The army major and captain involved didn't know who I was. Next thing we were up there over Auckland dodging searchlights and going into stall turns. The gunnery officer took me down the fuselage and showed me how to be a belly gunner. As the gunnery position was lowered I thought I would slide out into space. I was not too keen on that.

'Then I climbed into the rear turret. I didn't like that either; it was too damn cold. It was ever so lonely in a bubble with Auckland all around me. I felt what it might have been like to be an air gunner, like my brother. I could also understand why they were getting popped off like nobody's business. Finally, I was strapped into the co-pilot's seat.

'The pilot said, "How are you getting on?" When I said, "Fine," he said, "No you're not. You're scared and you're going to be sick."

'He then asked after the others. "Oh they're no good," replied the gunner. "One of the Army chaps is down in the can. The other went down to the belly gun when it was still open. With everything being tossed around he thought he was going to fall out. He's on the navigator's bunk. Neither of them are able to do any observing."

'Next thing a friendly hand reaches over and is holding mine in a fatherly way. Three weeks later we were married. My colleagues said, "Fancy getting married. It won't last." I had had proposals, but I always knew there would be someone who would really matter.

'Fred Lucas was aged 28, five years older than I was. Owing to his war experience, he was an old 28. And, he was taller than me — just.'

POPEYE WAS A nickname Fred Lucas inherited soon after being posted to the RAF No 10 Flying Training School in Yorkshire. Lorie said he had to have his teeth out before he could pass his medical. He had grown up with the poor dental care that was typical in New Zealand rural areas.

'He had this act at boozy parties. He would rotate his false teeth without removing them from his mouth. During one of these toothabatic exercises his facial expression, with his large nose and jutting jaw, made him look for all the world like Popeye. Next thing a Popeye character appeared on his aeroplane, and the name stuck.

'When we were married they tried to call me Olive Oil, after Popeye's wife. I was able to nip that one in the bud, but ever since, people in aviation have always known Fred as "Popeye".'

NOT LONG BEFORE they married, Popeye got himself into an incident that was typical of the spirit that had once won the RAF selectors' approval. He was to form No 40 Transport Squadron to provide an important supply line between New Zealand and the Pacific war.

In March 1943 the Americans delivered the first Douglas Dakota C-47 (the military version of the famous DC-3 airliner) to the RNZAF. The aeroplane, No 3501, was brand new and for many days it sat on the tarmac in what Popeye described as a 'lonely splendour'.

'A Major Ross, one of the Americans, was supposed to have checked Fred out but he didn't turn up. In the meantime Fred had been looking at the handbook left on the seat. He then rang up Squadron Leader Bill Tacon and asked if he would be "second dickie" as they tried a little taxiing — just to see how the aeroplane handled.

'Next thing they were lined up, into the wind, at the end of the runway. Popeye opened the throttles and they were airborne. I knew nothing of this until, all of a sudden, I heard there was an emergency on. I was on duty on the ambulance. The fire tender came screaming around and I was waiting with the ambulance engine going. Then I heard, "Popeye's in trouble. He's up in the Dakota and he's going to crash-land." Of course everyone was out to have a look. Not so long before, an American B-17 bomber had crashed at Whenuapai.

'Overhead, Popeye was doing a circuit, preparing for a belly landing. He couldn't get the undercart down. In the end it was nothing. A warning light was on and a horn alarm was blaring. Fred and Bill were up there with the book that said, it might be this, it might be that, or it might just be an electrical fault in the warning system.

'Fred had decided to land anyway and as the aeroplane slowed on the ground Bill jumped out and placed locking pins in the undercarriage legs. Later Popeye said he had never seen anyone run so fast. The scare was over. I went back to my job, the fire tender went back to the fire station and everyone went back to work again.

'Next day they were again flying the C-47, this time going as far as Dunedin with about 12 passengers. Nothing about it appeared in the newspapers. Then, a couple of days later, the major arrived and took Fred up. Unbeknown to him, Fred had already done 13 hours.

'He eventually took Fred up for some night flying. Of course Fred had always come in without using landing lights while flying in England, so he didn't bother with them on this occasion either. The major then told Fred to go up again, with the landing lights on. Fred did, and made a mess of his landing.

'Yes, in things like that Fred was a bit of a wag. And he always wore his cap at a rakish angle. But he was also very fussy about doing things properly as far as flying was concerned. He was RAF trained, and meticulous about his responsibilities. I think a lot that has been said about him being reckless is folklore. He never had any patience for pilots who cut corners, or who drank before flying.

'The only aeroplane he ever successfully pranged was a Gipsy Moth while making a shorter than normal final approach during his first solo flight at Taieri. He had cut the motor to avoid high-tension lines but for some reason forgot to push the stick forward. His normally placid flying instructor became quite agitated and shook his fists before getting Fred back into the air again.

'Later Popeye did a lot of things some aviation people thought were hairbrained, especially when he opened up strips at Milford Sound and Martins Bay.'

The Dakota C-47 (DC-3), 3501, displaying the famous Popeye character.
LORIE LUCAS

SOON AFTER THEY were married, Popeye was on his way back to England to join No 487 Mosquito Squadron. It was a very worrying time for Lorie. Fred was low flying, often at treetop to dodge radar detection. The Mosquito pilots were looking for rocket-launching sites the Germans were thought to be building during the build-up to D-day. At that height, items on the ground flashed past. On one occasion he shot up a German staff car and, next day, read a report about some well-known general being killed. He believed the general must have been in that car. He once had an engine shot out, but was able to make it back to England.

'I never knew if he would come back. It is different today with counselling and all sorts of things. I believe people were stronger those days. It had not been that long ago when people had come out to New Zealand on sailing ships. Your husband could be bumped off in a Maori war, or be drowned in a river. It was just part of life. That was the way it was. You just picked up the reins and carried on, especially if there were children to care for.'

IN 1968 *POPEYE Lucas Queenstown* was published. The author is acknowledged as FJ Lucas, but I suspect Lorie did much of the work. By then Fred and Lorie, and their five children, were living at Cecil Peak Station.

'Fred never liked writing. He was a poor correspondent, even when his old wartime colleagues tried to keep in touch. He was also impatient and would tell you something in as few words as possible. He could never remember dates. In the end I tried sending Fred off to bed with this old-fashioned tape recorder. I used to like staying up

A 1943 night flight in a Lockheed Hudson, over Auckland, produced the ingredients for an enduring partnership. Popeye was the pilot, and Lorie an unofficial passenger.

Popeye Lucas and Lorie leave All Saints Anglican Church at Three Lamps, Ponsonby, after their wedding on 20 April 1943. NZ HERALD

late, catching up on all the bookwork. At 2 am one morning I turned on the light and saw the whole tape was used up. Oh good, I thought. But when I went to play the tape there were only about two sentences, followed by some silence, some deep breathing, then snoring. Having been through all his wartime night flying, Fred could drop off to sleep anywhere.

'We didn't like the book at first. But it was reprinted several times. I don't think Popeye ever read it.'

Popeye Lucas Queenstown is a delightful tale of New Zealand pioneering in a wonderful Central Otago lakeside setting. It records a time of short-sighted officialdom that stifled post-war initiative and enterprise. But its coverage of Popeye's war years is skimpy and needed to be addressed.

'When the book was being written wartime stories weren't all that popular. Fred didn't really talk much about it,' Lorie recalled. 'I was always a bit of a tomboy. I always liked men's talk about engines, aeroplanes, dogs on the sheep station, and so on. In the end I had to find most of it out for myself. I answered all his letters and started filing cards of information from this correspondence.

'Popeye's lack of interest in his war was all the more maddening because he was a great raconteur. He could convincingly take off a Scotsman or an Irishman when telling a story.

'A tourist visiting Queenstown from Dusseldorf had once asked Popeye if he had ever visited Germany. Popeye replied, "Oh yes. On several occasions, but only ever at night!"

'Whenever one of his old wartime mates turned up, out would come the whisky bottle. And the top would never go back on. But whenever I tried to find out more about his trips, necessarily recorded so briefly in his Pilot Logbooks, he was never very helpful. We would get out maps, measure distances, and work out flying hours. I would then say, "It must have been to either Nuremberg or Munich?" But he would never remember.

'Popeye was also very off-hand about his own gongs. He always said there were hundreds of others who weren't there at the right time, or nobody bothered to put their names forward. He never felt he was someone special. As a CO he was popular and that was unusual. He would shout for everyone down at the mess, and sometimes our mess bills were considerable.

'But young pilots always worried him. In England they would turn up with about 150 hours, and only 16 hours on a twin-engine fighter bomber, that's all. They were aged 18 to 20. I would look through his logbooks and diaries, and see the names of pilots. Three weeks later they would be gone. An aircraft hadn't returned. They never had a chance, and nobody even remembered their names, or anything. Mothers never knew what happened to their sons. They were gone — just like smoke. Fred felt very deeply for these lads.'

Towards the end of his life Popeye was keen for something to be written about some of these pilots, even if just some of their names were mentioned. His grandchildren were also curious and regarded their grandfather as some sort of wartime guru.

Popeye's War was published in 1996, some time after my visit to Motueka's back-blocks. As my car bumped over the rough farm track leading back to the road I knew I had discovered a different Popeye Lucas from the one I had anticipated earlier in the day as *Black Magic* was steadily winning the Americas Cup.

One of the RAF de Havilland Mosquito fighter bombers flown by Popeye when he was attached to No 487 Squadron in 1944.
Lorie Lucas

Post-war, the DC-3 civil version of the Dakota C-47 became a familiar sight in New Zealand skies. In recent years several DC-3s have been returned to duty as vintage recreation aircraft. This one, at the December 1994 Hokitika air show, is flown by the New Zealand Warbirds Association.
ROY SINCLAIR

'Popeye was not really the unruly larrikin many people believed him to be,' Lorie had told me over one last cup of coffee. 'He was certainly anti-bureaucrat. His father, Charlie Lucas, was known as a staunch old Tory. Fred was not a Tory. He wasn't a socialist either. He got on well with everybody. He was quite deep-thinking about a lot of things.'

As I headed back to Nelson I could still hear Lorie chuckling as she had told me that Popeye was 'Not a bit like the ideal man of my dreams. But we were like-minded. We worked as a team. He used to make the bullets and I would fire them.

'I never discouraged his flying. I was always keen on flying myself and didn't want to stop him, even if he was going to bump himself off next day. A lot of girls met a flyer and then wanted him to get a job in a drapery because it was safer.

'And I never used to argue, or have a good row and end up not speaking. I never knew when he might not come back. But I always knew there were times when I could have kicked his . . . kicked him, because I was being taken for granted.'

ON A HOT summer's day at Mt Cook airport a Japanese tourist, smiling ear to ear, thrust a huge snowball into my hands. He then made a hurried departure, presumably to board the awaiting ATR flight to Queenstown. In the heat the snowball, which merely minutes before had been scooped from the Tasman Glacier, started to drip, the ice water evaporating almost before it touched the hot pavement.

The Japanese tourist had been flown to the glacier in one of the famed ski-planes operated by Mount Cook Airline. His pilot had been 34-year-old Brent Turner, the eldest grandson of 'Popeye' Lucas. Brent's mother, Wendy Turner, was Popeye's only child from his first marriage.

'Grandad and I were the best of mates. I feel very proud to have had such a well-known grandfather who is a legend in aviation circles,' Brent tells me during the few minutes before his next glacier flight.

'I can remember the days when I visited him at Motueka, long after he had given up flying. He was a great home-brew maker. He would grab a bottle and say, "I've got nothing else to drink so we will have to have one of these." Then he would get out his logbooks and he would soon be telling me a long story associated with each brief entry.

'One of my early ambitions was to take him for a flight. The big day came in 1986. There we were, sitting in the Cessna 152 about to take off from Motueka to fly to Westport. I had less than 200 hours' flying and Grandad had about 15,000 hours. But he no longer had a pilot's licence.

'The funny thing about it was that Grandad never liked flying somewhere just for the fun of it. There always had to be a purpose for the flight. On this occasion, while I was doing my pre-flight

Brent Turner, grandson of Popeye Lucas and a Mount Cook ski-plane pilot, flies tourists to the Tasman Glacier. 'This is my dream job,' he says. 'Sometimes I feel Popeye is sitting behind me, watching me, as I fly the Pilatus Porter.'
ROY SINCLAIR

inspection, I looked up and saw him limping along with this huge wheelbarrow full of apples. The limp was the result of a wall falling on him when he was building a hangar at Frankton airport near Queenstown.

'He told me we were going to take the apples to my uncle's place at Westport. We certainly took off with an all-up weight. And we ate apples all the way to Westport.'

THESE DAYS BRENT Turner flies a Swiss-made Pilatus Porter. Flying ski-planes is his dream job. He is not interested in moving on to the airlines. He enjoys meeting the tourists, especially the Japanese, who talk about the 'rubbery pirate' (lovely pilot), and thank him for the safe 'fright' (flight). His uncle, Marty Lucas (a son of Lorie and Popeye), spent eight years flying ski-planes at Mount Cook before taking a job flying Pilatus Porters for Zimex, a Swiss charter company.

'It's quite strange working for Mount Cook when, in the 1950s, Popeye's Southern Scenic Airways at Queenstown was in competition with Harry Wigley's aviation ventures. Harry Wigley pioneered ski-plane landings on the glaciers and, eventually, established the Mount Cook Airline.

'Harry Wigley was always saying, "Keep that bastard Lucas away from the Mount Cook airstrip. He's taking passengers from our Mount Cook road coaches." On back-country airstrips Popeye Lucas and Harry Wigley used to look out for one another's wheel marks from their respective Austers. Had one, or the other, been in there first? They were both great aviation pioneers.'

Brent Turner can recall from an early age sitting on his Grandad's knee listening to one story after another. He says a lot was made of Popeye's military career but there was more to him than that.

'I was always interested in his New Zealand flying. Back in the 1930s he would cycle more than 30 kilometres to the Balclutha Aero Club only to hear the instructor tell him the weather was too bad for a flying lesson. Often he would cycle all the way home in the rain or even sleet.

'After the war, when it was difficult to get people to fly, he used to joke about it to put any timid passengers at ease. He was a real people's person but from his joking he got a reputation for being a bit slap-happy. That was a misconception. He was always thorough with his check-lists even though he could fly his Auster by the seat of his pants. He would never compromise safety with hooning.

'He would always say that if you act the goat up there, "the pilot will be the only one who gets a buzz out of it. Your passengers, whether they are your family or strangers, will never fly with you again."

'One day he was flying some people on the West Coast. He had made a lot of effort to give them a smooth flight. But when he hit a little turbulence and the aeroplane bumped, a lady in the rear seat tapped him on the shoulder and said, "Naughty naughty!"

'Marty took him for a fly in an Auster one day. Grandad had not flown an Auster for 20 years. Marty said, "You can have a play if you like." Popeye reached up for the trim and took control almost as if he had never stopped flying. He then greased down onto the home paddock, making a perfect final approach between two poplar trees. Next day Marty took to the trees with a chainsaw saying, "That approach is too tight for me!"

'Grandad's old Auster ZK-APO is hanging up in a garage somewhere in Alexandra. One day I hope it will be restored and I will get to fly it.

'When Grandad died in 1993 Marty and I went up to scatter his ashes over his Motueka West Bank farm. Marty and I shared the flying. Marty owned a high-winged Maule then. When we landed we were dismayed to see that most of the ashes appeared to be stuck along the side of the aeroplane. Marty said he would wash them off when he flew back to Mt Cook. He was flying ski-planes then. In the end, the ashes fell off all over the Southern Alps. There's bits of Popeye everywhere.

'Sometimes I feel he's sitting behind me, watching me, as I fly the Pilatus Porter up to the Tasman Glacier. He had a tremendous influence on me. In my mind he was always a careful pilot. But he had a wicked grin.'

Mount Cook Airline Cessna ski-planes on the Tasman Glacier in 1973.
Roy Sinclair

CHAPTER 14

Landing Amidst a Slipstream of Adventure

A truly magical experience — flying with Cathy Pegg above Melbourne's Port Philip Bay. The aeroplane, VH-JDI, is a Piper Warrior II.

Roy Sinclair

I often hear people talking about flying a small aeroplane, solo, across the Tasman Sea to New Zealand. It's the weirdest thing. I never say anything to them but to myself I say, I've done that. I know what it is like.

Cathy Pegg

WHENEVER CATHY PEGG drives onto one of Melbourne's freeways she heads her 1970 Mercedes Benz towards the fast lane. The classic car, named 'The Baroness May' — after her mother — is the second love of her life. Her first love, and one that involves all her passion, is flying. But Cathy Pegg is no ordinary aviator. She is Maori. And, as a symbol of wealth, the distinctive Mercedes Benz emblem on her $4000 car is as phoney as are the bullet-hole transfers on the rear windscreen. Her upbringing in New Zealand is the sort of stuff that inspired Alan Duff's *Once Were Warriors*. Her father, 'a violent womanising alcoholic', was far from being the ideal family man. She grew up on the Whenuapai Air Force Base where her father was stationed, and eventually graduated from Auckland's Massey High School, near Henderson, as the 'school dope'.

Aged 21, and a trained nurse, in 1977 she escaped to Australia and subsequently, at the Point Cook Royal Australian Air Force Base, met and married her former husband, Phillip. Late in December 1993 she returned to New Zealand for the first time to see her much-loved mother. She flew herself in a single-engine Cessna 182 via Lord Howe and Norfolk islands, becoming the first Maori woman to fly the Tasman Sea solo. The momentous event, which also included a return flight to Australia, went almost unnoticed in New Zealand. In Australia, Dick Smith, the entrepreneurial aviator and founder of *Australian Geographic* magazine, claimed Cathy's trans-Tasman flights as a double aviation record.

Cathy Pegg in a reflective pose at Point Cook airfield, south-west of Melbourne. Almost unknown in New Zealand, her trans-Tasman flights in December 1993 and January 1994 were claimed, in Australia, as a double aviation record.
ROY SINCLAIR

In May 1997 I met Cathy Pegg and the Baroness May, simultaneously. I am not sure which I noticed first. Both were impressive. Both promised to be as forthright as they were intriguing. I had tracked Cathy Pegg through *Australian Geographic* and the generous help from the editorial staff. I wrote to her and in return she phoned me. We spoke for five minutes and I knew a deserving story was ready for the telling. Next day I was peering through travel agents' windows, checking out the best deal for a return flight to Melbourne. A few short weeks later and I had arrived, unprepared for the verbal adventure of my life.

'I love this old classic car. When I am driving it my friends call me Cathy von Pegg,' she told me as we pounded along in the fast lane. Yet, despite an inherent fear of fast cars, I felt secure with the Baroness May and its exuberant driver. And we did spend a lot of time criss-crossing Melbourne's freeways during the three days it took to build my story. We were either on our way to Point Cook airfield, located near Melbourne's outer western suburbs, or to Moorabbin's general aviation airport south-east of the city. And for three days we talked, and talked, and talked — mostly about flying and aviators. Cathy had taken a week's leave from her job in the publications department at the Laverton RAAF Base.

We were two excited Kiwis inextricably caught up in a huge Australian metropolis, one in which we had a shared affinity. In 20 years Melbourne, unlike her native New Zealand, had shown Cathy Pegg some kindness. Perhaps, too, I could make a similar claim. Many years previously, in Melbourne, I had met the first love of my life when, as an uninformed and clownish 23-year-old, I made my first tentative venture away from home.

Cathy, I soon discovered, had experienced 42 years of life that had been as poignant as it was quirky. She does not know self-pity. The greater part of her conversation is spiced with genuine laughter, although she unashamedly admits to knowing how to cry — a lot — whenever she is overwhelmed. Her more poignant experiences include a temptation, as an unemployed young nurse, to street walk in St Kilda's notorious red light district when money ran short. 'I was desperate and prepared to do anything — well almost. But I couldn't imagine allowing any man to be up to his nuts in my guts for any amount of money.' She then landed a fortuitous job at the Freemasons Hospital in South Melbourne.

On another occasion, a tragedy at Point Cook had her hauling a young Air Force flying officer from a burning Tiger Moth that had spun into the ground. At the time she was learning to fly herself. Most student pilots would have given flying away after such a shocking experience. For myself, I had wimpishly let young and short-tempered flying instructors destroy my ambition to fly. I told Cathy about it, and I felt ashamed.

'FLYING TO NEW Zealand was an ambition for as long as I can remember,' she said. 'It was something I used to fantasise about. I remember telling someone that I was going to be the first Maori woman to fly the Tasman Sea. I never thought it would happen. It did happen. I was successful. It nearly killed me.'

Cathy Pegg was looking for an adventure, one that would give a private pilot the same sort of satisfaction a mountaineer gets on the summit of Mt Everest. It all started when, as a dutiful wife, she joined her husband clay-pigeon shooting at the RAAF Point Cook Gun Club.

'Phil never forced me to do anything I didn't like to do but I thought it was my duty to accompany him rigorously every weekend, a spare Browning slung over my shoulder, as he skilfully blew multitudes of clay birds out of the sky, one after the other. God, how I hated

Her first trip home in 15 years, Cathy Pegg flew herself in a Cessna 182 VH-EKF. Here, at Gisborne, she enjoys her accomplishment as the first Maori woman to fly the Tasman Sea, solo. 'All I did was to fly home to see my Mum,' she says.
GISBORNE HERALD

the place. It was a wasted weekend but anything was better than the routine of housework and mowing lawns, the weekend highlight of every woman married to the defence force.'

To escape the talk of the other women comparing the unlikely qualities of their respective offspring, Cathy would walk the short distance to the perimeter of the airfield. From there she loved the sight of Melbourne's skyscrapers, but more enthralling were the small aeroplanes and their student pilots attempting to take off and land with some degree of precision.

'I could watch them for hours. I imagined I was one of those pilots, swooping down over the gun club, my left fist jammed hard against the windscreen and my middle finger jutting upright at those pathetic clay targets that made me play second fiddle to my marriage.

'Then, late one Saturday afternoon, on our way home, we passed the RAAF Flying Club as one of the aircraft was taxiing in after a late flight. I shouted for Phillip to stop the car. I got out and went so close I could almost touch the Piper Tomahawk. I was so excited I thought I might have an orgasm — that was something that didn't happen to many women at the gun club. Phillip had sensed my excitement and suggested I visit the flying club, which I did.'

Cathy's first flying lesson was booked for 28 June 1987. From her first step into the flying club she had found a home away from home, and new friends. Her instructor was Jack Edwards, a man in his mid-sixties who had flown several years for Ansett Australia following his discharge from RAAF flying.

'He was incredibly patient, and he had to be, the poor man. Aged 32 I was known as old "Flossy", and I was about the worst student pilot God had ever put on this earth. They told me that flying was the most fun anyone could have outside the bedroom, but what they neglected to tell me was I had to learn how to fly the bloody aeroplane first.

'That first lesson was a nightmare. We lined up on runway 17 and gave the Tomahawk VH-PCF full throttle. No matter how hard I tried I could not keep that aeroplane straight on the runway. That day, I really made Ding Duck look like Tom Cruise flying those fighter jets in the *Top Gun* movie. As I struggled to battle the rudder pedals, my fantasies of giving the gun club the majestic royal salute soon went out the window.'

Cathy persevered. Jack was always encouraging and she got to love VH-PCF. Then one day, while waiting for her flying lesson, she heard a May Day call on the clubhouse radio. PCF had had an engine failure. The instructor and his student pilot were looking for a paddock to land in. The paddock had long grass that hid a large hump. The Tomahawk flipped. The occupants, lucky not to have been killed, suffered back and neck injuries. WH-PCF was wrecked, beyond repair.

She continued her lessons in other two-seat trainers: a Cessna 150 Aerobat and a Beechcraft Skipper. Both were almost the same to fly as the Tomahawk. On 6 September, when she had 8 hours in her log-book, Jack decided Cathy would fly solo.

'Jack had booked the Skipper VH-UMX for my lesson. There was nothing out of the ordinary to suggest what Jack had in mind. We took off from runway 17, flew three circuits, and on the third touch-down Jack told me to pull over to the edge of the runway. I thought I had done something very wrong and braced myself to have my poor bum kicked from one end of the runway to the other.

'Jack calmly undid his safety belt, opened the door, and stepped out onto the wing. He then shouted, "THIS IS YOUR FIRST SOLO. GOOD LUCK AND DON'T FORGET TO FLARE." With that, he slammed the door.

'And I said, "SHIT!"

'I lined up and pushed the throttle forward. UMX started to roll and, without Jack's added weight, the Skipper leapt into the air. Did I feel great!!! — until I turned to base and realised I had to land the thing all on my own. I trimmed the aeroplane to 65 knots, put on flap as required and did my utmost to stop myself from pooing my pants. As I got closer to the ground, I pulled the throttle to idle, eased the control column back, held my breath and waited for the crash. To my great astonishment UMX greased onto the runway and came to a gentle stop on the centre line. Jack was smiling as he waited for me. I was shaking in disbelief.'

Cathy continued to fly solo, building up confidence and experience. She then went through a rigorous exercise learning how to recover from a spin. At 6000 feet Jack told her to put the carbie heat on, pull the throttle back to 1500 RPM and gently pull the nose above the horizon until the plane, with wings shuddering, stalled. He then reduced power to idle, eased the control column back as far as it would go, and gave the weight of his boot to the left rudder. At 45 knots the stall warning screamed, the left wing dropped, the tail went up and the nose went down.

'I had never in my life felt so scared. The Skipper spun towards the earth. I opened my mouth to scream but nothing came out. Meanwhile, Jack was talking me through the recovery. I was more concerned about recovering from throwing up. We spent hour after hour trying to recover from spins.

'Next weekend I was booked to fly the Aerobat VH-WXS. On my own Jack had told me to practise my stalling. As I climbed to 6000 feet I told myself to forget about stalling; it was simply far too dangerous and whoever invented stalling needed a damn good slapping about! Still, if I wanted to fly I had to master stall recovery. At 6000 feet I secured everything, satisfied myself there were no other aircraft about, and went through the familiar routine.

'For a first try I was only going to stall, as Jack had instructed me to do. But as I dropped the nose to recover, the left wing dropped and WXS spun. This time I was on my own. I went into shock, freezing at the controls. The altimeter passed through 4000 feet before I gained control of myself. At that point I realised I would have to do something quickly if I were to survive.

'I went through everything Jack had taught me, and spoke each instruction as if he had been there. WXS recovered 2500 feet above the ground. Still shocked and shaken I flew back to Point Cook and landed on Runway 17. I shut down the engine where I stopped in the middle of the airstrip, got out and, with my back to the wheel spat, put my face in my hands and sobbed. Three other aeroplanes could not land because I was blocking the runway. I had spun WXS seven times before recovering.

'The club members, and especially Jack, were very understanding, and in no time they had me back training. After 70 hours' flying I was

Bonnie Quintal, an accomplished aviator and 'character' of Norfolk Island', tries out the pilot's seat of VH-EKF. 'Bonnie is one of my best friends in aviation,' says Cathy. CATHY PEGG

put before the Chief Flying Instructor to do my Restricted Private Pilot's test. I passed the test on 15 April 1989. This time Jack was not there to congratulate me. Five days earlier he had died of cancer of the liver. That was one of the biggest losses of my life. Jack had been the father to me I never had. He had always been there when things went wrong. He would say, "Flossy, this is all right; it's not as bad as it seems. Stick at it." I miss him very much.'

An elated Cathy Pegg, having cheated death on the New Zealand to Norfolk Island leg of her return flight, celebrates being safely on land.
BONNIE QUINTAL

It was time for Cathy to do her cross-country training for her full Private Pilot's Licence. She asked one of the RAAF pilots from the Number One Flying Training School to help. He was Flying Officer Mark Thoresen, a New Zealander and a C-130 Hercules pilot. Like Jack, he was an excellent instructor. As a friend, he also taught Cathy some military manoeuvres, and the tricks aeroplanes could do. One of these was later to save her life while she was flying in New Zealand.

'The poor man didn't know what he was letting himself in for. I was flying the Piper Warrior VH-GWD and although I had become a competent solo flier, I had the rare ability to become lost almost as soon as the wheels of GWD left the ground. My new instructor and I never came to loggerheads about anything in particular but we did frustrate the shit out of each other. Mark would sit beside me in the next seat and if he wasn't rolling his eyes he would be shaking his head. They were the only ways he could express his utter disbelief at some of the things I did. Then one day he let me loose to fly the skies of Victoria on my own. I couldn't believe he would do such a stupid thing.'

Her first solo cross-country flight, in a Cessna 172, went very well. Her next one didn't. It ended with her becoming hopelessly lost somewhere over Phillip Island.

'I was flying the Warrior VH-GWD again. I flew east through Melbourne's controlled airspace. As I did so I called up, in succession, the Melbourne Radar Advisory Service, the Essendon Airport tower and the Moorabbin tower. The sun was behind me and the day couldn't have been more wonderful. But when I turned west to find my way back to Point Cook the sun was streaming into my eyes, and the city was lost in smog. Visibility quickly reduced until I had to squint even to see the prop arch, just the short distance beyond the windscreen.

'I tried to hold my westerly heading for the time required for the leg I was flying, but I already knew I had lost the plot. I went into a slight panic, knowing I would end up flying aimlessly until my fuel ran out, resulting in a forced landing and, possibly, a wrecked aeroplane, or worse. I couldn't believe I had allowed myself to become lost so quickly, and in such a small area.

'I had a gut feeling that Phillip Island airfield was probably somewhere close but because I could not pinpoint my exact position there was no chance of a diversion. So I took control of myself and starting looking for somewhere to land — on a road or in a field.

'From 2000 feet I spotted what looked like a small racecourse and flew over to check it out. Yep, it was a private racecourse. It looked small but I was desperate. I felt that, maybe, I could land even if I couldn't take off again. I took GWD down to 500 feet, put out the first stage of flap and flew over again to check out the surface and the length. I couldn't see any power lines or any other obstruction, so I went down to 200 feet for a closer look. Satisfied, I set GWD up for the landing and brought her over the fence at 60 knots. With full flap and a light load she touched down on the stall to a fairy kiss landing and, enveloped in a cloud of dust kicked up from the track, stopped safely in a short distance.

'As I shut down the engine I saw an old gent approaching. The expression on his face was one of surprise and amusement. When I opened the door he asked, "Got a problem lady?"

'All I could say was, "I'd love a cuppa!"

'With that, he showed me into a little shed and put the kettle on. Then, to my utter embarrassment, he pointed a crooked withered finger in a southerly direction and said, "Most fliers round here land on a little grass strip about a kilometre from here."

'In my panic I had flown over the Phillip Island airstrip and not seen it. My father's words, telling me that I was nothing to him but a failure and an embarrassment, came back to haunt me once again. I could have cried but I had to maintain my composure in front of this old man who, fortunately, didn't know an aviation stuff-up even when it hit him in the face. Appearing to be cheerful, I finished my cup of tea, got my bearings, checked the length of the field, and planned my flight back to Point Cook.

'With full throttle, and feet planted hard on the brakes until the RMP registered 2700, and 10 degree of flap, I made a perfect short-field takeoff, leaving the race course at 60 knots with loads of strip to spare. An hour later I landed at Point Cook, glad to be back and telling my friends, who were concerned by my late arrival, about my landing at Phillip Island owing to poor visibility. I did not add that I had not quite made it to the airstrip!'

After a few more hours of dual cross-country flying, Mark Thoresen thought it was time for Cathy to do her flight test. He arranged for the Chief Flying Instructor to fly with her on her next cross-country to check out her navigation. The CFI did not tell Cathy it was a flight test. If it did not go well he was not going to say anything. The flight would merely be entered in her logbook as just another dual cross-country.

'I was the only person in the flying club that day who did not know what was happening. Imagine my surprise when I arrived back to a round of applause. That was yet another occasion when I was moved to tears.

'Next Saturday morning I was up early. So was Phillip. He was at the gun club. I was at the flying club. No one else was about as I slid open the hangar door, pulled out VH-WXS, and methodically went through my pre-flight checks.

'At 100 feet I held her level above Runway 17 and let her gain speed. We rushed over the "piano key" markings of Runway 35, banked to the right and headed straight for that damnable clay-pigeon shooting range. Phillip was setting up for the day. I had spent two years of slow, frustrating learning but when, with my middle finger raised against the windscreen, I gave that gun club the promised royal salute, nothing had ever felt so sweet. I pulled the nose up and over to the left, into a wing over, and landed. Yeah, it was a great start to the day!'

CATHY PEGG DRIVES the Baroness May to the furthest part of the former RAAF Point Cook Base. When we stop, Cathy is looking pleased with herself. With the demise of the airfield as an operating RAAF base, many of the buildings have been rearranged, partly in an effort to establish the National Aviation and Space Museum of Australia. For Cathy, however, the most auspicious change was when the gun club became the Point Cook Flying Club.

The clubhouse and its surrounds have become a temporary film set for Moby Dick Productions. Cathy shows me the former clay-pigeon site now occupied by a replica sailing ship embedded in a huge pond. The pond is fitted with railings on which a fake white whale, hunted by Melville's demented Captain Ahab, will soon perform for the cameras. Inside the flying club I am approached by a man with a softly spoken Scottish voice. His hand is outstretched.

'I have not met you,' he says, and I introduce myself. His name is Patrick Stewart, an actor, of *Star Trek* fame. I know, as a journalist, I should be spending longer talking to him but I am already absorbed by another story; one about a Maori woman who flies, and who speaks to me with a wonderful, almost musical, Australian accent one hears only in Melbourne.

Later, Cathy talks about her Maori heritage and the little she knows about it. 'It was taken from us in the 1960s. At school, in Whenuapai, we were threatened with the strap if we were heard speaking our Maori language in the playground.' She shows me the Maori bone carving she wears, always. 'It hangs close to my heart. I don't really know what it represents, but it is something very precious.'

Only a month or so before my visit she had seen the film *Once Were Warriors*. 'I was shocked and stunned. I cried for a long time. It was as if someone had made a movie of a day in my own life when I was growing up in New Zealand.'

She then talks with some melancholy about the recent demise of her marriage to Phillip, forced by an over-long separation when the RAAF posted him to New South Wales. 'He was the most honest man I will ever know,' she says.

We talk about people who have become famous, what drives them, and the accolades history has awarded them. She has a great admiration for the pioneer aviators, Charles Kingsford Smith and, especially, Jean Batten. Indigenous people, she says, are either great failures or they believe they have to work so hard to prove something, to themselves, and to others.

'When I flew to New Zealand, I did it for me.'

She talks quietly about a day in November 1991 when she was at Point Cook — the day when the Tiger Moth crashed. It was being flown by Group Captain Mike Birks. His passenger was a younger flying officer, Rick Davies.

'I would never condemn any pilot for making a mistake. I have made a lot myself. But if you do not do it properly, aviation will bite you. It doesn't matter who you are, or how good you are. I have lost some very dear friends to air accidents.'

When the Tiger Moth spun into the ground, Cathy ran out to the burning aeroplane. One pilot was on fire and appeared to have a broken neck. He was probably already dead. She hauled the younger man out, and away from the crash. He gained consciousness, realised what had happened, and went to save his companion.

'I was not going to see two men die so I ran after him and brought him down with a rugby tackle that ought to have got me into the All Blacks. Later, when I visited Rick in hospital, I met his wife. She was pregnant.'

Cathy shows me a beautifully presented note Rick had written and sent to her. 'Rick and his wife really appreciated what I did that day. That means a lot to me. Whenever I hear of someone getting an OBE or some other big award, I think of this note from Rick.'

We sit for a time in silence, thinking about our conversation, which has embraced a lost heritage and another tragedy. Before I had left

A departing glimpse of Lord Howe Island is caught by Cathy Pegg's compact camera as she climbs VH-EKF for the final ocean sector, to Coffs Harbour, and the completion of her trans-Tasman flights.

home, an understanding friend, Hettie Wells, who is known worldwide for her Hettie's Rock Shop in Beckenham, Christchurch, had given me a small piece of greenstone to take to Cathy. I had told Hettie that Cathy is Maori. A piece of gifted greenstone — the treasured stone of Maori people — is a gesture for good luck, and friendship. Cathy holds the greenstone between the palms of her hands. And her beautiful hands gently enclosing the stone are held in an attitude of prayer.

A few moments later, she jolts me from my reverie with, 'Gosh, I have absolutely nothing we can drink!' I come to the rescue with a 375 ml bottle of Pegasus Bay Noble, a late harvest Semillon Sauvignon from North Canterbury. Cathy says the wine is indeed excellent — so good in fact she accuses me of having covert motives, and she roars with laughter when I appear offended by her facetious comments.

'Regrettably, such a small bottle between two does not go very far,' I reply. 'Besides, tomorrow you will take me flying!'

IN 1993 CATHY Pegg was saving for an airline ticket to New Zealand. She phoned a friend from the flying club and told him about it. Unimpressed, he said, 'You're saving money to give to an airline? You are a pilot, Cathy. Why don't you bloody well fly yourself?'

‘I thought that was really not such a bad idea so I phoned a friend in Queensland. He was Jimmy Connor and he had a Sud-Horizon, a small French aeroplane. I came straight to the point and said, ‘Jimmy, how would you feel about lending me your aeroplane to fly to New Zealand?’

‘He said, “Cath, what a damn great idea.”

‘It would have eased my mind had he said, “No.” The idea of flying over all that ocean terrified me. I knew I would be carrying a spare pair of undies, and they wouldn’t be lace!’

Cathy was told to make preparations for a late December departure. But just a few weeks later the aeroplane was wrecked by a hailstorm. The huge hailstones demolished all the control surfaces — the ailerons, flaps, and elevators.

‘I thought it was all over. Then John Laming, a retired RAAF squadron leader, told me he knew of a little twin-engine Piper Comanche that would be available for my flight. John even offered to see me through my twin endorsement, for nothing. Just a few weeks before departure the owner asked for $10,000 up front. I was truly pissed off. I didn’t have that sort of money. I was annoyed that he had waited until I had made most of my preparations before dropping the bombshell. I used ample choice expletives to express my utter disappointment. I was almost ready to throw all my charts in the rubbish. I had had two chances, and you don’t usually get a third.

‘Then, John rang again. He said, “I have found the perfect aeroplane for you.”

‘I thought, “Doesn’t this man ever give up?” To John, I said, “Shit. It’s on again. I’ve got to face that bloody ocean.”’

The use of the Cessna 182, Victor Hotel-Echo Kilo Foxtrot was going to cost Cathy $4000. That was her budget. Fuel would cost another $1000, which could go on her Mastercard. The Cessna was overhauled thoroughly two weeks prior to takeoff. The engine was found to have a cracked cylinder.

‘An overhaul was not due for some time, and a cracked cylinder might not normally be found in the usual 100-hour check. Had I flown as it was I think the cylinder would have cracked wide open and I would have ditched.’

The RAAF helped with providing survival equipment, which included a Uvic flying suit, one-man life raft, life jacket, emergency locator beacon, flares, and two-way radio. Cathy was taken on RAAF training courses and shown how to use the equipment. She was put into a decompression chamber and taken up to a simulated 28,000 feet to demonstrate the effects of hypoxia.

'The RAAF was very supportive, and it was great fun jumping off Zodiacs and being rescued by helicopters. I was also shown how to use the Pyrotechnics, the flares and sea dyes. I even spoke to Squadron Leader Garley, in Canberra. He is also a pilot. "If we can help a fellow aviator, we will," he told me. That was brilliant, and it was very encouraging to be backed by a defence force.'

Members of the Australian Women's Pilots Association wrote letters seeking sponsorship. *Australian Geographic* publisher, Dick Smith, was impressed by Cathy's meticulous preparation and her commitment to the RAAF safety training. He donated $1000 to foot the fuel bill.

Later, Dick Smith, under the heading 'Landing an aviation record' wrote:

> *In a feat worthy of more experienced pilots, Cathy flew from the Royal Australian Air Force base at Point Cook, south-west of Melbourne, to her homeland, via Lord Howe and Norfolk islands . . . with just 200 hours' flying experience and only two other cross-country flights under her belt . . . All the support and planning in the world, including advice from around-the-world fliers Gabby Kennard and Peter Norvill, could not prepare her for the dramas she experienced.*

SHE WAS ISLAND-HOPPING, starting across the ocean from Coffs Harbour in New South Wales. It was the reverse of Francis Chichester's trans-Tasman Gipsy Moth seaplane flight of 1931. Cathy even studied Chichester's basic navigation involving wind drift calculations that had enabled him, with very basic instruments, to pinpoint a small island in a vast ocean.

'I was not a bit confident when I set out. I was certainly scared. I had thought I was well prepared but I did not have an instrument or night rating, and that almost cost me my life. I was reluctant to have anyone with me. I didn't know what was going to happen. My biggest fear was surviving a serious mishap, and my passenger dying. I could not have coped with that. I did take my Teddy bear given to me for the trip by my half-brother, William. I call the bear Charles Kingsford Smith.'

Cathy started flying across the ocean on 30 December. Her Cessna, laden with fuel, tie-down kit, and emergency gear, struggled into the air and flew with its tail down and nose up. With standard fuel tanks, the Cessna could hang in the air for five and a half hours.

'I kept looking down at the water thinking that I would soon be down there and it would all be over. But after half an hour I relaxed. You become very accepting of what might happen. I stopped worrying and just flew.'

The flight of 316 nautical miles took two and a half hours, and was almost uneventful. The Cessna had twin ADF (Automatic Direction Finder) needles on the one dial to assist with the compass navigation. Once the ADF needles were aligned to the appropriate NDB (Non Directional Beacon) ground stations, at the departure and arrival points, it was easy to see if the aeroplane drifted off its course. Cathy also had her own Global Positioning System, a Garmin 55. It plugged into the cigarette lighter.

Memories of Francis Chichester's 1931 trans-Tasman flight are kept in a small museum on Lord Howe Island. As Cathy Pegg gazed at photographs of Chichester and his fragile Gipsy Moth floatplane she drew comfort from knowing she was not 'the only idiot to fly the Tasman Sea alone.'

'At the time there were no GPS units approved for Australian aviation. Some pilots say a GPS is cheating on navigation because it is so simple to use. If it is set correctly it will always take you right above where you want to be. A GPS will also count down the nautical miles remaining to fly, and will indicate the aeroplane's ground speed. When flying over a featureless ocean I believe a pilot should use every means of navigation available. My GPS is a very basic model, with nothing outrageous about it. It got me all the way to New Zealand and back.

'You always feel confident you will find your island. But it was a beautiful sight seeing those twin peaks of Lord Howe framed in my windscreen. I was 100 miles out, flying at 8000 feet. As I got closer the picture just got bigger and bigger.'

THAT NIGHT CATHY stayed on the island. She had a dream: Her older sister was flying a Cessna across an ocean. Cathy pleaded with her, 'Mary, don't do this. This is a very silly thing to do.' But she went off and did fly over the ocean — and the Cessna crashed.

'It did worry me. Then I thought, if I go back, or if I go on, either way I will be flying over water. I could have caught a commercial flight back to Australia. Someone would have had to fly the Cessna back to Australia and I would have spent the rest of my life not knowing how my flight might have turned out. So I decided to fly on. I had made my Last Will and Testament before I left home, and not told anyone. Phillip would have found it when he went through my things.'

Next morning Cathy was preparing for the 480 nautical mile flight to Norfolk, expected to take just over three and a half hours. Dressed in her all-weather flying gear, which included thermal underwear in case she ditched, she was sweltering. The Cessna had been refuelled the previous day so all she had to do, apart from the usual pre-flight checks, was to recheck the fuel levels and do a fuel drain in case condensation overnight had left water in the tanks.

'I did a drain of the wing tanks and they were OK. The Cessna 182 also has an engine drain but that one is very awkward. I couldn't reach the top of the fuel drain inside the engine cowling, pull a little plug, and also put a drain under the engine. My arms, encased as they were in all the flying gear, just weren't long enough. I thought I wouldn't bother. Then I realised I'd better do it properly if I was going to fly over water. Perhaps I was still thinking about that disturbing dream?

'I managed to jam a jar under the cowling flap, and pulled off two full jars of water. Had I not done the drain properly, the engine might

The Cessna 182 VH-EKF at Melbourne's Essenden airport. 'After returning from New Zealand I was so attached to the Cessna I hid it in a hangar for a week — until someone reminded me it had to be returned to its owner.'
CATHY PEGG

have got me into the air over the sea and stopped. I would have landed in the sea, and it would simply have been bad airmanship.'

Flying on from Lord Howe becomes an international flight, involving clearing customs and filing an International Flight Plan. She had been told that she could fly on an Australian domestic flight plan but New Zealand said, 'No.'

'I said, "Shit!" The flight plan was important should a search and rescue be necessary. While I was contemplating what to do, a Dash 8 landed. I ran out waving my arms crying, "Please, Captain. Have you got an International Flight Plan?"

'He gave me one but I didn't even know how to fill it in. I felt a dork. He showed me, and he even filed it in to Auckland International Airport. He took off for Norfolk half an hour after me, and much later passed me again on his way back to Lord Howe, long before I arrived at my next island.'

Again, the ocean flight had been almost uneventful apart from minor visibility problems caused by the smoke from New South Wales bush fires drifting out across the Tasman. She was met at Norfolk by Bonnie Quintal, one of the island's characters and an accomplished private pilot who has flown around Australia, twice, in a Cessna 172, and around America in a Piper Warrior.

'Bonnie told me she had cancelled my motel booking and I was to stay with her. She is a beautifully spoken woman aged in her sixties. We went up to her house where she had afternoon tea set out ready. The cake was all cut up nicely. She sat me down at the kitchen table. I was feeling sweaty and uncomfortable in all my flying gear. She passed me a cup and said, "Here you are dear. Have a nice cup of tea and a piece of cake. After that long flight you must be feeling fucked." My jaw dropped.

'That night Bonnie took me out on the town and I soon discovered she was prepared to make the most of it. I was decidedly worse for wear when we arrived home. Bonnie then said, "Do you want another spot, dear?"

'Having been out on the town with Bonnie, it seemed I was known by everyone on the island as I prepared to take off next morning. The customs officer even knew me. Knowing Bonnie certainly made all the formalities simple. Bonnie helped with my flight plan and had it faxed to Auckland. She has since been one of my best friends in aviation.'

Norfolk to Kerikeri is almost the same distance as from Lord Howe to Norfolk, but not quite so difficult. The last part of the flight, for some distance, is over land. Much of Cathy's flight was made at 8000 feet, but during the first hour she climbed to 11,000 and suffered from mild hypoxia.

'Auckland wanted to know where I was along that leg. They couldn't contact me, nor I them. I was operating VHF radio. So they asked a Qantas jet to try and contact me, which they did on the 1215 emergency frequency I was operating on while flying over the ocean.

'The Qantas captain called Echo Kilo Foxtrot, twice. Suddenly I realised that was me. Who wants me in the middle of all this ocean? He then told me Auckland wanted to know my arrival time into Kerikeri. I was operating on Melbourne's Eastern Standard Time. Flying operates on UTC Greenwich time. For me, the time is one hour forward, and evening becomes morning. But I couldn't work it out. It didn't occur to me something was wrong.

'Then the Qantas captain said, "For Christ's sake, just tell them how long it's going to take you."

'And I said, "Three hours."

'He was very nice even though he must have thought I was a bit dopey. He then said to me, "You are a woman; in a single-engine aeroplane, flying from Australia to New Zealand?"

'I said, "That's right." He said, "Bloody women. Only a woman would want to do that!" To this day, I have no idea who he was.'

'Realising I was probably suffering from hypoxia I double-checked my compass alignment. I knew then that something was desperately wrong. If what I was seeing was correct, I should have been flying backwards. I was reading my compass backwards! I thought, ever so casually, I had better do something about this. I descended to a lower, and safer, altitude but it didn't make much difference. I continued to read my compass backwards.'

Approaching New Zealand, Cathy saw one of the most dramatic sights she had ever seen from the air. Beyond the tip of Northland the sea appeared to be boiling where the Tasman Sea and Pacific Ocean met. 'It went on for miles and miles. It was magnificent; I just wanted to keep on looking down at the angry currents.'

Another beautiful sight was the cloud covering the land. 'I knew then why New Zealand was always known to Maori people as Aotearoa, the Land of the Long White Cloud. I wanted to fly above the cloud but I knew I had to descend and fly under it, and fly south to my arrival at Kerikeri.'

Cathy Pegg landed at Kerikeri early in the afternoon. It was New Year's Day, 1994. 'I was pleased I had arrived within my estimated time. I thought I might have felt more emotional. But I was just feeling an overwhelming relief at making it.

'The inside of the aeroplane had to be sprayed before the customs people would allow me out. They handed me the spray can and told me to do it myself. I didn't know how much to use so I must have almost emptied the entire can. I was coughing and spluttering, and they were tapping on the window saying, "That's enough, that's enough!" I was almost suffocated.'

Maria Stewart, a friend with whom she had done her nursing training in Auckland, was there to meet her. They celebrated with a huge meal of seafood. But the seafood was too rich for Cathy's stomach and next day she was unwell.

'After all my years in Australia I was unable to cope with New Zealand seafood. I wanted to stay in Kerikeri until I felt better, rather than fly on to my home in Gisborne. But I had been led to believe that my mother was in hospital and she was anxious to see me. I had come all this way and was worried about my mother, so I decided to fly on.

'As I flew over the ranges from Opotiki I was feeling worse and knew I should not have been flying on my own. I was flying in a space of about 50 feet between the mountains and the cloud base, and that was a really silly thing to be doing.

'When I called inbound to the Gisborne tower I was told to hold west of the field because of a helicopter operating over the vicinity. I was feeling so sick I never really heard what I had just been asked to do. It went in one ear, and out the other. I just wanted to be down on the ground. I flew over the airfield and almost collided with the bloody helicopter.

'Realising I was about to be killed, along with those in the helicopter, I instinctively put the Cessna into an initial and pitch manoeuvre which banks the aeroplane into the circuit at top speed. With the wings almost 90 degrees to the ground, you bank crosswind and then bank in the opposite direction to fly down wind. Having the wings at 90 degrees means the speed washes off as the aeroplane turns. It was one of those little tricks Mark Thoresen had taught me and I did not think a Cessna would do it. I was chronically ill but in aviation you take responsibility for whatever you do.

'Once I was on the ground the controller called me to the tower. I knew I was going to have my arse kicked red raw from one end of the strip to the other. We both knew I was in the wrong. When he saw my RAAF flying suit with the flying officer's stripe on the shoulder all he said was, "In civilian street we do what the air traffic controller tells us to do." I was let off very lightly.

'My mother was there to meet me. She had not been in hospital at all. My father was there, too, but he walked away without speaking to me. I tied the plane down, threw up and went home to my mother's house where I passed out, and slept, for the next 24 hours.'

Cathy Pegg and her 1970 Mercedes Benz, the 'Baroness May.' Both are impressive.
ROY SINCLAIR

CATHY PEGG SPENT the next week in New Zealand, catching up with her mother and several sisters. She loved being with her mother, who had always been the strength of the family, and she loved being in Gisborne. It was a beautiful place, and the Gisborne Aero Club put on a celebratory barbecue. 'That was a tremendous surprise.'

Everyone involved in aviation treated her exceptionally well. 'If you fly, it does not matter where you go in the world, you're going to be looked after and treated nicely,' she said.

She felt more confident about tackling her homeward flight to Australia. Back in Kerikeri she met up with Nigel Strange, an instructor at the aero club. When she had arrived in New Zealand Nigel had lent her New Zealand maps and a rule to measure nautical miles. The measurements on the rule were a little different from her equivalent Australian equipment. He had also helped her calibrate the Cessna's instruments for New Zealand flying.

'Nigel took me home for the night. Unbeknown to me, he was still living with his parents. They lived in an enormous house. I played their piano and Nigel's mother treated us as if we were a couple of kids. It was really wonderful.

'In the morning Nigel took me to the airport and I packed the aeroplane, faxed my flight plan to Auckland, and prepared for the flight to Norfolk. It was going to be the most devastating day of my trans-Tasman flights.'

Difficulties started with the flight plan, which indicated Cathy was flying by Visual Flight Rules. The Auckland people told Cathy that, under New Zealand regulations, a private pilot without an instrument rating was not allowed to fly more than 100 nautical miles off the coast.

'They had let me fly into New Zealand, but they weren't going to let me go. I pointed this out to them. They said they would ring me back. I told Nigel I was going to fly out no matter what they said. I couldn't imagine the Royal New Zealand Air Force being sent out to shoot me down.

'Fortunately, they did let me go. They had been in touch with Australia and decided that, because I was an Australian pilot flying an Australian-registered aircraft, I could fly according to Australian regulations. They wished me a good trip.

'I said, "Thank you very much; see ya later alligator."

The Auckland Air Traffic Control Centre vectored her flight over

Kaitaia, which meant she had to fly a dog leg and then intercept her planned course. The change also added a little distance to the flight, but not too much.

'At 8000 feet I was encountering shocking headwinds. My GPS indicated a ground speed of only 80 knots. I knew that at that speed I could never reach Norfolk before running out of fuel. Auckland called me up and asked me to confirm my ground speed. I told them it was 120 knots. I was still flying over land, and I did not want to be told to return.

'I had already decided to fly 100 nautical miles off the coast and if my ground speed had not increased sufficiently, I would turn back.'

At that crucial stage the Cessna was achieving 100 knots over the sea. Cathy was hoping for 130 knots, but she believed she would reach Norfolk. At exactly the half-way point the cloud came in and she decided to turn back. With a strong tail wind she knew she had ample fuel to return to New Zealand, but when she looked behind the aeroplane the weather had encircled her. She knew she was trapped.

'Not being instrument rated I tried to fly under the cloud and continue on to Norfolk. I got down to 900 feet and by squinting I could just see the ocean. The rain was so loud on the upper wing I couldn't even hear the engine. I knew that one decent downdraft would put me down in the sea and the flight would be over. I also knew that, as a VFR pilot, I had been really stupid to allow myself to get caught in this weather. Then things got worse.'

Any pilot, unable to fly on instruments, who has inadvertently flown into cloud knows what it is like. The pilot suddenly becomes completely disorientated, shaking his or her head in an attempt to get a grip, then looks out again, towards the water or the ground, trying to make some sense of an environment that is without a horizon or any other reference point. More often than not the pilot ends up dead.

'I was having difficulty keeping the aeroplane in the right flying attitude. I was completely confused as I scanned the instruments, trying to fly on them. But I could not do it. With an altitude of only 900 feet I was so close to the sea I knew I would soon fly into the water. Then, as I scanned the instruments, I noticed the engine manifold pressure gauge was flicking, and the RPM started to drop back. I was picking up carburettor ice, starving the engine's fuel supply.

'In all the years of flying in Australia, I had never picked up carburettor ice. For a time I didn't even realise what was happening. As I watched, the manifold pressure kept dropping and, even though I

Urms Wright, of Moorabin's Valight Training Services, took Cathy Pegg through the ground subjects for her Private Pilot's Licence. Gruff and outspoken, Urms presents a rare passion for a professional standard of flying (aero) club instructing. 'He's one of the nicest people in Australian aviation,' says Cathy.
ROY SINCLAIR

could not hear the engine, when the nose started to drop I knew it was losing power. I pulled on the carbie heat in an effort to blast hot air through the carburettor. Then, I started to feel prickly. I knew this was it; I was going to ditch in the ocean in bad weather. I started to cry. The tears streamed down my face, and down the front of my flying suit. As I watched the altimeter fall another 300 feet, towards the unfriendly ocean, I was demented with a feeling of failure and self-pity.'

JUST OVER THREE years later, Cathy pauses as she tells me the story. In the sudden silence, I hear the soft whirring of my tape recorder. We share the remaining exquisite contents from the bottle of Pegasus Bay Noble. Cathy looks at me, and smiles. I cannot think of anything appropriate to say.

'Once you have accepted what is going to happen to you, you can suddenly think very clearly, and everything appears to be happening in slow motion,' she tells me. 'I started thinking the most stupid things like, where am I going to go to the toilet in a one-man dinghy? And, how am I going to keep my lips moist without my chapstick? I was being really pathetic.

'I then realised that, in a high-wing aeroplane, I would be trapped once it landed on the water. The fuselage was going to sink quickly and I was not going to get out. The water was going to pour in and I was going to drown. I was a fucking idiot. It was as if I had let myself go from the safety of my mother's womb into God knows what. And even if I were lucky enough to get out, I would soon freeze to death.'

As LUCK WOULD have it, in pulling on the carburettor heat, Cathy had done the one thing left to save her life. As the tears flowed freely, and she wallowed in her grief, the ice was being turned to water and thrust beyond the cylinders to be spat out with the exhaust. Fuel was flowing through the carburettor. The engine sprang back to life.

'Suddenly I was looking at this turning propeller. I could not think what to do with it. What does a pilot do with a turning propeller? With power back in the engine, the nose started to rise. But I was still in bad weather, and I still could not see. But the altimeter was climbing and when it got to 900 feet I burst out into an eight-eighths blue sky. There was no wind. I had been in the cloud for just 10 minutes. When I flew out I had gone from one weather extreme to the next. On full power I climbed to 8000 feet and flew on to Norfolk, just as fast as I could.

'Bonnie Quintal was there waiting for me. She wanted to take me out on the town again. I was reluctant because I knew what she had been like the first time round. But we did have a lot to celebrate that night, so out on the town we went. And we did have a really wonderful time.

'Of course, I told Bon all about my flight. I told her how hard I had cried. As we celebrated I kept saying, "It's true, Bon! It's true, Bon!"

'And all Bon could say was, "Fuck, love!"'

THE NEXT DAY'S flying landed Cathy in yet another predicament, on Lord Howe Island. The flight from Norfolk had gone well despite the visibility being severely impaired by smoke from Australian bush fires that still drifted across the Tasman. The smoke became so dense there was no horizon to fly on, but Cathy did have a clear view of the ocean, enabling her to keep the aeroplane flying at the right attitude. At 5000 feet she could not see Lord Howe until she was only 15 nautical miles out and, even then, the island's twin peaks appeared as faint silhouettes.

'After battling the smoke, I was very tired by the time I arrived. I should have over-flown the island and checked out the runway but I didn't. Instead I flew straight in. As I was descending between the peaks I thought something was wrong. When the wheels were about 10 feet off the runway I turned round to check the windsock and realised I had about 20 knots of tail wind. The strip is also slightly downhill, and it's short.

'I was annoyed with myself. I had made too many mistakes during my New Zealand trip. I had been sick and I had been tired, but there are no excuses for bad airmanship.

'With the Cessna's nose up and tail down I had my feet absolutely hard on the brakes as soon as the wheels touched. I had full flap out and everything out, short of opening the doors. The Cessna settled onto its nose wheel as the main wheels squealed to a stop. Another 30 feet and I would have tipped over the end of the runway, into the sea. I had once again been very lucky, but I wanted to kick myself.'

Cathy taxied off the runway to discover the airfield was absolutely deserted — at three-thirty in the afternoon. She got on the radio only to be told the customs officer was out fishing.

'This man was out fishing, and I was told he would be back in an hour. Four messages had been sent to Lord Howe advising of my arrival and I was only 15 minutes late, which is not bad for a long ocean flight. Being the obedient sort of person I am, I said I would just sit in the aeroplane until the customs officer arrived.'

As the time passed Cathy became hotter and hotter until she could stand the tropical heat no longer. Somehow, she had to get out of her flying gear. The shorts and light shirt she had been wearing on Norfolk were handy, in the back of the aeroplane. In the cramped cabin she started to strip.

'I took off my life jacket, then my Uvic jacket, unzipped my flying jacket and managed to pull off my thermal singlet. At this stage I slipped and fell down between the rudder pedals on the passenger side of the cockpit. As I tried to push myself up on the pedals I started to panic. If someone turned up, I was literally flopping about half naked!

'Tangled up in what clothing I had left on, as well as that which I didn't have on, I was listening to the rudder going bang, bang, bang, as my frantic hands pounded the rudder pedals. Suddenly I heard a knocking at the window and someone was asking, "Are you all right?" All I could think was, "This is not happening."

'The customs officer merely said, "Take your time. Just get dressed." I was embarrassed. I was aged 38 but I could see he was not 38. He was somewhat blasé, wearing shorts and jandals. His open shirt showed a great hairy chest. He was extremely good looking. How dare they send a customs officer like that to me!

'I climbed out at last wearing my shorts and shirt, and he just said, "Are you feeling better now?" He stamped all my books and said, "You could have stepped out of the aeroplane while you were waiting!"

'People on Lord Howe do treat you very well considering their visitors are strangers who just drop in out of the sky. I stayed the night with Beth Wilson, the radio operator, and her husband. Next morning they lent me a bike to cycle around the island. I discovered a small museum with a wall of photographs of Francis Chichester's visit to Lord Howe Island from 1 April to 10 June 1931. His Gipsy Moth floatplane was sunk and wrecked by a storm while it was moored overnight in the lagoon. He was stranded on Lord Howe and spent all that time rebuilding his floatplane and getting to know the islanders, some very well apparently. Chichester made the first east to west solo flight across the Tasman Sea.

'I spent a little time gazing at the Chichester photographs. It gave me comfort to think that I had not been the only idiot to fly the Tasman Sea alone. He, too, had made a lot of mistakes, but so had I. I smiled to myself as I thought how I had got away with a lot more than he did. My plane hadn't been turned over and wrecked by a storm. I had experienced a few dramas that almost killed me, but not quite. My dramas had just brought a few tears — and changes of underwear.'

TWO DAYS LATER, on 13 January, Cathy Pegg landed back at Point Cook. She told me the Cessna had an auto-pilot but it had given so much trouble she didn't use it. It worked perfectly, however, during the last half hour of the flight from Coffs Harbour to Point Cook. 'I hand-flew that aeroplane all the way to New Zealand and back again.'

She hid the Cessna in the hangar for a week after the New Zealand flight — until someone reminded her it had to be returned to its owner.

'I felt so attached to that aeroplane. It is now a forlorn sight at Essenden airport, grounded with serious airframe problems.'

Cathy's next flight was her annual flight review to renew her Private Pilot's Licence. With the examiner she did one circuit and was told to land. He did not say anything, leaving Cathy to think, once again, that she had done something drastically wrong. Back at the clubhouse he casually asked for Cathy's logbook and entered the appropriate endorsements. When Cathy asked about the remaining part of the expected test — a cross-country flight to prove she could cope with navigation, and her ability to fly in controlled airspace, the examiner said, 'You have just returned from New Zealand. That is a magnificent achievement for any private pilot. If you had done something wrong during your flight tests I would have had to fail you. I could not have coped with that.'

Finally, I asked Cathy if she would do the trans-Tasman flight again. As she thoughtfully pushed a hand through her hair she replied, 'Yeah, I would. Of course I would. I would do it ten times more. I want to be the first Maori woman to fly around the world. But next time I would go with an instrument rating or, at the very least, a night rating. Anyone contemplating an ocean crossing without the ability to fly on instruments is a bigger idiot than I am.

Landing an aviation record for her New Zealand flight, she said, was a bonus. 'All I did was to fly home to see my Mum.'

NEXT DAY WE once again cross Melbourne in the Baroness May, this time to Moorabbin airfield. Cathy plays an Enya tape. Unbeknown to her it is one of my favourite Enya albums, and I know it is a good omen for the day. At the airfield we call in at Valight Training Services to meet Urms Wright, who took Cathy through all her ground subjects for her Private Pilot's Licence. A former flying instructor for the Royal Air Force in the United Kingdom, some years ago he set up his own flying school in Melbourne. His passion for flying and, especially, a professional standard of flying instruction is amazing. I wonder what he would have made of my own efforts to fly, discouraged by supposedly inept instructors, and with only six hours of flying recorded in my New Zealand Pilot Logbook. But I do not enlighten him. Urms has already given me an earbashing about fledgling instructors

Cathy Pegg prepares to take her newly found 'writer' friend for a flight from Melbourne's Moorabin's general aviation airport in May 1997.
ROY SINCLAIR

who take a job in a flying club merely to gain the necessary hours for an airline career. Cathy says Urms is one of the nicest people in Australian aviation.

'He is so frustrating. He continually took me to the edge of my ability, and got me through.'

A gruff and delightfully outspoken man, Urms appears not to suffer fools gladly. His heartfelt respect for Cathy's ability as an aviator, and her considerable achievements, is obvious.

Half an hour later Cathy is taking WH-JDI, A Piper Warrior II, off from Moorabbin's 13 Right runway. In the passenger seat I am relaxed as we bank towards Melbourne and set a course that will encircle Port Philip Bay. We fly over Williamstown where New Zealand's second ANZAC frigate has just been launched, and over-fly Point Cook airfield. Ahead lies 12 nautical miles of sea.

Cathy points to the dual control column in front of my seat. 'How long is it since you have flown, Roy?' she says, quietly.

I did not want to fly. Adjusting my seat, I reluctantly place my feet on the rudder pedals and, with freely sweating palms, take hold of the control column as Cathy appears to relax in her left-hand seat. With an anxiety I know only too well, I feel the aeroplane take charge of me. For a few moments I am overwhelmed. I look pleadingly at Cathy, hoping she will read the anguish in my face and take over. But Cathy has never given in to her own inability, and she is not about to let me give in to mine. With one of her reassuring smiles she indicates our next heading, at Portarlington — across the sea. Encouraged, I feel a glimmer of confidence — until I need to make a turn. I start into it tentatively with the ailerons, touching up with the rudder as we go. A quick glance to see the black ball nicely centred in the slip-and-turn indicator, and I know I have done it quite well. Cathy attends to the radio calls, and we listen to the companionable radio chatter from other aircraft flying in the same control zone. Occasionally she points to one of the instruments and I make the necessary correction to maintain the aeroplane's heading or attitude. Flying 2000 feet above the bay, we both look out for other air traffic. I am feeling great.

Another passable turn, at Point Lonsdale, and I am flying over the Port Philip Bay heads, turning again, inside the spit at Arthur's Seat, to avoid over-flying the military zone marked on our chart. Cathy is looking pleased with herself. She knows she has done something for me, and it is precious.

'It wouldn't take much to get you flying, Roy,' is all she says as she takes control over the Mornington Peninsula and prepares for the landing back on Moorabbin's 13 Right runway. The day has ended perfectly.

I HAVE A thing about saying goodbye. Cathy takes me to Spencer Street station. Having a little time to spare before returning to New Zealand I have promised to visit my in-laws near Camperdown, a train ride of about two and a half hours from Melbourne. I tell Cathy I would give her a huge hug if we weren't at a crowded railway station. 'Who cares about people?' is all she says.

Moments later she is walking away. She does not look back. I see her go until she is lost to the crowds. Even then, I still gaze at the spot where she vanished.

Unknown in her own country, she is truly remarkable. She is

Cathy Pegg tries out the cockpit of a veteran Miles Falcon monoplane at Point Cook. With her is Keith Hatfield, the aeroplane's owner. A retired Army colonel, Keith is also a keen aviation historian. He has met and spoken with many of the great pioneers of aviation, including Edgar Percival and New Zealand's Jean Batten. His own aspirations to join the RAAF were thwarted by colour blindness. 'I was offered a position in the sergeant's mess, peeling potatoes.' In 1969 he established his own flying school at Berwick. Cathy Pegg, he says, is an extraordinary young woman whose double crossing of the Tasman Sea, so early in her flying career, was 'an outstanding feat in any man's language'.

ROY SINCLAIR

courageous. She is outrageous. She is a survivor. Yet, for all she has achieved as an Australian-trained aviator, she is still one of us, a New Zealander. And, one day, New Zealanders may be proud to know who Cathy Pegg is.

Earlier the same day, the Baroness May had taken us on one last trip to the Point Cook Flying Club. We were to meet Keith Hatfield, a one-time Army colonel and Cathy's good friend. He kept two veteran aeroplanes at Point Cook — a Miles Falcon and a de Havilland Leopard Moth. He wanted me to see them.

'Soon I will be stone motherless broke,' Cathy had told me as we pounded down the Point Cook road. 'I don't even know where I will be living soon, but I know I will be on my own. Each pay day will always be a great day. I will buy my food, pay my rent, and fill up the Baroness May. After that, there will be just enough to pay for an hour's flying.

'I will be in the sky high above Melbourne's western suburbs. And as I look down I will be wondering what a poor person will be doing on a day like this. I will then say, My God! The poor person is a Maori girl and she's up here — flying!'

BIBLIOGRAPHY

Annabell, Ross. *A Shower of Spray and We're Away! Fred Ladd* (AH & AW Reed, 1971)

Chorley, WR. *RAF Bomber Command Losses of the Second World War* (Midland Counties Publications, 1992)

Bain, Gordon. *De Havilland, a Pictorial Tribute* (Promotional Reprint Co Ltd, 1995)

Brown, Gerald. *Delivery Diary 'Aotearoa'* (Solent Flying Boat Preservation Society, 1989)

Chichester, Francis. *The Lonely Sea and the Sky* (Hodder & Stoughton, 1964).

Fenwick, KE. *Flying Training Manual* (revised edn, 1994)

Hawkins, Nigel. *Man on the Move* (RD Press, 1992)

Hodgkinson, Vic. *Beachcomber, the Story of a Sandringham* (Southampton's Hall of Aviation, 1989)

Lainé, Shirley. *Silver Wings* (Grantham House, 1989)

Lucas, FJ. *Popeye Lucas Queenstown* (AH & AW Reed, 1972)

Maling, Peter. *Wanderlust: The Life of a Pioneer New Zealand Airwoman* (PB Maling, 1988)

Markham, Beryl. *West with the Night* (Welcome Enterprises, Inc. 1994)

New Zealand Wings Magazine (various issues)

Rennie, Neil. *Conquering Isolation* (Heinemann Reed, 1990)

Taylor, John (ed.). *The Lore of Flight* (Park Lane, 1990)